D1557430

# Transforming Shakespeare

# Transforming Shakespeare

## Contemporary Women's Re-Visions in Literature and Performance

*Edited by*

## Marianne Novy

St. Martin's Press
New York

ISBN 0–312–21472–3

Library of Congress Cataloging-in-Publication Data

    1. Shakespeare, William, 1564–1616—Adaptations.    2. Shakespeare,
William, 1564–1616—Film and video adaptations.    3. American
literature—Women authors—History and criticism.    4. English
literature—Women authors—History and criticism.    5. Shakespeare,
William, 1564–1616—Dramatic production.    6. Shakespeare,William,
1564–1616—Stage history—1950-    7. English drama—Adaptations—
History and criticism.    8. Women theatrical producers and
directors.    9. American literature—English influences.    10. Women
in the motion picture industry.    I. Novy, Marianne, 1945-    .
PR2880.A1T71999
820.9'9287'0904—dc2198–37271
CIP

Internal design and typesetting by Letra Libre

First edition: March, 1999
10  9  8  7  6  5  4  3  2  1

# Contents

# Acknowledgments

I am grateful, first of all, to the International Shakespeare Association for inviting me to lead a seminar on women writers rewriting Shakespeare at the 1996 International Shakespeare Congress (which was devoted to the theme of Shakespeare and the Twentieth Century) and to Gillian Beer for agreeing to be the co-leader of the seminar and for her intellectual energy. I would also like to acknowledge the significant contributions of the members of the seminar whose papers couldn't be included here—Rebecca Bach, Carla Dente Baschiera, Jennifer Carrell, Pilar Hidalgo, Megan Isaac, Phyllis McBride, Mary Janell Metzger, and Meghan Nieman—as well as the contributions of the auditors who participated in the discussion, in particular the person whose comment prompted Jane Smiley to rethink her whole approach to Lear in *A Thousand Acres,* as the appendix to her essay discusses.

Some of the contributions to this anthology have appeared previously. I am grateful to Laurence Goldstein, editor of the *Michigan Quarterly Review,* for permission to reprint, with a few changes, Linda Bamber's story, which appears in the Fall 1998 issue. I am also grateful to Jill Levenson, Jonathan Bate, and Dieter Mehl, editors of *Shakespeare and the Twentieth Century: Selected Proceedings of the International Shakespeare Association World Congress, Los Angeles, 1996* (Newark: University of Delaware Press, 1998), for permission to reprint the essays by Jane Smiley and Penny Gay, again with a few changes. The essay that appears here as the appendix to Jane Smiley's "Shakespeare in Iceland" first appeared in the *Washington Post Book World,* June 21, 1998, p. 1. The Museum Mayer van den Bergh and the Institut Royal Du Patrimoine Artistique-Koninklijk Instituut voor Kunspatrimonium, Brussels have kindly given permission to print a reproduction of Bruegel's *Dulle Griet,* and the Shakespeare Birthplace Trust shared photographs of Katie Mitchell's production of *Henry VI: The Battle for the Throne.* Rita Dove has given permission to quote from her poetry.

For many other kinds of support in assembling this anthology and bringing it to publication, I am grateful to Jill Levenson, Kim Hall, Barbara Bowen, Jean Howard, Michael Bristol, Valerie Wayne, Valerie Traub, Dympna Callaghan, Peter Erickson, and Roger Pringle. Pat Renkiewicz helped with typing. My husband, David Carrier, and my daughter, Liz Carrier, cheerfully took telephone messages and supplemented my computer skills.

# Introduction

*Marianne Novy*

The late twentieth century has seen an explosion of literature in which women rewrite Shakespeare. Many new opportunities have emerged for women directors and performers to stage Shakespeare in the theater and on the screen. This anthology explores some of this recent writing and performance. It discusses late-twentieth-century women who often talk back aggressively to Shakespeare's plays, to earlier interpretations of them, and to patriarchal and colonialist attitudes that the plays have come to symbolize.[1] Using fiction as a form of criticism, they let characters escape plots that doom them to an oppressive marriage or to death; as writers, performers, and directors, they demythologize myths about male heroism and also about female martyrdom, and they imagine stories for figures who are silent or demonized in Shakespeare's version. Jane Smiley's *A Thousand Acres* reimagines *King Lear* in 1970s America with the father a secretly incestuous childbeater; Marina Warner's *Indigo* rewrites *The Tempest* giving a voice and a history for Sycorax.

Not all the women discussed here would consider themselves feminist, and those who do exemplify a range of attitudes. All however have been touched by the feminist desire to imagine women as subjects and not simply as objects. Furthermore, all of them live in a society in which the possibilities for women are far different than those in Shakespeare's day, partly because of the legal, social, political, and cultural activities of feminists, and these different possibilities are inevitably part of the horizon of our subjects' writing and performances. But these writers and directors are concerned with many other issues in addition to gender. Colonialism, race, class, nationalism, militarism, environmental issues, and sexuality are among the many concerns that their transformations of Shakespeare address.

In many different dimensions, then, these women's perspectives lead them to new energies in creation and in criticism of earlier literature, as explained by Adrienne Rich in the essay that contributes to the title of this collection:

> Re-vision—the act of looking back, of seeing with fresh eyes, of entering an old text from a new critical direction—is for us more than a chapter in cultural history: it is an act of survival. Until we can understand the assumptions in which we are drenched we cannot know ourselves. . . . We need to know the writing of the past, and know it differently than we have ever known it; not to pass on a tradition but to break its hold over us.[2]

The women whose works are explored in this collection are not simply looking to break with Shakespeare, however. Often, like the writers and performers from subordinate groups (including women) discussed by Susan Bennett and Kate Chedgzoy, their interest is in how to use transformed versions of Shakespeare on their own behalf.[3] Their concern may be to meditate on the links of the past to the present; sometimes the use of Shakespeare dramatizes a link among what Diana Brydon, in her essay in this volume, calls "multiple intersecting pasts," and thus helps us to understand a condition of cultural hybridity. It is partly for this reason that *The Tempest* and *King Lear*—plays of fathers and daughters that make it possible to criticize patriarchal heritage as well as colonial heritage—have been especially prominent in recent rewritings.

Women of the late twentieth century are certainly not the first to write about their responses to Shakespeare, to rewrite some of his plots in their own work, or to re-imagine his writings in their performances. As my contributors and I have shown in previous books, from the late seventeenth century on—the time that women began to act in Shakespeare—Aphra Behn, Margaret Cavendish, Jane Austen, Charlotte Brontë, George Eliot and many lesser known women have engaged in a kind of dialogue with Shakespeare. Often, these women writers analyzed Shakespeare's portrayal of women to claim him as a supporter.[4] This interest in claiming Shakespeare on behalf of women began—with Behn and Cavendish—before Shakespeare was a culture hero; his rise in status in the eighteenth and nineteenth centuries surely heightened it. Women have often been especially interested in cultural constructions of Shakespeare that have affinities to cultural constructions of women: the outsider, the artist of wide-ranging identification and sympathy, and the actor. When Jane Smiley, in her essay in this collection, summarizes the qualities in Shakespeare that she admires, her image of him as "a person of wide-ranging interests . . . a writer who used his instrument to explore the world and not himself" fits in this tradition.

However, in the twentieth century, many women writers, unlike earlier ones, have emphasized that—no matter how much their attraction to Shakespeare—they do not find his works universal. This explicit critique began during the first wave of feminism in the early twentieth century. In Dorothy Richardson's experimental novel *Pilgrimage* (1910), for example, Miriam thinks, "there was no reality in any of Shakespeare's women. They please men because they show women as men see them," and no voice in the novel disagrees.[5] Even though Virginia Woolf praised Shakespeare for his androgyny and objectivity in *A Room of One's Own* (1927), she commented that his women were shown mainly in relation to men and wondered about a possibility he didn't seem to have considered: a friendship between Cleopatra and Octavia.[6] And although H. D., in *By Avon River* (1949), imagined Shakespeare as an androgynous father-muse with a special affinity for his daughters literal and literary, she nevertheless identified with his offstage, silent character Claribel and gave her a voice.[7]

With the second feminist wave, beginning in the 1960s, such critiques were no longer exceptional but rather part of an interpretive community in which writers, scholars, and performers all participated.[8] Most of the subjects and essayists in this collection, who similarly find a lack of universality in Shakespeare, developed out of this interpretive community.

Not every allusion to Shakespeare, of course, is significant enough to make a work a rewriting; nor is every rewriting a significant enough variant of Shakespeare's perspective to be considered a transformation.[9] The comparison of a female suspect to Lady Macbeth, for example, a shorthand characterization Susan Baker has shown abounds in detective stories, simply enlists Shakespeare as "authority on motivation."[10] This practice is the opposite to the way most of the works discussed in this anthology question received interpretations of Shakespeare and challenge his authority.

In one sense, a twentieth-century writer who uses a Shakespearean reference always transforms it to some extent, since the modern context is so different. Even Baker's detective stories make a transformative leap in comparing twentieth-century middle-class women to Lady Macbeth, but their focus is on similarities rather than on differences. The rewritings discussed in this book, however, involve more of what Ann Rosalind Jones describes as an "oppositional" response to their Shakespearean predecessor—"the ideological message and force of the reigning code is . . . pulled out of its dominant frame of reference and subversively inserted into an 'alternative frame of reference.'"[11] On the other hand, in many Shakespeare plays the "ideological message" itself includes contradictions, and hints of an "alternative frame of reference" are already present, so even an oppositional rewriting may develop possibilities at least latent in the "polyphonic" Shakespearean text.[12] And even an underlining of a contrast, such as the assertion that a novel is not going to end like a Shakespearean romance, suggests that the comparison between the two is relevant. In Warner's *Indigo,* indeed, the statement its Miranda makes about not living in the reconciliatory world of the *Tempest* turns out to be complicated as the plot eventually gives her a reconciliation of her own.

While each of Shakespeare's plays has been of interest to some twentieth-century women, there are genre- and play-related differences in the kind and level of interest. Shakespeare's history plays, for example, have been least considered by women rewriters of Shakespeare, as by feminist Shakespeare critics, since there are few large roles for women in the best known of them, *Henry IV, Parts 1* and *2,* and *Henry V.*[13] Ironically it appears that some history plays, perhaps because of their relative unfamiliarity, have emerged as an area of greater opportunity for women directors.[14] In this collection, Barbara Hodgdon analyzes a production of *3 Henry VI* directed by Katie Mitchell and finds that women's voices resonate more in her production than in history plays directed by men, but also that her production deals critically with nationalism and militarism as much as with gender issues.

Shakespeare's comedies—especially those with cross-dressing and/or talkative heroines—have often been celebrated as an area of relative visibility and power for women. For different reasons, *As You Like It* and *The Taming of the Shrew* have had special meanings among the comedies. Rosalind's witty resourcefulness, especially when disguised as a boy, has held particular interest; consider, for example, Angela Carter's comparison of the freedom Rosalind's disguise gave her to that conferred by new styles in 1960s clothing: "Rosalind in disguise in the Forest of Arden could pretend to be a boy pretending to be a seductress, satisfying innumerable atavistic desires in the audience of the play."[15] Feminist critics such as Peter Erickson and Clara Claiborne Park have pointed out that male power still remains in *As You Like It;* Patricia Lennox's essay in this volume shows that when a recent woman director focuses on more of the female characters in the play and undercuts the play's closure, the production conveys a criticism of the final marriages.[16] *The Taming of the Shrew* has often seemed the paradigmatic comedy for feminist rewriting, since more dramatically than any other it shows a spirited woman forced into an accommodation with her husband and her society.[17] Some rewritings/revisionary productions of this play have tried to make the accommodation one in which she still holds power; others have turned the play into a tragedy, as in one Turkish version in which Kate commits suicide at the end.[18] Here, Penny Gay shows how Australian directors, female and male, have recreated the play in terms of their own culture's gender relations, with Gale Edwards alone focusing the final scene on Kate, who looks up as if in protest to the heavens.

It is, however, Shakespeare's tragedies that have the most cultural force overall; accordingly, they have been most often rewritten by women as well as by men and occupy the most space in this anthology. *Othello,* with its unusually explicit discussion of gender issues, has been of special interest to feminist critics, and the two plays discussed in my article clearly—though not always straightforwardly—deal with its feminist concerns. *Othello* is also the Shakespearean work most specifically important to Rita Dove and to many other African-Americans. Peter Erickson's article about Dove—in whose responses to Shakespeare race seems more important than gender—permits us to examine also the history of African-American appropriations of Shakespeare. Francesca T. Royster shows a different history of African-American women performers in relation to Cleopatra, up to Tamara Dobson's performance as Cleopatra Jones.

Perhaps partly because the relation of women writers to the past has often been thematized as a daughter-father issue, *King Lear* has been of increasing interest to women in recent years.[19] Jane Smiley's *A Thousand Acres,* for example, follows *Lear's* plot amazingly closely in some respects (her essay in this volume discusses going through the play scene by scene) although it ultimately presents a very different picture. This anthology gives heavy representation to discussions of *A Thousand Acres* because of its current prominence (it won the Pulitzer Prize in 1992 and was made into a feature film in 1997), its accessibility for discussion together with *Lear* in the classroom, and the differences among the three essays included. Here Barbara Mathieson demonstrates how environmentally sensitive criticism makes *A Thousand Acres* look even bleaker, Iska Alter focuses on genre and the issue of narrative unreliability, and Smiley provides unusually thorough autobiographical reflections on her earlier responses to *Lear* and Shakespeare as well as the various stages in the writing of her novel—including an appendix in which she discusses how drastically her view of both *Lear* and her novel have changed since she wrote the essay. In contrast to these essays, Suzanne Raitt discusses Margaret Atwood's *Cat's Eye,* a novel that rereads *Lear,* in a very different way, in relation to Canada's colonial past.

This anthology also includes several different contributions involving rewritings of *The Tempest*—a prominence that, again, represents how many modern authors have been drawn to revisit this play, which, like *Lear,* includes an important father-daughter motif. Interest in rethinking *The Tempest* has heightened under the influence of postcolonialism. Ngugi wa Thiong'o's novel *A Grain of Wheat* (1967), Aimé Césaire's play *Une Tempête*

(1969) and Roberto Fernandez Retamar's essay *Caliban* (1972) all rewrite *The Tempest* to analyze and challenge its image of colonial mastery; as women writers in English become more global and more globally conscious, *The Tempest* becomes a place to deal with colonial and racial issues as well as gender. Here, Diana Brydon analyzes the re-imagining of Canada's history in *Plainsong* by Nancy Huston, a Canadian expatriate living in France, and Caroline Cakebread discusses *Indigo,* in which the British novelist Marina Warner reenvisions Sycorax while coming to terms with her own family's colonial past in the West Indies. Although these two novels deal with exploitation by European settlers more thoroughly than does Shakespeare, both of them, like *The Tempest* itself, end with at least some reconciliation. A similar move occurs at the end of the last contribution to this anthology, a fictional piece by Linda Bamber, author of *Comic Women, Tragic Men.* Exemplifying the link between criticism and fiction so often analyzed in these essays, Bamber creates another version of Miranda and the other characters in *The Tempest* and imagines her Miranda seeing a dramatic presentation of her story (somewhat as Marina Warner's Miranda does in *Indigo*) and dealing with a Shakespeare theme park that parodies the cultural nostalgia discussed by Susan Bennett. Bamber's Miranda has a comic insouciance about some issues raised in feminist Shakespeare criticism, as well as an eye for some of the ambiguities in literary treatments of race, rape, and rape fantasies (a link with *A Thousand Acres* as well).

The essayists in this collection find many variations in the ways that these late twentieth century women use Shakespeare to meditate on the relation of contemporary cultures to traditions. While Smiley rewrites *Lear* to expose the problems of our dominant cultural tradition, Raitt argues that *Cat's Eye* uses *Lear* in a very different manner: Atwood's desolate, haunted use of the name Cordelia is simply "a cultural postscript" that "adds another dimension of incoherence." While Mathieson focuses on the tragedy of the loss of nature in *A Thousand Acres,* Lennox shows how Edzard replaces the usual forest in *As You Like It* with an abandoned dockyard that offers liberation in its own way. While my chapter shows how Ann-Marie MacDonald dramatizes the escape of women from Shakespeare's tragic plots, Hodgdon shows that Mitchell makes the roles of women as mourners a link between the deaths in *Henry VI* and the mass deaths in late-twentieth-century Europe. Erickson discusses how Rita Dove associates Shakespeare with her family home and reunion while imagining an expatriate jazz musician whose Shakespeare allusions mark his alienation; Royster shows how the transformation of Cleopatra into Tamara Dobson's Cleopatra Jones exemplifies African-American appropriation of Shakespeare to address social and cultural marginality.

The revisiting of Shakespeare in these works links most of them, however, with the sort of postmodernism discussed by Linda Hutcheon, which involves "repetition with critical distance that allows ironic signaling of difference at the very heart of similarity."[20] Huston, Warner, Atwood, and MacDonald are all reflexive and metafictional, thematizing the woman writer or (in Atwood) the woman artist.[21] Analogously, Dove focuses not only on her own relation to Shakespeare but also on that of a black musician. Though Smiley's novel has no writer or artist within, its concern with conflicting memories, its first-person narrator who ends the novel by discussing her quest for understanding, and the constant intertext between her story and the very different interpretation of similar events in *King Lear* give *A Thousand Acres* a metafictional, self-conscious element as well. Smiley even gives her narrator/main character an explicit critique of what the character's husband calls "real history" that is very much in the spirit of much postmodernist metafiction: "You see this grand history, but I see blows. I see taking what you want because you want it, then making something up that justifies what you did."[22] Similarly, Bamber's Miranda confronts both the official story of Prospero's role on the island and the guerrilla theater version, and briefly becomes a playwright who can tell the story in her own way.

As this anthology suggests, the novel has long been the privileged place for women writers to rethink Shakespeare's plays. The late twentieth century has seen many novelistic rewritings by authors who include Margaret Drabble, Angela Carter, Gloria Naylor, Margaret Laurence, A. S. Byatt, Nadine Gordimer, Fay Weldon, Michelle Cliff, Valerie Miner, Ann Tyler, Erica Jong, Rachel Ingalls, Elizabeth Jolley, Barbara Trapido, Iris Murdoch, Constance Beresford Howe, and Catherine Clement.[23] Shakespeare has figured less in the work of recent women poets, although Marilyn Hacker's sonnet sequence *Love, Death, and the Changing of the Seasons* uses Shakespearean epigraphs and reworkings to reflect on the growth and end of love between two women in the 1980s, and Suniti Namjoshi rethinks the Caliban/Miranda/Prospero relationship in her sequence *Snapshots of Caliban*.[24] Women playwrights have been fewer by far than women in other genres; beyond those discussed here, others who have rewritten Shakespeare are Melissa Murray (*Ophelia*), Alison Lyssa (*Pinball*) and Elaine Feinstein (*Lear's Daughters,* co-authored with the Women's Theatre Group).[25]

Women otherwise involved in the theater are rethinking Shakespeare in some ways very similar to the writers I have discussed. While women who have acted in Shakespeare in England in the late twentieth century have been interviewed by Carol Rutter, women directors' thoughts on Shakespeare, or analyses of their work, are harder to find.[26] This is largely because women who have directed Shakespeare at the most prestigious sites are still few. This volume's treatment of women directors in England needs to be supplemented with an awareness of their colleagues around the globe—from Ariane Mnouchkine in Paris to Janet Suzman in South Africa to Tina Packer at Shakespeare & Co. in Lenox, Massachusetts, to Audrey Stanley at the Santa Cruz and Berkeley Shakespeare Festivals, and many others as well.[27]

Once it might have been tempting to imagine that women's Shakespearean rewritings and performances in the late twentieth century would all be celebratory in tone, focusing on the new possibilities for women to survive or escape tragedy and reimagine comedy. But the new visions into which women have transformed Shakespearean themes have been much more complex than such generalizations would suggest. On the stage, women have played, for the first time, both Falstaff and the title role in *Lear;* in their writing, women have told contemporary tragedies as well as happier stories.[28] Women who reflect on Shakespeare are not necessarily complacent about how we are better off since his time, any more than they necessarily idealize that past. As Hodgdon quotes Mitchell, "Sometimes in portraying the women as the victims they are textually, it can actually awaken people to more sense of the need for equality." Portrayals of women as victims here are not the result of something inevitable in human nature, but, as in Paula Vogel's *Desdemona,* intended to shock us into change. Conversely, portrayals of women as transformed out of stories of victimhood, as in MacDonald's *Goodnight Desdemona,* can be particularly exuberant because empowerment is not something that can be taken for granted.

The transformations discussed here are part of a larger group of transformations which includes late twentieth-century works by men as well. The performance-oriented essays by Gay and Hodgdon have neatly shown specific contrasts, pointing out how the women's voices and viewpoints receive more emphasis in the productions directed by Gale Edwards and Katie Mitchell. But what should the comparison class be for the rewritings? Like Chedgzoy and Bennett, I find the most obvious comparisons from the late twentieth century are with rewritings by males from consciously oppositional perspectives.[29] It is often the treatment of a subordinate group in Shakespeare that mobilizes authors to re-visions. Tom Stoppard's play *Rosencrantz and Guildenstern are Dead* (1966) can be seen as a rewriting of *Hamlet* in terms of class—from the viewpoint of the attendants—as well as a recreation in the absurdist mode of Samuel Beckett. More obviously, Arnold Wesker's play *The Merchant* (1976) and Alan Isler's book of fictions *Op. Non Cit.* (1997) both rewrite the story of Shylock, contextualizing it with early modern Jewish history.[30] Salman Rushdie's novel *The Satanic Verses* (1988) rewrites *Othello.*

Caryl Phillips's novel *The Nature of Blood* (1997) reimagines both *Othello* and *The Merchant of Venice*. In the play *Overtime* (1996), A. R. Gurney, a white Anglo-Saxon Protestant heterosexual male who writes about the American upper class, though himself from no subordinate group, is influenced by oppositional perspectives—Jewish, feminist, gay, and African-American—which he tries to mediate when he reimagines a new American multicultural community in a sequel to *The Merchant of Venice*. While female characters figure in most of these rewritings, the question of how Shakespeare's plays help us think about the situation of women today and in history is, understandably, less central in them than it is in the women's writings discussed in this anthology (with the exception of Rita Dove's). Authors such as Isler, Rushdie, Gurney, and John Wideman, in whose novel *Philadelphia Fire* (1990) students perform *The Tempest,* are more interested in other dimensions of the relation of contemporary cultures to traditions.

Transformations of Shakespeare have flourished at the end of the twentieth century precisely because many writers of both sexes and many different racial and ethnic backgrounds are conscious of how different the stories they want to tell are from his. Similarly, directors and performers are imagining Shakespeare in ways that contrast with stage traditions. As Peter Erickson writes, "Shakespeare becomes a resource in a different sense as a richly complex reference point within the larger project of cultural change we are undergoing with regard to race, gender, and class."[31] His plays are too powerful to forget, but twentieth-century writers, directors, and performers can make us remember them differently.[32]

## Notes

1. For earlier discussions of such rewritings, see especially the discussion of Adrienne Rich, Gloria Naylor, and Maya Angelou in Peter Erickson, *Rewriting Shakespeare, Rewriting Ourselves* (Berkeley: University of California Press, 1991), 95–176, and the discussion of Margaret Laurence in Gayle Greene, *Changing the Story: Feminist Fiction and the Tradition* (Bloomington: Indiana University Press, 1991), 148–65, as well as essays in *Cross-Cultural Performances: Differences in Women's Re-Visions of Shakespeare,* ed. Marianne Novy (Urbana: University of Illinois Press, 1993), and the last two chapters of Marianne Novy, *Engaging with Shakespeare: Responses of George Eliot and Other Women Novelists* (Athens: University of Georgia Press, 1994; Iowa City: University of Iowa Press, 1998).

2. Adrienne Rich, "When We Dead Awaken: Writing as Re-Vision," in *On Lies, Secrets, and Silence* (New York: Norton, 1979), 35. This essay was first delivered as a talk at the Modern Language Association Convention in 1971.

3. Susan Bennett, *Performing Nostalgia: Shifting Shakespeare and the Contemporary Past* (New York: Routledge, 1996); Kate Chedgzoy, *Shakespeare's Queer Children: Sexual Politics and Contemporary Culture* (Manchester: Manchester University Press, 1995).

4. For further discussion of this history, see *Women's Re-Visions of Shakespeare: On Responses of Dickinson, Woolf, Rich, H. D., George Eliot, and Others,* ed. Marianne Novy (Urbana: University of Illinois Press, 1990), as well as Novy, *Engaging with Shakespeare.*

5. Dorothy Richardson, *Pilgrimage* (1910: reprint, London: J. M. Dent, 1967), 2:188.

6. Virginia Woolf, *A Room of One's Own* (New York: Harcourt, Brace, 1927), 86–87. Woolf's interest in Shakespeare, and H. D.'s, can also be contextualized within modernism's fascination with him, recently discussed by Richard Halpern, *Shakespeare Among the Moderns* (Ithaca, NY: Cornell University Press, 1997).

7. H. D. [Hilda Doolittle], *By Avon River* (New York: Macmillan, 1949). See also Susan Stanford Friedman, "Remembering Shakespeare Differently: H. D.'s *By Avon River,*" in Novy, ed., *Women's Re-Visions,* 143–64.

8. On feminist interpretive communities, see Annette Kolodny, "Dancing Through the Minefield: Some Observations on the Theory, Practice, and Politics of a Feminist Literary Criticism," *Feminist Studies* 6 (1980): 1–25, and Patrocinio P. Schweickart, "Reading Ourselves: Toward a Feminist Theory of Reading," in *Gender and Reading,* ed. Elizabeth A. Flynn and Patrocinio P. Schweickart (Baltimore, MD: Johns Hopkins University Press, 1986), 31–62.

9. Ruby Cohn, *Modern Shakespeare Offshoots* (Princeton, NJ: Princeton University Press, 1976), distinguishing from adaptations, says that "In transformations Shakespearean characters move through a partly or wholly non-Shakespearean plot," 4. Martha Rozett writes, "The author of a transformation is engaged in dismantling, rearranging, sometimes fracturing the text, sometimes adding to or updating it; sometimes parodying or inverting it, and then reassembling it into a recognizable re-imagining of the play as we know it." Martha Rozett, *Talking Back to Shakespeare* (Newark: University of Delaware Press, 1994), 8. The productions directed by Gale Edwards, Katie Mitchell, and Christine Edzard (discussed in this volume by Penny Gay, Barbara Hodgdon, and Patricia Lennox) would probably not be included under these definitions of transformation, though, Rozett admits the "blurring of the distinctions among transformations, interpretations, and performances," as well as adaptations and offshoots. Ibid., 9. Nevertheless these productions do significantly deviate from dominant performance traditions.

10. Susan Baker, "Shakespearean Authority in the Classic Detective Story," *Shakespeare Quarterly* 1995 (46): 424–448; quotation is from 434, where she gives eight examples.

11. Ann Rosalind Jones, *The Currency of Eros: Women's Love Lyric in Europe, 1540–1620* (Bloomington: Indiana University Press, 1990), 5–6. Jones is quoting Christine Gledhill, "Pleasurable Negotiations," in *Female Spectators: Looking at Film and Television,* ed. Deirdre Pribram (London: Verso, 1988), 67.

12. The word "polyphonic" comes from Ania Loomba's discussion of this issue in *Gender, Race, Renaissance Drama* (New York: Manchester University Press, 1989), 146.

13. See the discussion of this absence in Jean Howard and Phyllis Rackin, *Engendering a Nation: A Feminist Account of Shakespeare's English Histories* (New York: Routledge, 1997), esp. 20–25. Howard and Rackin note the recent interest of feminist critics, and the importance of women, in the three *Henry VI* plays.

14. Notable productions of *Richard II* have been directed by Joan Littlewood (1954), Ariane Mnouchkine (1981), and Elizabeth Huddle (1981). The New York Shakespeare Festival had its second woman director overall, Jane Howell, for *Richard III* in 1983. See *Shakespeare Around the Globe: A Guide to Notable Postwar Revivals,* ed. Samuel L. Leiter (New York: Greenwood Press, 1986), pp. 577, 589, 571, 619.

15. Angela Carter, "Notes for a Theory of Sixties Style," reprinted in *Nothing Sacred* (London: Virago, 1987), 87. See also Marjorie Garber on Rosalind as "the favorite among Shakespeare's cross-dressers, the shorthand term for benign female-to-male cross-dressing in literature and culture," in *Vested Interests: Cross-Dressing and Cultural Anxiety* (New York: Routledge, 1992), 76.

16. Peter Erickson, *Patriarchal Structures in Shakespeare's Drama* (Berkeley: University of California Press, 1985); Clara Claiborne Park, "As We Like It: How a Girl Can Be Smart and Still Popular," *American Scholar* 42 (Spring 1973): 262–78; reprinted in *The Woman's Part: Feminist Criticism of Shakespeare,* ed. Carolyn Ruth Swift Lenz, Gayle Greene, and Carol Thomas Neely (Urbana: University of Illinois Press, 1980).

17. Some British feminists published a magazine called *Shrew,* surely with this play as well as the traditional meaning of the word in mind.

18. This production, directed by Yücel Erten in the late 1980s, is discussed by Zeynep Oral in *Is Shakespeare Still our Contemporary?* ed. John Elsom (London: Routledge, 1989), 74–75.

19. Considering works up to 1973, Ruby Cohn wrote, "No important fiction has embraced *Lear* as it has *Hamlet,* and very few dramatists have used *Lear* as a springboard for their own plays." Cohn, *Modern Shakespeare Offshoots,* 232. This is clearly no longer true.

20. Linda Hutcheon, *A Poetics of Postmodernism: History, Theory, Fiction* (New York: Routledge, 1988), 26. This is Hutcheon's redefinition of parody, which she believes is central to postmodernism and distinguishes from ridiculing imitation.

21. On metafiction in feminist fiction, see especially Greene, *Changing the Story.*
22. Jane Smiley, *A Thousand Acres* (New York: Ballantine, 1991), 342–43.
23. See Novy, *Engaging with Shakespeare,* for a detailed discussion of this tradition in the novel.
24. On Namjoshi, see Diana Brydon, "Sister Letters: Miranda's *Tempest* in Canada," in Novy, ed., *Cross-Cultural Performances,* 178–181.
25. In 1998, the American repertory company The Acting Company commissioned seven playwrights, including Marsha Norman, Ntozake Shange, and Wendy Wasserstein, to write *Love's Fire,* a set of short works responding to Shakespeare's sonnets. See "Aspects of Love: Seven Playwrights on the Sonnets," *New York Times,* May 31, 1998, sect. 2, 4. More spontaneously, the playwright-performer Anna Deavere Smith compares her role—"the mimic [who] has opened up a new way of seeing"—to that of the "all licensed Fool" in *King Lear.* See Anna Deavere Smith, "Inside the Political Mimic's Fun-House Mirror," *New York Times,* August 16, 1992, sect. 2, 20.
26. Carol Rutter, et al., *Clamorous Voices* (London: Women's Press, 1988); see also Penny Gay, *As She Likes It: Shakespeare's Unruly Women* (New York: Routledge, 1994).
27. For a comprehensive international overview that includes scores of women directors among the many whose productions it discusses, see Leiter, ed., *Shakespeare Around the Globe.* See also Peter S. Donaldson, "'Haply for I am Black': Liz White's *Othello*," in *Shakespearean Films/Shakespearean Directors* (Boston: Unwin Hyman, 1990), 127–44.
28. On Marianne Hoppe in Robert Wilson's *Lear* in Frankfurt, see Arthur Holmberg, "'Lear' Girds for a Remarkable Episode," *New York Times,* May 20, 1990, sect. 2, 7; on Ruth Maleczech in Lee Breuer's *Lear* at Mabou Mines, see Margaret Spillane, "King Lear, Queen for a Day," *In These Times* 14, no. 11 (Jan. 31-Feb. 6, 1960): 24.
29. Bennett discusses some rewritings whose perspective is not oppositional: for instance, Howard Barker's play *Seven Lears* (1989), in which Barker is not "concerned to re-member the Mother; he wants only, but slightly differently, to insist on her discipline and punishment." Bennett, *Performing Nostalgia,* 50. Edward Bond's play *Lear* (1971) takes an oppositional stand in terms of class and power politics, but not particularly in terms of gender. See also Novy, *Engaging with Shakespeare,* 187.
30. Rozett, who has an extended discussion of Wesker's and earlier rewritings of *The Merchant of Venice,* also notes that much of the "talking back to Shakespeare" of transformations "comes from marginalized groups." Rozett, *Talking Back to Shakespeare,* 5.
31. Erickson, *Patriarchal Structures,* 176.
32. I have adapted this last phrase from H. D. and from the title of Susan Friedman's essay about her; see H. D., *By Avon River,* 31; Friedman, "Remembering Shakespeare Differently: H. D.'s *By Avon River.*"

# 1

---

# Making it New: Katie Mitchell
# Refashions Shakespeare-History

## Barbara Hodgdon

I begin with a familiar text, Thomas Heywood's rave review of "our domesticke hystories":

> What English blood, seeing the person of any bold
> English man presented and doth not hugge his fame,
> and hunnye at his valor, pursuing him in his enterprise
> with his best wishes, and as being wrapt in contemplation,
> offers to him in his hart all prosperous performance, as if
> the Personator were the man Personated, so bewitching a
> thing is lively and well spirited action, that it hath power
> to new mold the harts of the spectators and fashion them
> to the shape of any noble and notable attempt.[1]

Heywood accords theatrical representation a doubled power: it not only makes the dead live again but also refashions spectators into subjects who identify with a specifically *English* heritage, one premised on and inspired by their forefathers' "noble and notable" deeds. Addressed primarily to male spectators, Heywood's comments serve as a touchstone for recent narratives about the power and popularity of Shakespeare's histories on the early modern stage. More specifically, his words ground conjectures about how those plays functioned within the social imaginary, both to remasculinize late Elizabethan culture and to participate in the patriotic project of nation-building that characterized the late 1590s and early 1600s.[2]

Although it risks collapsing one history into another, it is not entirely ir-responsible to argue that "Shakespeare-history" serves a similar function in the twentieth-century social imaginary, especially in Britain since World War II, where stagings of the plays repeatedly have been aligned with celebrations of national identity. What immediately comes to mind, of course, is Laurence Olivier's 1944 film of *Henry V.* As though explicitly evoking Hey-wood's ghost, Olivier dedicated his film to "the Commandoes and Airborne Troops of Great Britain, the spirit of whose ancestors it has been humbly at-tempted to recapture"; in representing an especially timely vision of an Eng-land "peopled with heroes" and led by a hero-king, the film invites its spectators to identify with, even to emulate, the patriotic ideals it puts on offer.[3] Several years later, Stratford's Shakespeare Memorial Theatre staged *1* and *2 Henry IV* and *Henry V* in conjunction with the 1951 Festival of Britain, inaugurating a tradition that has consistently linked stagings of the histories with nationally subsidized theatrical companies, especially but not exclusively the Royal Shakespeare Company, whose (male) artistic directors have repeatedly mobilized the plays to mark moments in their own profes-sional and institutional histories. Peter Hall and John Barton's *The Wars of the Roses* (1964), for instance, restructured the long-neglected early histories into three well-made plays; in the mid- to late 1970s, Terry Hands marked the histories with a structuralist stamp; and Trevor Nunn chose *1* and *2 Henry IV* to celebrate the 1982 opening of the RSC's new London home at the Barbican Theatre.[4] The most recent attempt to fit the early histories into dominant tetralogy thinking generated several monumental theatrical marathons, among them Adrian Noble's *The Plantagenets* (1988), a compi-lation in the Barton-Hall tradition of slimmed-down, reconstituted narra-tives subscribing to the myth of linear historical movement and representing early modern English history as a pictorial discourse. Evoking the aura of nineteenth-century theatrical representation, Noble's productions reified the past as a fancy-dress pageant filled with neo-chivalric tableaux, drum-and-trumpet marches, splendid costumes, and RSC signature stage smoke, and shot through with notable performances showcasing exemplary figures.[5] Widely praised, his achievement is perhaps best summed up by Richard Ed-monds, who saw it as an exercise in historical reconstruction that generated "a sense of England itself singing the clear tunes of its history."[6]

I rehearse these histories in order to situate the subject of this essay: Katie Mitchell's 1994 staging of *3 Henry VI* in Stratford's smallest theater, The Other Place, a performance that breaks with the traditions of theatri-cal representation I have just mapped out. To invoke Heywood once again, it "new molds" both narrative and spectator-subjects to refashion a differ-

ent history and a different spectatorial economy. Such refashioning, I will
argue, aligns with a newly historicized viewing pleasure. In exploring what
that means, I want to map its traces in several ways. One strand of my argument points to those features that distinguish Mitchell's staging from
previous productions of the histories; another marks how women's bodies
and voices intervene in, even disrupt, a narrative centered on constructing
masculine kings and re-engendering a dynastic heritage. How, I want to
ask, do women's performative bodies function as levers to decenter those
narratives? How do such performances serve to open up spaces in which alternative histories can be discerned and to offer sites from which spectators
can re-perform those histories? In addressing these questions, I contextual-
ize my own responses as a historically situated spectator in relation to the
review discourse surrounding the performance—a move that, at least in
part, will demonstrate how individual spectators' accounts are empowered
and restricted in unique ways.

Given the present climate of cultural critique, many automatically assume that stagings mounted by women directors, especially those who, like
Mitchell, have publicly espoused ideals of social and economic equality and
have attracted notice within a primarily masculinist theatrical meritocracy,
will be "feminist" productions. Speaking to this point, Gale Edwards, director of the RSC's recent *The Taming of the Shrew* (1995), remarked in an interview with Kate Alderson: "People don't think, gee, a man is going to
direct *King Lear,* this'll be really good because a man is directing. . . . It's part
of what [*Shrew*] is about, isn't it?"[7] Although *3 Henry VI* offers fewer opportunities than *Shrew* for a potentially deconstructive staging, news of
Mitchell's project spawned assumptions that she might tease feminist scenarios from the plays, might retell Shakespeare's history as the story of *her*
feminism.[8] Yet this was not precisely the case. Speaking several years after the
production of her anxieties about engaging with the sexism of early modern
drama, Mitchell explains: "I think ultimately the best way of approaching it
is to put the woman in the historical context, be as true to that as is possible, even if it is offensive, because sometimes in portraying the women as the
victims they are textually, it can actually awaken people to more sense of the
need for equality."[9] Situating the play in its prefeminist world, then, opens
up a space for the director and her actors, as well as for spectators, to perform a cultural materialist, or materialist feminist critique. Indeed, by "attending to women" historically (to invoke the title of a notable University of
Maryland conference), Mitchell's *Henry VI* uses Shakespeare's text to interrogate structures of hierarchy, especially those concerning gender and class
relations, in a prevailingly masculinist culture. To borrow Lisa Jardine's

evocative metaphor, Mitchell reweaves the historical tapestry inherited from her theatrical predecessors.[10] Marking a radical shift from past as well as present stagings of Shakespeare's histories—notably Matthew Warchus's *Henry V*, which occupied Stratford's main stage the same year—Mitchell's production is less interested in memorializing national history than in releasing different ways of responding to traumatic national, and global, memories.

## Looking Back from Now

Mitchell's choice of *3 Henry VI* for her first Shakespeare project seemed an odd one for a rising directorial star whose RSC career as an assistant director had included work on *Much Ado About Nothing, King Lear,* and Deborah Warner's groundbreaking *Titus Andronicus;* and, as a director, acclaimed productions of Heywood's *A Woman Killed with Kindness* and Ibsen's *Ghosts.*[11] Admitting to not being "smitten" by most of Shakespeare, Mitchell was drawn to *3 Henry VI* for several reasons. Part of its appeal was that it had never been performed on its own in Stratford. "That's very liberating for a director," remarked Mitchell, "a great Shakespearean play without any 'production luggage' along with it. Audiences—and actors—don't come weighted down by the way it's been performed before. . . . [Y]ou start with a clean slate, which is very exciting."[12] Although by staging the play that made the youthful Shakespeare's reputation (in Robert Greene's famous accusation, a "tiger's heart wrapped in a player's hide") she affiliates herself with the RSC's house dramatist, Mitchell sidestepped that potential connection: "I am interested in art for change's sake, not art for art's sake, and certainly not art for my ego's sake." When questioned further, however, she admitted a hidden agenda:

> I very much wanted to respond to the situation[s] in Bosnia and Rwanda. . . . I wanted to present a civil war . . . which occurred on our own turf. Maybe this will help us view similar conflicts abroad with a cooler perspective. We need to re-observe the world through a new pair of glasses. That is why I did not want to update the play, or stuff it with graphic images from the television or newspapers. We are completely immune to modern reports of human horror anyway.[13]

Certainly this was not the first time that a state-subsidized production of one of Shakespeare's histories had sought to make connections with contemporary events, either by staging their traces or through accidents of historical reception. Both the London press and academic critics quickly labeled

Adrian Noble's *Henry V* (1984) an anti-war, post-Falklands staging; when the production reached London, the scrim backing the final tableau was inscribed with the names of the Agincourt dead, paying specific homage to Maya Lin's Vietnam War memorial, which had been recently unveiled in Washington.[14] More recently, Ian McKellen reports that the Royal National Theatre's *Richard III* (1992), set in an imaginary 1930s black-shirt regime, prompted audiences in Bucharest to cheer at Richard's death in memory of their recent freedom from Ceauşescu's tyranny.[15] In Mitchell's case, however, even more directly personal as well as topical connections influenced her decision. Noting that "forty percent of the play takes the form of direct audience address, as the characters manipulate opinion in a dramatic debate about civil war," she discerned, in the play's formal structures, an opportunity to address nontheatrical events she had observed during her research on Eastern European theater as the holder of a 1989 Winston Churchill Memorial Trust Fellowship, experiences that had also energized her staging of *A Woman Killed With Kindness*. Speaking of herself as a "closet anthropologist," Mitchell emphasized her ability to think and feel her way into "alien cultures, value systems, and social atmosphere" and, especially, her interest in the ways in which cultural minorities, Catholic as well as Russian Orthodox, cling to religion as a way of giving form and structure to their lives.[16]

Significantly, however, Mitchell does not mobilize Shakespeare's play to tell the history of another culture, nor does her staging make any attempt to turn the struggle it dramatizes into a universal phenomenon. Retitled as *Henry VI: The Battle for the Throne* to mark its reappearance in isolation as a "new" story, one engendered and energized by present-day contexts that demand such a retelling, Mitchell's staging offers an ethnography of England's own genocidal struggle, premised on Brechtian notions of historicized theatrical representation. As Brecht writes:

> We must leave [social structures] their distinguishing marks and keep their impermanence always before our eyes, so that our own period can be seen to be impermanent too. . . ."Historical conditions" must of course not be imagined (nor . . . constructed) as mysterious Powers (in the background); on the contrary, they are created and maintained by men (and will in due course be altered by them): it is the actions taking place before us that allow us to see what they are.[17]

In several ways, the production announced its debt to Brechtian methods. Rather than subscribing to the usual practice of privileging characters' names and ordering them in relation to each other, the production's program lists the actors' names first, in alphabetical order, followed by those of the character or characters each plays. In print, then, the actors stand apart from their roles—a move that not only erases myths of royal (and gender) hierarchies but also serves to demystify the illusion that the player is identical with the character and the performance with the actual event.[18] Moreover, in advocating a type of theater that "not only releases the feelings, insights and impulses possible within the particular historical field of human relations in which the action takes place, but employs and encourages those thoughts and feelings which help transform the field itself,"[19] Brecht suggests the need for practitioners to understand historical differences in order to respond to them, a practice that aligns with Mitchell's own research methods, which resemble those of the alternative theater company Joint Stock, a collective ensemble committed to creating political theater, more than the traditionally director-oriented practices of the RSC.[20] Her passion for giving drama direct access to non-theatrical life surfaces in several interviews with *Henry VI*'s actors. Jonathan Firth, who played Henry VI, mentions a preparation period of historical readings on the period, and Liz Kettle, who played Lady Grey, recalls how, before going into rehearsal, the actors also went to York and Tewkesbury to visit the locales of the play's bloodiest battles. "Until then," she observes, "I hadn't really realized that England had killing fields of its own . . . these fields that looked like any other were in fact places where 30,000 men had died." Connecting that to her own experience as a production assistant on a BBC documentary in Ethiopia, where she saw firsthand the brutal aftermath of war, with rusting tanks by the side of the road, Kettle speaks of keeping these images in mind as she worked.[21]

This insistence on exploring material history links Mitchell's practice, within theatrical culture, to that of Deborah Warner, whose *Titus Andronicus* and *King John* (as well as her 1995 *Richard II* for the Royal National Theatre) model a similar attention to physical, tactile detail in order to evoke an "authentic" and "true-to-life" sense of cultural differences. Almost unanimously, reviewers praised Mitchell's production's precisely articulated recreation of a historical past. Although critics' thorough documentation of the set, props, costumes, lighting, and sound design can be attributed in part to the "close up and personal" circumstances of any staging in The Other Place, many remarked on what Nick Curtis called a "brooding, intense vision . . . [that] concentrates on the complexities of text and on acting" to evoke a late medieval world of ordered ceremony and gesture that, at the time of the events dramatized, was in crisis.[22] Even those who, like the *Sunday Times*'s critic, mourned the loss of "blood-soaked pageantry . . . huge events rocking and wrecking the country" and missed the "grand theatrical lyricism of the writing, the sense of big public passions [and] Tudor spectacle," mentioned how, in this "symphony played by a small ensemble," the actors' clear articulation of speeches and their ability to speak Shakespeare's early verse "as though it were modern prose" turned dynastic politics into personal arguments, conveyed with clarity and precision.[23]

Especially striking, however, was how critics spoke about the significant features of Mitchell's staging in terms of a sensory, even *sensual,* experience. Mentioning in particular the music of shawms and bagpipes, the offstage drumming and clamor that signified battle engagements, and the repetitive tolling of the bell that hung above the massive upstage doors, they were also alert to other sounds: the rushing winds and the cries of wolves and dogs baying that echoed the animalistic behavior of the mortals. Repeatedly, reviewers recalled the sound of birdsong heard in the pause before the climactic battle, evoking a natural world that counterpointed the butcheries that would cut off Lancastrian succession. Moreover, Mitchell's staging prompted critics to write their own ethnographies of mise-en-scène: the wood-bark shavings covering a rough-boarded floor, the upstage barn doors closed with a huge iron bar and dominated by a fading Bayeux tapestry-like image of St. George, and the equally faded banners, hanging right and left stage, emblazoned with the cross of St. George—signs of the realm as slaughterhouse, a farmyard milieu in which the characters themselves have become the dragons of a lost English Eden, where falling leaves, swirling snow, and a single pine tree mark seasonal cycles and the passage of time.[24] Once again, Brecht offers a useful gloss: "Our enjoyment of old plays becomes greater, the more we can give ourselves up to the new kind of pleasures better suited to our time. To that end we need to develop the historical sense . . . into a real sensual delight. When our theatres perform plays of other periods they like to annihilate distance, fill in the gap, gloss over the differences. But what comes then of our delight in comparisons, in distance, in dissimilarity—which is at the same time a delight in what is close and proper to ourselves?"[25]

Clearly missing the familiar spectacle of royal packaging, Benedict Nightingale cites the irony of the play's subtitle ("The Battle for the Throne") in relation to the item of furniture to which it refers: "what the characters battle to obtain is a squat, chunky lump, more desirable than the wooden chairs beside it only because it has arms and some rudimentary carving at the top. It goes very well with the crown, which is a flimsy band of metal with a tiny cross pathetically protruding from its front."[26] But whereas Nightingale silently evoked Peter Brook to read the production's "down-at-heel" approach as "rough theater," others aligned Mitchell's simplified, near-diagrammatic stage space with the stark, emblematic staging of medieval morality plays.[27] That connection was especially obvious in the play's allegorical signature, the molehill scene, in which Henry VI wears a symbolic crown of thorns and in which the corpses of the father killed by his son and the son killed by his father are represented by the roses of the opposing faction. As Paul Taylor writes, "when murdering kin stare with horror at what they are holding in their hands, the fragile beauty of the flower brings home . . . its incongruity as the logo for war and butchery."[28]

Further signs of that incongruity appeared in the production's strong religious overtones, enhanced by anthems and chants sung in Latin, and in a series of powerful stage images juxtaposing Catholic ritual, ceremony, and gesture with rituals of killing. All wear armor over a kind of monastic smock that becomes increasingly broken down, stained with mud and blood, as if to symbolize the nobles' desecration of the religious ideals they pretend to espouse. Yet these warriors retain some residual memory of the Christian idealism that they constantly violate: Lancastrians and Yorkists alike swear oaths on a Bible placed on a small table, each calling for God to sanction the cyclical blood revenges that pattern the action. And, in an extraordinary moment, both sides become their own clergy as they kneel before the weathered, broken-down icon of St. George, joining together briefly to sing a Latin anthem at the walls of Coventry before drums interrupt the chant and they hack each other to pieces. If there is a presiding deity here, he exists only in the memory that links Henry V to St. George, a memory far in the past that emphasizes how, in a war that has degenerated into personal vendettas, national interests are increasingly overlooked.[29] To drive the point home, the clergy themselves enact their own rituals at the edges of the action. After York's assassination on the molehill, a priest kneels and prays silently at a tiny double-doored shrine containing a pietà icon, in which the Virgin's head, wreathed with holly leaves and red berries, affords a single spot of bright color in the production's otherwise monochromatic palette; the priest carries a bowl, which catches the blood dripping from York's (unseen) head on the battlements, perhaps collecting relics of his martyrdom, either for posterity or out of his own self-interest. Similarly, a half-naked man kneels to pray before the shrine in the French scene, chanting in Latin throughout the action, as though to mark the difference between one nation and another, between faith and its absence.

Another sense in which the production engages with history or, perhaps more appropriately, enables spectators to fix its theatrical signs in relation to what Janet Staiger calls an "historical real" is by situating its aura of authenticity in relation to other texts and discourses.[30] One of these is the discourse of art history. The figure of Bruegel's *Dulle Griet,* her eyes flashing fire and carrying a long sword, graces the program cover as the production's apocalyptic "muse," and several other details depicting monstrous creatures from the same painting appear on its inner pages, signs of a world gripped by terror. Not only do the painting's browns and rusts echo in the rough-timbered set and the armor, but Mad Meg's costume—armor worn over a loose undergarment—appears to have inspired the costume worn by Yorkists and Lancastrians alike. Even Queen Margaret, whose white smock and cropped hair enhances her resemblance to Henry VI, wears laced-up boots, marking her aggressive, even transgressive, behavior. A kind of sixteenth-century *Guernica,* Bruegel's painting, which represents the horrors of foreign occupation during the religious wars between Flemish patriots and Spanish soldiers, seems an especially appropriate emblem for this performance, not only because it documents a history that negotiates between that of Shakespeare's play and contemporary genocidal struggles but also because its representational style echoes that of a medieval mystery play.[31]

Two other intertexts are equally crucial to mapping the production's intersections with early modern history. Although this is only a conjecture, it seems probable that some of the readings Jonathan Firth mentions were *The Paston Letters,* four excerpts of which appear in the program.[32] In one, John Paston, the head of the family and a major figure in Norfolk, writes to his brother about the September 1471 outbreak of plague ("the most universal death that ever I knew in England") and warns him "to be careful of your behaviour and especially of your language, so that henceforth no man may perceive by your language that you favour any person contrary to the King's pleasure." In another Margaret Paston writes to her husband, soliciting his help in obtaining "cross-bows and grappling irons to bind them with, and quarrels [metal arrows] . . . pole-axes . . . and as many jacks as you may" so as to fortify her house. And in a second letter to John, dated October 27, 1465, Margaret writes of the destruction of Hellesdon Manor by the Duke of Suffolk's men:

> [They] ransacked the church and bore away all the goods that were left there, both of ours and of our tenants, and even stood upon the high altar and ransacked the images and took away those that they could find. . . . As for lead, brass, pewter, iron, doors, gates and other stuff of the house, men from Costessey and Cawston have it, and what they might not carry away they have hewn asunder in the most spiteful manner.

The final excerpt, from John Paston II to his mother, lists the nobles and esquires who lost their lives at the Battle of Barnet and, after reporting that

*Dulle Griet*, by Pieter Bruegel the Elder. Photograph courtesy of Museum Mayer van den Bergh, Antwerp, Belgium. Copyright IRPA-KIK, Brussels.

Queen Margaret, Henry VI, soldier and Edward, Prince of Wales, prepare for battle. Ruth Mitchell, Jonathan Firth, Tam Williams and Tom Walker in *Henry VI: The Battle for the Throne*, dir. Katie Mitchell. Photograph courtesy of The Shakespeare Birthplace Trust, Stratford-upon-Avon.

"the Queen Margaret is verily landed with her son in the West Country, and I believe that tomorrow or else the next day the King Edward will depart from here towards her to drive her out again," expresses a somewhat uneasy providentialism: "God has shown Himself marvellously like Him that made all things and can undo again when He pleases, and I can think that in all likelihood He will show Himself as marvellous again, and that in short time." Appropriately, given Mitchell's emphasis on the relations between secular and sacred histories and on how religious sanctions are brought forward to justify familial revenge, these voices are juxtaposed, however ironically, to selections from Ecclesiastes: "To every thing there is a season, and a time to every purpose under the heavens . . . A time to love, and a time to hate; a time of war, and a time of peace"; and "One generation passeth away, and another generation cometh: but the earth abideth for ever. . . . The thing that hath been, it is that which shall be; and that which is done is that which shall be done: and there is no new thing under the sun."

### Material Women

If Mitchell's staging gave the events related in the *Paston Letters* a precisely sustained theatrical life, the balanced phrases of the Ecclesiastes poet—"A time to be born, and a time to die . . . A time to weep . . . a time to mourn"—offer a kind of mantra for the production, made intensely visible in the ritual ceremonies that accompanied each death, beginning with that of York's youngest son, Rutland. Dressed in black, her head covered by a pall reminiscent of those worn by Muslim women, a woman enters and begins to chant, a cappella, a *miserere;* the lament is taken up by the noble warriors and a priest, and together they raise Rutland up and lead him off the stage, through the audience. Following York's death, the procession recurs: as the smell of incense again fills the theater, this time the chant is a *kyrie,* and the woman holds in her hand the bloodied napkin with which Margaret has taunted York. Similarly, after Henry VI's murder, she carries a feather and a rosary, signs of his failed pacifist regime. After each death, a small cross of ragged sticks bound together and bearing a red or white rose is placed in the rim of earth framing the playing space; at play's end, thirteen frail crosses are all that remain.

Setting Mitchell's strategies beside those of Matthew Warchus's mainstage *Henry V* highlights how each director incorporated tropes of memorialization and images of traumatic memory. Using *Henry V*'s previous theatrical and cinematic histories as touchstones, Warchus's staging explored how Henry's life and his history has become a national—and theatrical—myth.

From time to time, an onstage audience, primarily of women and boys dressed in 1940s costumes, gathered behind red-velvet-roped stanchions familiar from museum displays to listen to Henry's famously rousing speeches. Agincourt's battle, played out on a steeply raked platform inscribed with the dates of Henry's birth and death (1387–1422), appeared to be taking place across his gravestone. Scribes seated at each side of the platform wrote the battle into chronicle, while rows of poppies surrounding the platform conflated two very different histories—those of Agincourt and World War I—into one. In this *Henry V,* women and children have a liminal status: consigned to the margins of the stage, they bear witness to the wartime losses of husbands and fathers; simultaneously, however, their silence in the face of Henry's rhetoric appears to acknowledge, even sustain, the impression that his words have become synonymous with patriotic and national agendas and with educational protocols.[33] Warchus's representation of Agincourt recounts a history of great deeds enacted and recorded by men, one in which the echo of Flanders Field appears as an entirely gratuitous overlay, an attempt to collapse war into a universal phenomenon.

By contrast, Mitchell's ceremonial processions of mourners and emblematic crosses not only make the universal particular—both in historical and theatrical terms—but also offer a more precisely articulated critique. Continuing its debt to Brechtian techniques of distantiation, the performance stages a tension between the actors' dignity and the characters' lack of it: whereas the *characters* repeatedly mock and insult the dying, the actors, stepping out of their characters and allegiances with kinship, join together as mourners to eulogize the dead.[34] Curiously, only one critic, Peter Holland, noted that it is a *woman* who leads these processions.[35] Yet to me, as to Holland, including women's *voices* as well as presences seemed one of the production's most crucial, and resonant, choices. On the one hand, such inclusion clearly marks their *exclusion* from a history that centers on retelling and memorializing masculine deeds. On the other, in that these moments open up a potential spectatorial position for women on an otherwise homosocial stage, they work not only to give weight and value to women's experience of war but to evoke connections between the dramatic situations crafted by Shakespeare and those recorded and pictured in contemporary news stories about Yugoslavia.[36]

Perhaps the best way of marking the difference between each production's gender politics would be to say that whereas *Henry V* stages a phallic war, one enhanced by spectacular tableaux that, as Holland notes, might have come from a *Boys' Own* history book,[37] *Henry VI: The Battle for the Throne* stages an erotic one. In part, the latter's perspective derives from a scripted emphasis on the dangers of femininity, especially insofar as it mars the war-like man. Although, as Jean Howard and Phyllis Rackin observe, that po-tential threat is not as fully developed in *3 Henry VI* as it will be in Shakespeare's later plays (notably *1 Henry IV, Henry V,* and *Troilus and Cres-sida*), it undergirds the play's central domestic relationship, that between Henry VI and Margaret, and is crucial to understanding Margaret's contra-dictory ideological position. "The scandal," Howard and Rackin write, " . . . is not that a woman is a general but that a man, and an anointed king to boot, can perform none of the actions expected of father and king. He is less fit to rule than his French-born wife."[38] Set beside Henry's quiet, rational, near-androgynous presence, Margaret has often appeared, in the theater as well as in critical discourse, as the "she-wolf" warrior queen or "monstrous" mother, an early study for the transgressive Lady Macbeth. A small, slight figure, Mitchell's Margaret (Ruth Mitchell) plays against this Amazonian stereotype: although perceived by the other characters as undermining the Lancastrian dynasty, she becomes its most aggressive and eloquent defender, upholding her son's claim to the throne. Driven by her knowledge of what she will lose if she does not look out for herself, all her energies appear di-rected toward preserving her son and toward her own sense of national in-terests: when, just before his death on the molehill, York turns on Margaret, she crosses quickly to stand in front of Ned, protecting him from York's curses; later, shackled to a tree, she listens helplessly to a son who borrows her language to taunt the Yorkist brothers and swoons as they turn on him with their swords.

Elsewhere, however, Mitchell's staging represents war as a homosocial, even homoerotic, affair. Here, Klaus Theweleit provides a useful gloss on Shakespeare's play and on this performance. Observing that the need to conquer femininity and the feminine undergirds the culture of war, Theweleit observes how the "idea of 'woman'" merges with representations of violence, a violence that stems, in his view, from a fear of dissolution through union with a woman and thus propels man—or, to evoke Julia Kristeva, abjects him—into a homosocial relation with other men.[39] Time after time in Mitchell's *Henry VI*, the nobles cling to each other as they die in one another's arms: Clifford cuts the white-robed young Rutland's throat during a smiling, *sotto voce* embrace; later, as Edward and his broth-ers drag Clifford's body center stage to mock his corpse, Richard caps their elaborate cruelties with a kiss before slinging him over his shoulder. Fi-nally, at Henry VI's murder, Richard draws his dagger, runs at Henry and sits astride his struggling figure, killing him in an orgy of sexual violence. Costumed, like Rutland, in a pure white monastic garment that enhances his passive, pacifist stance, Henry represents a feminized presence, and his death at the hands of a Richard who resembles a neo-Nazi skinhead thug offers perhaps the most blatant instance of how Mitchell's staging weaves together masculinist wartime aggression and sexual domination. For me, the moment recalled the climactic sequence of Stanley Kubrick's *Full Metal Jacket* (1987) in which the marines, thinking that they are besieged by an entire enemy force, discover that they are up against a single sniper who turns out to be a young Vietnamese woman. If, as Tania Modleski writes, "the moral of [that] encounter might be summarized, 'We have met the enemy and she is us,'"[40] that "moral" offers an equally pertinent gloss for Mitchell's scenario, in which Henry VI's murder is driven by a need to kill the woman in the king.

An equally apt subtitle for Mitchell's staging of *Henry VI,* in that it evokes the feminine as that which threatens the integrity of the masculine subject, might be "A War of Wives and Roses."[41] Aside from Margaret, the play's most visible wife, the woman who achieves particular prominence is Lady Elizabeth Grey, played by Liz Kettle, who also leads the ritual processions of mourning. Howard and Rackin offer a pertinent reading of the scene in which Edward IV "woos" Lady Grey, mapping how its staging signifies "the new power dynamics that are evolving at Edward's court." Here, rather than surrounding the king at center stage as wise counselors or warlike brothers, Clarence and Richard are consigned to the margins, from which they mock their brother-king as he seduces a woman "who has neither high rank nor great wealth to recommend her as a king's bride."[42] In Mitchell's staging, Edward sits on the crude throne, one leg thrown over its arm, exposing both legs and one thigh, a sign both of his sensualism and his disregard for the crown's meaning. As though showing off his power, Edward snaps his fingers at the black-gowned Grey, who lies prostrate before him as she asks for the return of her lands lost in the war. Reminiscent of a similar encounter between Isabella and Angelo in *Measure for Measure,* the scene unfolds as a clash between two competing discourses in which the tension between masculinity and femininity is played out for Edward's brothers' enjoyment. Crossing casually to the now-kneeling Grey, Edward lifts up his smock as though inviting her to perform fellatio. When she turns away, he forces her onto her back and gets on top of her, holding her arms outstretched at either side to pin her to the floor. But he stops just short of rape: deciding, on the spur of the moment, to make her his queen, Edward yanks her to a standing position, seats her on the throne and jams the crown on her head. Interrupted by the business of war, he then shoos her out the upstage door and follows her, smirking over his shoulder at Clarence and Richard.

Edward IV attempts to rape Lady Elizabeth Grey. Lloyd Owen and Liz Kettle in *Henry VI: The Battle for the Throne,* dir. Katie Mitchell. Photograph courtesy of The Shakespeare Birthplace Trust, Stratford-upon-Avon.

At one performance, Grey still wore the crown at her exit; at another, Edward angrily snatched it back. Either choice reveals how, in appropriating the sacred crown to secular, and sexual, use, Edward initiates a break in the circle of male alliances that has supported the Yorkist claims.[43] Later, his marriage to Lady Grey becomes the sticking point that separates him from his brothers: Clarence refuses Edward's hearty offer to find him a wife; and Richard seeks the crown for himself. As the scene ends, with Edward vowing to keep the realm safe and all kneeling together to swear fealty, Queen Elizabeth glances at her wedding ring and moves aside uneasily, as though knowingly aware, in the face of this brotherly dissension, of the fragile bond it represents.

Significantly, Elizabeth's awareness recurs at the play's close, where once again her presence, voice, and her double role as mourner, energizes *Henry VI*'s final image. In Mitchell's staging, the last scene presents an unsettled, and unsettling, Yorkist victory celebration, powerfully reworked as a kind of epilogue. As the bell tolls once again, this time heralding both the crowning of a new king and the birth of his heir, strong light coming from behind the upstage doors illuminates the stage, where white and red roses are joined together on the Bible, as though anticipating a future Tudor narrative, beyond this play and beyond this stage with its thirteen rude crosses of the war dead. Carrying the young prince in her arms, Queen Elizabeth steps onto the stage from the aisle and stands to one side as Edward turns his back on war, banishes Margaret to France and proclaims domestic peace by calling for "drums, trumpets and shows." Little is made of Richard's Judas kiss, often the centerpiece gesture of this scene, especially in productions that purposefully drive forward to Richard's own play and to history's next chapter. Taking his newborn child in his arms, Edward exits, followed by Clarence and Richard. Alone, her son appropriated by her husband and his brothers, Bess stands, her empty arms extended, looking after the three. Then, kneeling at center stage, she takes off her crown in a gesture reminiscent of Cleopatra who, at Antony's death, proclaims herself "no more but e'en a woman" and who, at her own, figures herself as wife and mother. As Elizabeth begins a final *kyrie,* the others return, as before, to kneel behind her; but it is her solo voice, once again evoking an absent God and backed by the others' humming, that echoes in the darkening space as the lights fade and go out. In these moments, the player Queen, already mourning for the death of a son that is presaged here but will occur (at Richard's hands) in the future, merges with the figure whose voice remains unheard except through prayer—in a language other than English, occurring at the margins of the text. Fused into one, she speaks for the losses of this war and to spectators' own traumatic memories of this, and other, global genocides. Offering a brutal glimpse of a world that consumes women, one in which sado-masochistic behaviors are perpetuated by a male comradeship that allies the father against the mother, Mitchell's staging relegates the signs of that world to an offstage position. What remains at the center is a figure capable of voicing another, equally authoritative history, one that offers to claim, or reclaim, a right to speak, not as an "enemy" but as a survivor.

In conclusion, I would like to add an epilogue of my own, one that brings full circle Mitchell's desire to make her staging of *3 Henry VI* intersect with and address contemporary events. The Commission of Experts appointed in October 1992 by Boutros Boutros-Ghali "to examine and analyze information gathered with a view to providing the Secretary-General with its conclusions on the evidence of grave breaches of the Geneva Conventions and other violations of international humanitarian law committed in the territory of the former Yugoslavia" describes the cultural forces motivating the "ethnic cleansing" occurring in Bosnia-Herzegovina and Croatia:

> [T]he Commission confirms its earlier view that "ethnic cleansing" is a purposeful policy designed by one ethnic or religious group to remove by violent and terror-inspiring means the civilian population of another ethnic or religious group from certain geographic areas. To a large extent, *it is carried out in the name of misguided nationalism, historic grievances, and a powerful driving sense of revenge. This purpose appears to be the occupation of territory to the exclusion of the purged group or groups.*[44]

As Eric Hobsbawm writes, "no serious historian of nations and nationalism can be a committed political nationalist" because "nationalism requires too much belief in what is patently not so." Hobsbaum goes on to quote Renan, the father of European critical discourse on nationalism, who remarked, "Getting its history wrong is part of being a nation."[45] In refusing to stage Shakespeare's history as complicit with such agendas, Mitchell's *Henry VI: The Battle for the Throne* offers a critical rewriting of nationalism's project. At least from where I sat, she seems to have gotten (her) history right.

### Notes

1. Thomas Heywood, *Apology for Actors* (N. Okes, 1612), I: Sig B4r.
2. See, for instance, Jean E. Howard and Phyllis Rackin, *Engendering a Nation: A Feminist Account of Shakespeare's English Histories* (London: Routledge, 1997); and Richard Helgerson, *Forms of Nationhood: The Elizabethan Writing of England* (Chicago: University of Chicago Press, 1992).

3. See Barbara Hodgdon, *The End Crowns All: Closure and Contradiction in Shakespeare's History* (Princeton, NJ: Princeton University Press, 1991), 195.

4. See Barbara Hodgdon, *Henry IV, Part 2* (Manchester: Manchester University Press, 1993), 90–91.

5. See Hodgdon, *End Crowns All,* 87–88. Notably, *The Wars of the Roses* (1986–89), directed by Michael Bogdanov and Michael Pennington for the English Shakespeare Company, represents a staging that goes against the grain of RSC practice.

6. Richard Edmonds, "A Haunting, Horrifying Marathon," *Birmingham Evening Mail,* October 24, 1988. All reviews cited from clippings books in the Shakespeare Centre Library.

7. Kate Alderson, "Interview with Gale Edwards," *Times* [London], April 21, 1995.

8. See Ellen Rooney, "What's the Story? Feminist Theory, Narrative, Address," *Differences* 8.1 (1996): esp. 10–11.

9. Katie Mitchell, quoted in Katie Normington, "Little Acts of Faith: Katie Mitchell's 'The Mysteries,'" *New Theatre Quarterly* 54 (May 1998): 105.

10. See Lisa Jardine, *Reading Shakespeare Historically* (London: Routledge, 1996), 132–33.

11. In addition to her stagings for the RSC, Mitchell has also worked with Paines Plough, The Writers' Company, The Tron Theatre Glasgow, The Abbey Theatre, and The Gate.

12. Marion McMullen, "Hooray Henry," *Manchester Evening News,* September 30, 1994.

13. Alfred Hickling, "Choice Part for Katie," *Yorkshire Post* October 12, 1994.

14. See Hodgdon, *End Crowns All,* 209.

15. See Ian McKellen, *William Shakespeare's Richard III* (London: Doubleday, 1996), 13.

16. See Paul Taylor, "An Eye for the Small Print," *Independent,* October 10, 1994.

17. Bertolt Brecht, *Brecht on Theatre: The Development of an Aesthetic,* ed. and trans. John Willett (New York: Hill and Wang, 1966), 190.

18. Ibid., 195. See also Rod Dungate, "*Henry VI, Part III,*" *Plays and Players* (September-October 1994): 31.

19. Brecht, *Brecht on Theatre,* 190.

20. On Joint Stock, especially in relation to Caryl Churchill's plays, see Helene Keyssar, *Feminist Theatre: An Introduction to Plays of Contemporary British and American Women* (London: Macmillan, 1984), 86–90; and Elin Diamond, *Unmaking Mimesis: Essays on Feminism and Theater* (London: Routledge, 1997), 88.

21. Liz Kettle, quoted in "Killing Fields of England," *Hartlepool Mail,* September 26, 1994. See also Alan Hamilton, "Tewkesbury 1471: Slaughter in the Abbey," *Times* [London], August 4, 1994. Hamilton's article was part of

"The *Times* Guide to Battlefields of Britain," which appeared as Mitchell's production opened.

22. Nick Curtis, "Strife Assurance," *Evening Standard,* October 11, 1994.

23. *Sunday Times,* October 14, 1994.

24. See, for instance, Michael Billington, "The Power, the Pain and the Pity," *Guardian* October 11, 1994; Paul Taylor, "The Horror, the Horror," *Independent,* October 12, 1994; Ann Fitzgerald, "Henry VI," *Stage,* October 1, 1994; and Margaret Ingram, "Young Company in a Restrained *Henry VI* Entitled to Travel Hopefully," *Stratford Herald,* September 18, 1994.

25. Brecht, *Brecht on Theatre,* 276.

26. Benedict Nightingale, "Rough Theatre, Rough Times," *Times* [London] August 12, 1994.

27. Taylor, "The Horror, the Horror."

28. Ibid.

29. See Billington, "The Power, the Pain and the Pity"; and Taylor, "The Horror, the Horror."

30. See Janet Staiger, "Securing the Fictional Narrative as a Tale of the Historical Real," *South Atlantic Quarterly* 88 (Spring 1989): esp. 395–96, 400–402.

31. See Robert L. Delevoy, *Bruegel,* trans. Stuart Gilbert (Cleveland, OH: World Publishing Company, 1959), 70–75.

32. See Norman Davis, ed., *The Paston Letters and Papers of the Fifteenth Century* (Oxford: Clarendon Press, 1971).

33. Such agendas and protocols are not exclusively English. William J. Bennett, the former head of the National Endowment for the Humanities and ex-drug czar, includes Henry V's St. Crispin's Day Speech as an example of perseverance in *The Book of Virtues: A Treasury of Great Moral Stories* (New York: Simon and Schuster, 1993), 514–16. Bennett notes that the speech is the model for football coaches' locker-room addresses to their players, a suggestion appropriated, whether consciously or unconsciously, during the pregame show of the 1997 Super Bowl, in which the speech, as it appears in Kenneth Branagh's 1989 film, appeared on the screen while Branagh's voice-over glossed the pseudo-heraldic insignia of both teams.

34. See Dungate, "*Henry VI, Part III,*" 31.

35. Peter Holland, "In a World with No Use for Goodness," *Times Literary Supplement,* August 26, 1994.

36. For example, the *New York Times International* reported on March 28, 1998, that in Kosovo Province, 5,000 ethnic Albanians buried two men, cousins aged 19 and 21, who were killed during an eleven-hour gun battle between Serbian police officers and ethnic Albanians. The picture accompanying the report shows the two men's bodies in open coffins, draped with Albanian flags and surrounded by some 20 women mourners, some of whom held up photographs of the dead.

37. See Peter Holland's review of *Henry V* in *English Shakespeares: Shakespeare on the English Stage in the 1990s* (Cambridge: Cambridge University Press, 1997), 194–99. See also Nicola Barker, "Not a Trouser in Sight," *Observer,* August 14, 1996.
38. See Howard and Rackin, *Engendering a Nation,* 85–86.
39. Klaus Theweleit is discussed in Tania Modleski, *Feminism Without Women: Culture and Criticism in a "Postfeminist" Age* (New York: Routledge, 1991), 62–63.
40. Ibid., 62.
41. I adapted the title of Carole Woddis's review, "Wars of Wives and Roses," *Glasgow Herald,* September 7, 1994.
42. Howard and Rackin, *Engendering a Nation,* 91–92.
43. Ibid., 93.
44. This document, called the Bassiouni Report, is cited in Beverly Allen, *Rape Warfare: The Hidden Genocide in Bosnia-Herzegovina and Croatia* (Minneapolis, MN: University of Minneapolis Press, 1996), 44 (emphasis added).
45. See Eric Hobsbawm, *Nations and Nationalism Since 1780: Programme, Myth, Reality* (Cambridge: Cambridge University Press, 1990), 12.

# 2

# Recent Australian *Shrews:*
# The "Larrikin Element"

*Penny Gay*

"There is something inescapably antipodean about the style of Gale Edwards' *Shrew,* not least its irreverence, and this, in the centre of the RSC's heartland, in Stratford," wrote the Australian academic and newspaper theater critic, Helen Thomson.[1] She went on to talk about the production's "exaggerations, its colourful vulgarity, its raw emotion." Gale Edwards is the first Australian woman—a double-whammy, this—to direct a play on the Royal Shakespeare Company's main stage—and *this* play, of course, is to modern sensibilities one of the most problematic in the canon. In this essay I will look at the ways in which *The Taming of the Shrew* has been made to speak from an identifiably Australian position, as I believe the RSC's 1995 production does, and what the implications might be for theories of critical appraisal and reception of Shakespearean performance in the late twentieth century.

As in other ex-British colonies, "Shakespeare" in Australia has been an instrument of imperial/patriarchal hegemony—"educative" rather than carnivalesque until, say, the last quarter-century. The Australian Elizabethan Theatre Trust, named after the young queen in the 1950s, was the last in a line of touring companies bringing "the Bard" in traditional "English" style to theaters, church halls, and Mechanics' Institutes all over the country.[2] Following the renaissance of Australian drama in the late 1960s there developed an interest in the possibility for Australian actors to perform classic plays, particularly Shakespeare, in their own idiom. The Nimrod

Theatre in Sydney under John Bell's direction pioneered the use of Australian speech patterns and accent in speaking the Shakespearean text: Bell spoke of the need to find "ways of speaking that will accord with our view of our own society."[3] Bell sought particularly to "localize" Shakespeare's comedies for the obvious reasons that a satirical target will be more easily recognized if it is embodied in a specific cultural referent, and that there are native traditions of comedy in virtually all cultures that can be fruitfully drawn upon. Twenty years later, Bell is still working in this tradition, with a lively awareness of how contemporary Australia defines itself. Here are some characteristic terms of that self-definition: *larrikinism:* "characteristics of non-conformism, irreverence, impudence" deriving from the nineteenth-century term for young street rowdies,[4] hence other important characteristics: a streetwise relation with the world and especially with authority, mateship (a culture of male bonding based on the pioneer bushman's ethos), egalitarianism, hedonism, and an emphasis on physicality.

John Bell remarked in a 1996 directors' forum in Sydney with Michael Bogdanov that he liked being labeled a "vulgar" director of Shakespeare, if that meant uncovering the carnival and music-hall elements in the plays. In Bell's adoption of the "larrikin" position characteristic of the Aussie self-definition and in his reference to Australian cultural history there is an emphasis on *working-class* origins and energy, which accords with white Australians' knowledge of how we got to be here, on the edge of the civilized world.

If I call this consciousness "postcolonial" it is not without an awareness of the conflicted nature of that term in current critical discourse. The dominant high culture of white Australia is still Anglo-Celtic; European and Asian immigration has had little effect, so far, on (for example) the makeup of the state-subsidized theater companies. Aboriginal art in all forms is a growing force, but it resists assimilation into the mainstream culture. White Australia is a "settler" culture, only now accepting its guilt for its treatment of the original inhabitants of the land; but it is also, and peculiarly, locally, a country founded on the forced immigration of convicts—the rejected dregs of British society, who must be hidden away at the bottom of the world, silenced through distance. When the descendants of that huge cohort of rejects found their voice—and their feet on the streets of Sydney and in the bush—they defined themselves as essentially resistant to figures of authority. This is not to say that those locally in authority did not reproduce the institutions of empire—hence the invocation of Shakespeare in official culture and education throughout the first 150 years of white history—but the white subaltern class was much more ambivalent about authority and set about forging an alternative identity.

Following Stephen Slemon's reclaiming of "that neither/nor territory of white settler-colonial writing . . . as a groundwork for certain modes of anti-colonial work,"[5] I want to employ the metaphor of the "naughty but favored child" (rather than "subaltern")[6] to describe the resistant attitude of Australian-born white settlers to the authority structures of the British empire. The Australian "larrikin" identity thus formed contests the center/ periphery binarism of colonialism, insisting on the integrity and right to speak of these particular subaltern individuals and their alternative modes of social organization and expression. This is where a strong working-class culture, such as that drawn on by John Bell, is a powerful instrument of disruption and revision. Nevertheless, it is clear that the culture of resistance thus created in Australia was contaminated by that most insidious of imperialist institutions, patriarchy. Put simply, Australian "larrikin" culture is and has been, since its first cheeky steps on antipodean soil, overwhelmingly male and masculinist. Any enactment of gender relations that claims to be speaking from an Australian position has to take this historical situation as a given.

It is easy to see how the uneven battle between Katherine and Petruchio and Baptista has particular resonances for any (post)colonial society, since the actions and attitudes of the authoritative males (Baptista, Petruchio) are analogous to those of empire-building colonial founders, treating the feminine Other as an object simply to be taken over, (ab)used, governed. Thus the categories of women and indigenous people are conveniently conflated. The question for contemporary Australian productions of the play is what to make of the figure of Katherine given, on the one hand, the dominant masculinist ethos of "mateship," and on the other hand, a cultural ideal of resistance and egalitarianism. I would argue that any fully theorized postcolonial production of *The Shrew* must in some way subvert Katherine's "submission" at the end of the play, since it signifies (done "straight") submission both to patriarchy and to text-as-imperial-law, "Shakespeare" as hypostatized author of the words that valorize the dominant culture.[7] In the remainder of this essay, I assess three recent productions in this light.

## The Bell Shakespeare Company, 1994[8]

John Bell insists that his attitude to Shakespeare is "reverent,"[9] but by this he means that he will not cut or alter the text, except where necessary for practical reasons: the Shakespearean text, in all its difference, must be allowed a "fair go" (another Australian national belief). But his productions are anything but reverent. Bell has commented frequently on his conviction that the plays will work for a contemporary Australian audience only if they are cleared of the accretions of deadly tradition. He believes that directors must find in them issues and tensions that a modern Australian audience can recognize. Of his 1994 production of *The Shrew,* for example, he observes,

> One has to come to terms with the fact that there is a wide variety of Australian accents. That's to do with region, with income, with schooling. We can't pretend that we're the egalitarian society we often paint ourselves as. So there is room in Shakespeare's hierarchical structures to find Australian counterparts. . . . I chose not to do it as *commedia dell'arte,* or a period farce or anything that is remote from us. I thought that if the play is worth doing, it's worth looking at right here and now and saying, well, what are our values? Do women have the freedom they want, yet? Do we still think about money and property more than relationships?[10]

In this spirit Bell opened the performance not with the Christopher Sly induction but with a 15-minute "audience warmup" of the sort experienced by television sitcom audiences. There was a "chook raffle" (actors ad-libbed in the audience selling tickets for a genuine frozen chicken, to be picked up by the lucky winner at the end of the show); a theater organ arose from the pit to entertain us with banal tunes; there was a mind-reading act, and a talent show—a boy planted in the audience got up and performed (in Sydney at least) a creditable tap routine. The audience soon recognized that they had strayed not into a theater but into that bastion of working-class Aussie culture, the Returned Soldiers League [now generally known as "leagues"] club. Vulgarity reigned: we were prepared for a world which was crass and carnivalesque—and *not quite our own,* middle-class and cultured intellectuals that we were (Bell made the justifiable assumption that most of his audience would only have been in such a "club" in the company of parents or grandparents). As one critic remarked, "Bell has translated high culture, the theatre of the Bard, back into popular entertainment"[11]—and it was genuinely and unpatronizingly funny: the middle-class audience was invited painlessly and pleasurably to revisit its roots.

This opening positioned the audience to accept the story that was then performed for them as one dealing primarily with issues of class, not gender. Baptista and his family live "somewhere between the Gold Coast and Sylvania Waters"—"where you find men dealing in money and property all the time, where they don't seem to go to work, where there's a lot of leisure and a lot of sunshine"[12]—their lifestyle all vulgar ostentation and consumerism (mobile phones and computers featured as props). Katherine (Essie Davis) was clearly alienated by this relentless superficiality, as her sober black costume (variously described as by reviewers as grunge and gothic) showed against the garish colors of the others' expensive but inelegant outfits. Davis had played a very moving Juliet for the Bell company in the previous season and does not fit the physical assumptions usually made about Katherine as a gawky or raging termagant (the actress playing Bianca was, in fact, taller). By contrast, Petruchio (Christopher Stollery—a brilliantly mordant contemporary Hamlet in 1992–3) was tall and well-built, with a natural swagger. Most remarkable was the class coding suggested by his costume: long hair and beard, jeans and leather jacket, identifying him, as Bell described it, as a "Nimbin hippie"—i.e., a drop-out from the materialist society represented by Padua/the Gold Coast. He later arrived for his wedding in charity-shop ill-fitting tails and topper—a critique of the rituals of wealthy Australian high society, aping the British imperialists. When he and Katherine arrived home after the wedding, the audience saw a garage-style junk-heap in which could be spotted the ruins of a young Aussie materialist's lifestyle: a pink Volkswagen Beetle, a surfboard, skateboard, etc. The hippie commune was populated by an assortment of misfits, which John Bell described as "like Robin Hood's gang," outsiders to society's conventional expectations, who were looked after by the charismatic larrikin Petruchio (in fact the iconic Australian bushranger Ned Kelly and his gang might have been a more appropriate analogy). Thus Bell established very strongly what Stollery also said he was looking for, a Petruchio whom the audience could like, indeed prefer to the soulless display of Baptista's household: a "disarming" character, said Stollery,[13] he also is "humbled" at the end, he has learned that his "blokiness" isn't good enough.

Bell pulled no punches with the "taming" scenes, however (except that he insisted that Petruchio never uses actual violence). One could see the logic: Kate was being deprived of the material goods that she had taken for granted and was being taught that the behavior of a spoiled child would not do in the alternative society she had now joined. But the audience routinely gasped at the extent of this forced re-education and her bewilderment and despair: she stood center stage and wept as her food and expensive clothes were taken from her. She was left wearing the now soiled and torn wedding dress, which took on the appearance of a hippie's Indian-style long dress. At the end of the "sun and moon" scene Petruchio gently placed his leather jacket round her shoulders, thus signifying that she had joined the gang of outlaws (though it was he who had "snapped" in this scene—the game had gone on too long. But, being a "bloke" he had to indicate this through an inarticulate gesture, said Stollery). Together, and to looks of horror from the expensively dressed guests, they arrived at Baptista's party. Much of Katherine's long speech of "submission" was directed at the other males at the party, who were vulgarly drunk and clearly undeserving of respect, despite the fact that they held the positions of economic power in this society. A long pause followed Kate and Petruchio's exit from the stage (Kate leading); as one reviewer noted, "The deflation of the male braggadocios is the play's final note. Gone are male bombast and arrogance, bets have been made and lost, the hangover is to come."[14] Thus Hortensio's final comment, "Thou hast tamed a cursed shrew," had no weight at all with the audience—a repulsive figure with his heavy gold chains and beer belly, he clearly had no understanding of the emotional pact that had been hammered out between the two "drop-outs" with their superior conception of social responsibility. Bell's production had made a valid point through satire about some aspects of contemporary Australian society.

Nevertheless, as far as the actors were concerned, the gender issues would not go away. Essie Davis had serious reservations about accepting the part: "I didn't know if I could say those last lines." Finally she decided to "play it straight." "In the end it will be up to the audience to decide if 'it's wonderful because Kate is fulfilled and happy,' or 'it's terrible because her husband has broken her spirit.'"[15] "We fought all the time [in rehearsal] and life was a mirror of the play for a while," Davis said. "Like our parts, we have been through the gates of hell, but finally reached a balance," said Stollery. Yet they still perceived their roles differently. "For Davis, 24, hers is a serious role without any funny moments and leaves her feeling completely drained. Stollery, 28, however, rolls around in the comedy of his part, relishing each laugh he earns from the audience."[16] Nothing new here, and Davis's comment in an interview is revealing: "It's so strange even being one of four women in a fairly male company. In a way this rehearsal process has been quite a map of the play, in terms of fighting for some things and giving in some of the time."[17] She gave in, ultimately, to a left-liberal Australian male director's belief (not unusual in leftist thinking) that class issues subsume gender issues.

The production was a critical success as well as a popular one. Its reading of contemporary Australian society was recognizable but unthreatening, though one or two female critics still expressed disquiet about Kate's final speech, wanting at least a tongue-in-cheek rendition from such a spirited modern woman: they "left the theatre feeling the same sense of bewilderment that is expressed by the rest of the cast in the final tableaus."[18]

## The Queensland Theatre Company, 1989[19]

Aubrey Mellor's production also began with a very cheeky localization: Christopher Sly, a country bumpkin, was visiting the 1988 Brisbane World

Expo, and found himself, drunk, outside the Italian pavilion. His indignant line to the Hostess, "the Slys are no rogues" was followed by "we came with the First Fleet"—a particularly revealing genealogy, since most First Fleeters were convicts. John Wood's Petruchio was "crucial" casting, according to Mellor: he has "a long tradition of Oz chauvinist roles together with genuine warmth and appeal and masculinity."[20] A burly "bloke," he is attractive without being conventionally good-looking. His Petruchio's household was "totally male and dressed in Brisbane Broncos footy jerseys . . . [and included] a lot of male bonding rituals." Mellor thereby foregrounded the action of the play as being more to do with problematic constructions of masculinity (such as may be found in the Australian mythology of "mateship") than with the position of women. "I wanted Petruchio to learn something during the action," he said.

Inside the pavilion Sly found himself in Renaissance Padua, a "very Australian version" of the old continent's culture, with a huge and vulgar David on one side of the stage and a Venus on the other. The Taming—Sly's dream—was played as the *commedia dell'arte* farce, with the Ocker Sly becoming the dream-Petruchio. Mellor's solution to the play's problematic gender politics was to have Kate and Petruchio attracted to each other as "sparring partners" in a "natural" war of the sexes "which should not create enmity." This is a common enough reading of the play, though it downplays the distressing sadism of the taming/torture scenes at Petruchio's house. What is more interesting is what Mellor did with the end of the play, beginning with Petruchio's instruction to Kate to "throw under foot" the prized new cap. The pause before she obeyed was indicative of disbelief and sad disappointment, and the speech that she then gave in response to his demand that she tell the women of their duty to their husbands was delivered by Victoria Longley as a speech in which love dies. "She felt betrayed," said Veronica Neave, who played Bianca.[21] According to Mellor, "the focus went strongly onto Petruchio as Kate's speech progressed and it became clear that he had turned her into a hausfrau—her damaged clothes by now a mousy color. Petruchio's [Sly's] nightmare peaked. . . ." The Folio text was cut after "may it do him ease." Mellor claims that "[t]he biggest problem for me with the play is that he says 'Kiss me Kate' following her famous submission speech . . . the original [ending] can only be tragic, unless Kate is a masochist." So Kate's "speech was completed with a follow-through of stunned silence after she leant her forehead to Petruchio's foot; the moment was held and disturbed music underlined it before Petruchio pulled away and retreated," ashamed, "leaving Kate then head up [with] all the others looking at the gesture" before she exited separately. Petruchio had clearly lost his marriage, though he'd won the wager.

The stage silently cleared leaving Petruchio, now Sly, asleep, until Kate re-entered, doubling as Sly's wife visiting the Brisbane Expo, and speaking lines partly from the 1594 text, partly Shakespearean pastiche (composed by Mellor and members of the cast in improvisations up to opening night). She was "furious at his all-night binge," and her "restoration to the sparring partner [who] had captured his affections caused him to utter with great relief 'Why there's a wench. Come on and kiss me, Kate,'" before moving "gently" (according to the promptbook) into "Good morrow Kate, for that's your name I hear," and the "courtship" scene began again. The pair "improvised a dance together which developed from playfully butting and shoving each other as they cuffed, embraced, took the lead from each other, etc."

Mellor's audacious metatheatrical device here did allow the audience to have their cake and eat it too: to experience, in Victoria Longley's performance of Kate's speech, the twentieth-century truth that a successful marriage cannot be based on such an unequal relationship, then to see "love reborn" in just such a "rocky" marriage, as Sly and his wife use the play's sexually charged language to carry them offstage to their private outback world *playing* Kate and Petruchio (wherever that might lead them—from private intimacy to the image of many an Australian marriage in which the husband still periodically wishes he was one of the boys). Nevertheless the focus of this "irreverent, unsubtle, and vulgar" production belonged to Petruchio and a specifically Australian construction of masculinity: "boaster and braggart" supported by "all the camaraderie of male society."[22]

## Royal Shakespeare Company, 1995

Much of what I have just described of Aubrey Mellor's 1989 Brisbane production may sound familiar to those who saw Gale Edwards's 1995 production for the RSC (in London from April 1996). This hugely popular production also used the Sly induction (considerably cut) as a way of saying that the Taming—a *commedia* farce—was the drunk male's macho dream; it also concluded the Taming at the end of Kate's speech, cutting the men's responses as a shamed Petruchio metamorphosed back into Christopher Sly. Katherine/Mrs. Sly returned, and in a silent gesture the two were reconciled. Edwards had in fact talked to Mellor "at length" about the play, which she was initially reluctant to take on, and she clearly took her basic ideas about the framing and the play-within from him. But the mood of Edwards's ending was very different from that of Mellor's: Edwards's Kate, Josie Lawrence, wearily accepted Sly's kneeling embrace, like a mother with a froward child, as she looked to the stormy heavens as if to say "How long, O Lord, how long?" (Edwards had first come to the attention of the RSC directorate with her powerful production of *Saint Joan* in the West End in 1994.)

I shall describe some details of Edwards's production in order to show their congruence with the recognizably Australian aspects of the productions I have discussed and to show where, as a modern woman, she diverged from the work of her male compatriots, in what becomes finally an even more telling postcolonial reading of the play. But I need to begin by recounting the story of Gale Edwards's appointment to the role of director in the main house of the RSC. About to leave England, she answered a call from the director of the most prestigious classical company in the English-speaking world who offered her *The Taming of the Shrew*, take it or leave it. This was her one chance. Adrian Noble clearly wanted to indicate his and the RSC's liberal credentials. Edwards's comment on this is acute: "People don't think, gee, a man is going to direct *King Lear*, this'll be really good because a man is directing. . . . It's what part of [*The Shrew*] is about, isn't it? How strange it is to be a strong woman."[23]

Edwards's "first impulse was to reject the offer," said Mellor, but once she had accepted she was determined to treat it without simplifying the issues for a modern audience:[24] "Our Kate is a highly brilliant, beautiful and intelligent woman. Both she and Petruchio exist in a world of buffoons. Yes, her behaviour is shrewish, but it is also spontaneous and violent and naughty, and wicked and mischievous and confronting"—very much that of the brilliant child revolting against the authoritative parent, or the larrikin young colony against the masters of Empire. This is implicit in Edwards's further comment: "That black, black view of the play with Petruchio as such a horrible bastard and a Kate learning how to love violence and oppression would be completely abhorrent . . . not to mention completely unintelligent."[25]

The production began with a storm, and the storm-laden cyclorama remained throughout the play, a threatening presence; further thunder and lightning accompanied Kate's/Mrs Sly's reentrance and the mimed end of the play. This is no Utopian (or rural) comic vision of marriage, but a slice of social realism, the everyday world of the drunken yobbo Christopher Sly, who has his dream of macho domination turn into nightmare as he realizes how dependent he is on the strength and support of his wife. The Taming dream-play took place literally within a threateningly red proscenium-arch frame that was flown in as the dream began. A circus band marched through the set (and did so again on several occasions). The costumes of the characters were a bizarre mix of styles and periods, with a strong subliminal suggestion of *commedia dell'arte,* but a deliberate lack of consistency. This is characteristic of the dream-world, which refuses historical specificity and easy narrativization.

The casting of Josie Lawrence and Michael Siberry set a stamp on the production that cannot be ignored. Both tall, handsome, well-built people, with a strong stage presence, they are not of the usual RSC mold. Josie Lawrence comes from a very successful career in provincial and non-mainstream companies, and particularly from television comedy and improv shows. Michael Siberry is an Australian who has worked in England for a considerable time, but who began his career in the State Theatre Company of South Australia (Gale Edwards's home state). He was able to draw on a recognizably "Ocker" (vulgarly Australian) quality in his playing that is foreign to many RSC leading men. He was violent and rowdy without the class connotations that such behavior elicits in England: loud on the outside, but a softy on the inside—if only he can allow himself to be. This was also the line taken by Christopher Stollery for Bell and John Wood for Mellor.

Whereas Petruchio/Sly was able to join the boys' gang of buffoons in the wedding scene in his insultingly outrageous costume (just as it was all too easy to join in the wager at the end), Lawrence's Katherine remained relatively plainly dressed, first in midnight blue, then in a conventional white wedding gown, then in the red of power, which was finally covered up with a dark greatcoat and shawl as the dream-Katherine metamorphosed into the real world's (less apparently powerful) Mrs. Sly. Puzzlement, alienation, and anger were the notes of Lawrence's Katherine, a conventional shrew only in the action sequences (fights with Petruchio and her sister), where her frustrated energies found outlet. In the wedding scene, with everyone but Kate and Petruchio wearing black and carrying umbrellas (another surreal touch), she reacted strongly and with increasing anger to his speech "I will be master of what is mine own," repeating with incredulity, " . . . 'stuff'?!" Increasingly, from the first courtship scene onwards, Edwards ensured that Lawrence as the feminine Other would disturb the master's fantasy of ownership and conquest; and could never, in fact, be fully controlled by his dream.

In Part 2, which began with the arrival at Petruchio's house, we saw the dream beginning to turn to nightmare. The Lord's hunting retainers now became Petruchio's retainers, played and costumed as gothicly grotesque clowns—the fantasy of colonial-style domination continued to reproduce itself, but it was beginning to get out of control. Katherine arrived filthy and obviously distressed; she hid under the table, alienated and frightened, while Petruchio and the ghoulish servants threw food around.

The images of Katherine's realistic maltreatment became more graphic. While a cocky Petruchio was explaining to the audience "Thus have I politically begun my reign," Kate entered upstage and sat, framed by theatrical wings that formed a small prison-like cell, looking upstage and away in an attitude of misery. She held this pose during the next long scene (4.2) which was played downstage between Tranio, Hortensio, Bianca, Lucentio and the rest: the superficial *commedia* buffoons. A telling cut of one line (from Grumio) gave Katherine her own soliloquy, "The more my wrong, the more his spite appears." She begged Grumio for food pitiably, as though to a jailer. Near breaking point, her "I will be free in words" was ignored by Petruchio, who proceeded to rip the new red gown off a lifelike mannequin as though he were violating it—or her. Katherine walked over to the naked mannequin and sat on the floor by it, weeping, thus clearly associating herself with its violation. At the end of this scene she was left alone and she gave a determined nod, as if to say "I know what must be done"[26]—as we saw in the "sun and moon" scene, where with somewhat amused exasperation she humored Petruchio. Finally they did kiss for the first (and only) time, having found a temporary plateau of mutual pleasure in game-playing.

Edwards's directorial emphases and the strong presence of Josie Lawrence provided a psychologically convincing and realistic portrayal of the story of one woman married to a boor. The final scene clinched it. On Petruchio's first command Kate entered smilingly, but caught sight of the wager money as she exited, and registered the real situation—that she is an object of male exchange still. On the second command, "Off with that bauble—throw it underfoot" she demurred silently, begging not to have to spoil her new cap, but finally, doggedly, did it. The third command brought her to the point of no return. Josie Lawrence's Katherine threw Petruchio a look as if to say "I'll tell you what you want to hear, but you won't like it," and as she walked slowly downstage center, her delivery of the speech created the impression that she was gathering back into herself all the proud subjectivity that had been beaten out of her in the "taming" section of the play. Much of the speech was addressed to Petruchio with a mixture of angry contempt and despairing bitterness. As she offered her hand in angry challenge to Petruchio, he came across and knelt in mirror image, facing her, but he could not look at her or touch her—like Mellor's Petruchio he was clearly ashamed of what he had brought to pass. This tableau was held as the stage was cleared of the other characters and their proscenium-arch set; then Katherine exited upstage through a miniature proscenium-arch, casting one contemptuous look at Petruchio as she left. He appealed with one hand toward her, the money from the wager spilling onto the ground, then collapsed forward into the fetal position of the drunken Christopher Sly. The hunters and the Lord returned briefly to reclothe him as Sly, speaking some lines from the 1594 *A*

*Shrew,* and as thunder rolled, Lawrence, now in greatcoat and shawl, returned as Sly's wife to take him back home. Still on his knees, he hugged her
remorsefully; she looked up wearily as the lights went down on this tableau.

The effect of cutting all the lines of the Folio text after Kate's "May it do
him ease" was, to my ears, astonishingly powerful. It left the "last word" with
Kate, not with the crass male observers, who, to a man, slunk away. Edwards
then added her own version of the final Sly frame, very different in mood
from that devised by Mellor and his actors.[27] The focus was absolutely on
the woman from the beginning of her speech to the end of the performance;
although locked into an always-disappointing relation with the masculine—
*her* Other—she *was* "free in words."

"I think the critics who were outraged by it just did not think that a
woman—let alone an Australian woman—should go to work at the RSC
and tamper with Shakespeare. But it is sold out. You can't get a ticket," said
a gleeful Gale Edwards.[28] My own random surveys of members of the audience reveal that the production had many women very excited by its combination of bold theatricality and a powerfully realistic reading of the central
part. Most men were more ambivalent, when not downright condemnatory,
but their critiques were carefully aimed not at the reading of Katherine and
Petruchio's relationship, but at the "stylistic incoherence" of the production.
This is a curiously limited view, in these postmodernist days, of the possibilities of theater to disturb expected responses; these critics apparently *know*
how the play should be done, or "what Shakespeare intended." Most newspaper reviews were, in fact, positive, the notable exceptions being the dis-
proportionately influential male critics of *The Times, The Observer, The
Sunday Times,* and *The Sunday Telegraph.*

In a discussion of Robert Lepage's *Dream*—which was also taken from a
"postcolonial" society, French Canada, to a very problematic "center," London's Royal National Theatre, where it was predictably savaged by the
critics—Barbara Hodgdon points out that the production enacted a carnivalesque resistance: it "yoke[d] divergent cultural materials and identities
into pastiche, collage, and bricolage, [was] oppositional to the grand literary
and theatrical narratives that would draw national and cultural boundaries
around 'Shakespeare' and manage 'his' meanings."[29] Edwards's production
of *The Shrew* is clearly in the same mold. When she began work on the play
she commented in an interview that Australians did have something to offer
on the world stage. The terms in which she defines this indicate the resistant
postcolonial position of her popularly successful production: "Baz
Luhrmann's work [on the films *Strictly Ballroom* and *Romeo and Juliet*] is a
prime example of a new-world energy which is positive, inventive and bold.

Australians might be accused of lacking in finesse—although I don't agree—but we make up for that in passion, bravery and innocence, and that's going to identify our work. . . . Shakespeare wanted his plays to be entertaining, vibrant and provocative."[30]

Edwards's commitment to "provocativeness" might be read as the "favored child" cocking a snook at patriarchal authority through over-the-top comic carnival, an assertion of the validity of popular and working-class modes of performance (no one who saw it could forget Mark Lockyer's Tranio as Gary Glitter/Elvis/Prince). So far it shares in the dominant masculinist Australian ethos of the *larrikin*. But at the same time, and taking "stylistic inconsistency" beyond even this carnivalesque paradigm, Edwards refocused the play so that the feminine, colonized, objectified, and (for a while) silenced Other became the inescapably powerful center, causing a re-siting of all figures of the patriarchal establishment to the margins, and a position of comic—or pathetic—impotence.

## Notes

1. Helen Thomson, "Exuberant Expats Draw British Theatregoers," *The Age* (Melbourne), September 12, 1995, 15.

2. Alan Brissenden details the history of Allan Wilkie's early twentieth-century Australian Shakespearean touring company in "Shakespeare's Australian Travels," *Shakespeare and Cultural Traditions,* ed. Tetsuo Kishi, Roger Pringle, and Stanley Wells (Newark: University of Delaware Press, 1994), 205–15.

3. John Bell, interviewed by David Britton, "The Sound of the Shrew," *ABC Radio 24 Hours,* October 1994, 49.

4. G. A. Wilkes, *A Dictionary of Australian Colloquialisms,* 4th ed., s.v. "larrikin,"(Oxford: Oxford University Press, 1996).

5. Stephen Slemon, "Unsettling the Empire: Resistance Theory for the Second World," in *The Post-colonial Studies Reader,* ed. Bill Ashcroft, Gareth Griffiths, and Helen Tiffin (London: Routledge, 1995), 104. Slemon proposes that "like the term 'patriarchy,' which shares similar problems in definition, the concept of colonialism . . . remains crucial to a critique of past and present power relations in world affairs, and thus to a specifically *post*-colonial critical practice which attempts to understand the relation of literary writing to power and its contestations" (106).

6. Susan Morgan writes, "What kind of aggression is being performed on the insights of the Subaltern Studies group or on Spivak's somewhat different insights when we eliminate the historically located context of meaning for 'subaltern' and read it as an ahistoric category, signifying a generic subordinate or colonized person?" Susan Morgan, *Place Matters,* (New Brunswick:

Rutgers University Press, 1996), 22. Morgan's argument that "it may well be useful to associate concepts with specific histories, theory with place, instead of hungering for 'models' or metaconcepts and metahistories" (23) is particularly valuable to those of us trying to define the work of what Stephen Slemon calls Second-World texts. See Slemon, "Unsettling the Empire," 110.

7. A theoretically "pure" Australian postcolonial production, one that cast Kate as an Aboriginal woman in a 1940s country town, has been to my knowledge attempted only once, in an ambiguous piece of "color-blind" casting, that was tactfully ignored by all critics (director Sue Rider, La Boite Theatre, Brisbane, 1994). With Petruchio as an Aussie "digger" (soldier) embodying the principle of macho mateship, it could have been an inflammatory production, particularly in Queensland, which has a history of racism. But both the director and the audience apparently chose to overlook the challenging image of miscegenation that was implicit in the traditionally lively and comical production. This is an example of what Slemon argues: "The Second-World [i.e., settler] writer, the Second-World text . . . have always been complicit in colonialism's territorial appropriation of land, and voice, and agency, and this has been their inescapable condition even at those moments when they have promulgated their most strident and most spectacular figures of post-colonial resistance." Slemon, "Unsetting the Empire," 110. Performances are of course particular and local texts, and the performance/appropriation of the imperial figure "Shakespeare" has the potential to be *anything* on a spectrum from the most transgressive to the most conservative.

8. This production toured to Newcastle (NSW), Melbourne, Sydney, Canberra, and Perth in a five-month season in repertory with *Macbeth.*

9. Unsourced quotations from John Bell in the material that follows are drawn from a conversation with the author on March 15, 1996.

10. John Bell, "Sound of the Shrew."

11. Marea Mitchell, "From Bell, Silent Treatment is Fun," *The Australian,* May 3, 1994, 15.

12. John Bell, "Sound of the Shrew," Britton interview.

13. Christopher Stollery, interview with the author, January 24, 1996.

14. Marea Mitchell, "Silent Treatment," *The Australian,* 15.

15. Essie Davis, interviewed by Anabel Dean, "Taming of the Shrewd," *Sydney Morning Herald,* June 24, 1994, 20.

16. Catherine Lambert, "The Grungeing of the Shrew," interview with Stollery and Davis, *Sunday Herald Sun* (Melbourne), May 15, 1994, 119.

17. Essie Davis, "Taming of the Shrewd," 20. For the reflections of other women on their experiences playing Kate, see Penny Gay, *As She Like It: Shakespeare's Unruly Women* (New York: Routledge, 1994).

18. Rebecca Clarke, "Accessibility: Again Courtesy of Bell Shakespeare." *Theatre Australasia,* (June 1994): 17.

19. Roger Hodgman's production for the Melbourne Theatre Company in 1991, though heavily conscious of gender issues, avoided direct contemporary confrontation with them by setting the play in the 1950s. The set signaled strongly the American cultural imperialism that Australia along with the rest of the Western world experienced in the 1950s, so that apart from the actors' Australian accents it was impossible to tell if the production was set in Australia (if it was, it was at any rate the Australia of 40 years ago). The actors and director had read with enthusiasm Marilyn French's *Shakespeare's Division of Experience.* This somewhat essentialist reading of Shakespeare and gender issues provided a depoliticized solution or "path through the play." The Sly framework was thus considered not necessary, since what we were to witness was a conflict and rapprochement between "feminine and masculine principles," chaos and order. Nevertheless the play ended with Petruchio and Katherine riding off into a separatist sexual heaven, which left unresolved the questions of what social structure their new-discovered "harmony" was to illuminate, and if they are to be read as "outside the system," rebels, in what way their private contract revises the oppressive relation proposed by Petruchio in Act One and followed through in the action of the play. That is to say, Hodgman, for all his good intentions regarding feminist issues, in failing to make a political critique of the society that sanctions Petruchio's and Baptista's attitudes, was merely replicating imperialist ideology: woman is the chaotic Other who must for her own good enter into the higher masculine order/law of harmony. (I am grateful to Frances Devlin Glass for information about this production.)

20. All quotations from Aubrey Mellor are from a letter to the author, March 29, 1996. I am grateful to Mr. Mellor for his generous assistance and for permission to quote from his notes.

21. Veronica Neave, conversation with the author, January 24, 1996.

22. Alison Cotes, "Belly Laughs Aplenty at the Changing of the Bard," *Courier-Mail* (Brisbane), August 19, 1989, 7.

23. Gale Edwards interviewed by Kate Alderson, "Whose Shrew Is It Anyway?" *The Times* (London), April 21, 1995, 33.

24. The most cogent negative critique of this production was conveyed by several delegates at the International Shakespeare Association Congress (Los Angeles in 1996) who wondered why Bianca was still given such dismissive treatment by a so-called feminist director. My answer would have to be that the production did not seek to be unambiguously feminist—a totalizing position perhaps available only to theorists—but that it reflected the speaking/seeing position of *one Australian woman.* Those who could drag their eyes away from Kate at the end of her speech would have noticed that Bianca exited not with her husband but with the much more amusing and attractive servant Tranio.

25. Gale Edwards, "Whose Shrew," 33.

26. Josie Lawrence confirmed my reading of this gesture in conversation on September 28, 1995.

27. Observers were divided as to whether there was any dialogue after Kate's speech: this in itself is an interesting indication of its powerful performance. In fact the last spoken line was "Sly, awake for shame" from the 1594 text, spoken by the Lord with a strong emphasis on the word "*shame.*"

28. Gale Edwards, interviewed by Bob Evans, "West End Winner," *Panorama,* January 1996, 36.

29. Barbara Hodgdon, "Looking for Mr. Shakespeare After 'The Revolution': Robert Lepage's Intercultural *Dream* Machine," in *Shakespeare, Theory, and Performance,* ed. James C. Bulman (London: Routledge, 1996), 81. Linda Hutcheon further helpfully theorizes the relation between postmodernist practice and postcolonial theory, focusing on "irony as a discursive strategy of both": "irony, the trope that works from within a power field but still contests it, is a consistently useful strategy for post-colonial discourse." Linda Hutcheon, "Circling the Downspout of Empire," in *The Post-colonial Studies Reader,* ed. Ashcroft et al., 134.

30. Gale Edwards interviewed by Jane Cornwell, "Australian Tames Bard at Stratford," *Sydney Morning Herald,* March 28, 1995, 8.

*3*

—◦◦◦—

# A Girl's Got to Eat:
# Christine Edzard's
# Film of *As You Like It*

*Patricia Lennox*

When Christine Edzard, one of four women to have earned a screen credit as the director of a Shakespeare film, translated *As You Like It* to the screen in 1992, she placed the action squarely in the late twentieth century.[1] While this was not unusual in itself, Edzard went further, much to the critics' displeasure, by locating the Forest of Arden in the vacant lots of the Rotherhithe docklands outside of London. This Arden became a site that was both wasteland and, paradoxically, a place of open skies; an outpost of free urban space in England's post-Thatcher world of big-money high-rises. Equally "subversive" if less obvious to the critics, though many of them still seemed unsettled by it, was the way in which Edzard presented the play's female characters, Rosalind, Celia, Phebe, and Audrey, as uniquely individual women, each quite at home in the twentieth-century setting and each clearly formed by class-related gender identity. In this low-budget, carefully nuanced film, in which close attention is paid to the telling details of characterization, food becomes an important part of the subtle code of signifiers that define these characters' economic class. All of the women are introduced to the viewer in eating scenes that create a series of visual images "authorized" by Shakespeare's frequent use of food metaphors in the play: wine, fruit, meat, victuals, fasting, and feasting. Throughout the film, food works its way on to the screen as a way of exploring the contrasts between court

and country, between scenes of a corporate world of power fueled by cocktail parties and buffets and a world of the marginally poor, cheerfully making do with ketchup on white bread. In a play that bases much of its humor
on the circulation of poetic language, where Petrarchan attitudes are struck
by a working (or, in this case, out-of-work) shepherd, issues of social class
and economic power are always just under the festive surface, as are the
erotic tensions created by transgressive desires, tensions capable of permeat-
ing gender and class boundaries with a cheerfully polymorphous perversity.

Christine Edzard's *As You Like It* is unique by Shakespeare-film standards
in its retention of nearly all of the play's text, and it is equally singular, by
any standard, in its careful avoidance of stereotyped characterizations of the
women's parts. Both the sensitive use of literature and the careful rendition
of individual characters are consistent with the other films in Edzard's reper-
toire. Almost all of her productions have been based on literary works: stories by Beatrix Potter, Hans Christian Andersen, Henry Mayhew, and
Charles Dickens. Her best-known film is the two-part, six-hour version of
*Little Dorrit* (1987), lauded as the best Dickens film since David Lean's clas-
sics, *Great Expectations* and *Oliver Twist*. All of Edzard's films are produced
and manufactured in Britain by Sands Films, the company she and her husband, Richard Goodwin, founded in 1975. The Parisian-born Edzard met
Goodwin, who had grown up in Bombay, when she was in Rome in 1966
decorating sets for Franco Zeffirelli's film *Romeo and Juliet*. Twenty-one
years old, she had given up the university studies in economics insisted upon
by her German-Polish artist parents in order to work in theater and opera as
an assistant to designers Rostislav Doboujinsky and Lila di Nobili. It was di
Nobili who had encouraged her to accept the job with Zeffirelli. When
Edzard and Goodwin married they settled in London, where they entered
into their first collaboration in 1971: an EMI Elstree-financed film of Royal
Ballet choreographer Frederick Ashton's *Tales of Beatrix Potter*. Goodwin
produced the film and Edzard designed the sets and costumes, a project that
took her two years to complete. Her dancing "mice" and "pigs" have all the
wit and charm of the books' original drawings, and the designs retain Potter's delicate palette of colors. Although Edzard and Goodwin's next film,
*Murder on the Orient Express,* moved them toward Hollywood commercialism, they chose instead to use their profits from *Murder* to establish their
own film studio, Sands Films.

Primarily because of Edzard's work, Sands Films, though small, has become a well-respected member of England's film community. When compared to the massive movie production of Bombay, Hollywood, or Moscow,
British cinema has been called a "cottage film industry,"[2] and Sands Films

seems to epitomize this idea with its self-contained studio, housed in several eighteenth-century warehouses. Edzard prefers to produce films in a totally independent environment, a kind of William Morris home workshop where everything is done under one roof. Within the studio's warehouses Edzard has a complete production facility that can handle a film from start to finish, including set-building, making costumes, and shooting, printing, and editing the film. It is an atelier where members of the production team play multiple parts, particularly in the more complex productions, such as *Dorrit,* where a Sands accountant discovered that his forte was sewing Victorian waistcoats.[3]

Edzard filmed *Little Dorrit* and *As You Like It* "on location" outside the studio's door in the Rotherhithe dockyards, a once-flourishing shipping site that fell into disuse decades ago. Benign neglect helped to ensure that a number of original buildings still survive from Rotherhithe's heyday, a period that began with the departure of the Pilgrims' ship, the Mayflower, from its quays and continued through the nineteenth century. The area had long been abandoned by the time Edzard and Goodwin established their studio there in 1975, and its derelict buildings were affordable for the fledgling company. When they first moved Sands Films into the dilapidated warehouses on Grice's Wharf, the company also produced toys and dolls' houses (an offshoot of set designs) to help keep afloat. The choice of a decaying Victorian wharf and the production of dolls' houses all seem part of Edzard's demonstrated fondness for late-nineteenth-century and Edwardian children's literature, an interest seen in her designs for *Beatrix Potter.* In fact, Sands's earliest independent films, *Stories from a Flying Trunk* and an animated short *The Nightingale,* were versions of Hans Christian Andersen fairy tales. Their most recent release, written and directed by Edzard, was *The IMAX Nutcracker* (1997), based on E.T. A. Hoffmann's classic story.

Given this predilection, it is to her credit that for *As You Like It* Edzard did not follow the lead of turn-of-the-century illustrated editions of the play, such as those created by artists Hugh Thomson and Will H. Low, books that present a charming, storybook version of the play with Rosalind and Celia as fairy tale princesses (an image retained in the 1936 film).[4] Furthermore, in her previous films Edzard had shown great skill and inventiveness in creating a period aura, especially in the minutely realized Victorian sets and costumes for *Dorrit.* Edzard had even served an apprenticeship in Renaissance lushness under the tutelage of film director Franco Zeffirelli. Despite the lure of this background, Edzard chose to set her *As You Like It* deep in the middle of contemporary London because, beyond her love of period design, Edzard has an even stronger commitment to the belief that literature tells stories that are true not only for the author's time but for our own. Speaking of *Dorrit*, for example, she said it is "terribly close, in hundreds of ways, to today."[5] A similar sense of immediacy informs her interpretation of *As You Like It.* By setting Shakespeare's play in the late twentieth century, Edzard allowed it to comment on the disparities she saw around her in post-Thatcher England with its increasingly affluent elite and growing unemployed underclass. She also made it clear that the contrast of the Duke's palace with the Forest of Arden includes the difference between a closed power structure and open affection: exclusivity and mutuality.

Edzard drew on both her theater and film backgrounds to produce a film that, while cinematic, retains various static framing qualities of a stage production. Although this troubled some critics who predicted "the film isn't going to turn kids on in the way Kenneth Branagh's *Henry V* or Mel Gibson's *Hamlet* did,"[6] it keeps the focus on the play and dialogue, filling the screen with actors, rather than with cinematic spectacle. It is true that Edzard's main cinematic influence here seems closer to the BBC Shakespeare series, particularly Jane Howell and Elijah Moshinsky, than it does to Branagh's filmic tributes to Hollywood or to Zeffirelli's painterly splendors.[7] Edzard's *As You Like It* is theatrical rather than cinematic in that the sets are limited and the camera work, though inventive, relies heavily on close-ups, using relatively few wide-angle shots. The film makes use of only three primary sets: the city "court" of marble pillars and gilt mirrors, the open space of the empty dockyard with mud and puddles, and the cozy interior of the "shepherd's cote" inhabited by Celia and Rosalind. Part of this restraint could easily have been imposed by the necessity of staying within the small budget with which Sands Films traditionally works. However, since Edzard is noted for her ability to produce even complex films on minuscule budgets and has been called a "miracle worker" in this respect, financing does not seem to have been the determining factor in this case. The settings have a spare documentary quality, costumes are inexpensive-modern, and the cast, recognizable actors but none star-famous, doubles most of the roles, but there is nothing that says, "We are doing it this way because we could not afford anything better." Instead all these elements offer Edzard a chance to work with aspects of *As You Like It* that make the play seem immediate, accessible, and pertinent. There is an immediately recognizable quality to the image of men and women living in an urban wilderness, camping in tents made of sheets of plastic and cardboard, cooking over fires in oil drums. On the wind-chilled wharf, Duke Senior's banishment has a poignancy that no shaded green forest could ever convey; his becomes the plight of an older set of values displaced by the money-grabbing forces of development. Amiens's

"Blow, blow, thou winter wind . . . freeze, freeze, thou bitter sky" (2.7.173, 184) rings true. Duke Senior's followers look genuinely rough-edged and chilled, in spite of the duke's persistent cheerfulness about the educative values of natural living, "tongues in trees, books in the running brooks" (2.1.16). (We might even argue that Shakespeare's audience did not quite believe this piece of optimism any more than we do watching this film.) Of the three main sets, the dockyard is used the most frequently and provides a number of different backgrounds, some of urban desolation, others of natural beauty. Like the play's dichotomies of court/country, good Duke/bad Duke, good brother/bad brother, the Forest of Arden also has two conflicting faces: freedom and hardship. The docks area is spacious, but not vast, and in spite of the feeling that it goes on for miles, there is always the sense of the city crowding in, of tall, sky-shrouding buildings momentarily held back on the horizon, but moving forward with the slow, unstoppable momentum of an ice floe. In some of the camera shots there are high-rises in the distance, in others derelict blocks of buildings; even the occasional bulldozer is seen parked at the edge. Eventually, ruthlessly, the city will crowd forward and overtake open-spaced Arden with its high skies and displace those who have used it as a safe harbor. It is Jaques who knows that the holiday mood, like all the stages of life, is transitory and that those who have escaped to the freedom of Arden will eventually return to the city.

The second set, the shepherd's cottage taken over by Celia and Rosalind, is a green-painted workman's hut set on an expanse of tarmac. Inside, although it is as snug as a Beatrix Potter room, the bare furnishings and household objects hung on the cheerful yellow walls send the message that this place, as rustic as a cabin in the woods with its lack of running water and electricity, is equipped only for bohemian living, a style that liberates Celia as much as Rosalind's male attire releases her. Edzard avoids the classic cinematic moment of feminizing domesticity; there is no flurry of curtains and cushions, no prettifying. Instead things are left much as they are found, freeing Celia, in her own form of class-transvestism, to sit contentedly at the bare table, rolling a cigarette, far from the filter-tips she lit with a silver lighter in her days at her father's court.

In contrast, the opening scenes—Orlando's confrontation with Oliver, Celia and Rosalind's conversations with Touchstone, the wrestling match, and Adam's consoling speech—all occur within the mirrored halls and marble foyers of what is obviously a single building representing all of the Duke's palace settings, as well as Oliver's house. Celia's room in 1.3 is created by a red velvet couch placed in a room marked by the omnipresent massive columns, and in 2.3, Adam's workbench is located in a darker version of a similar space. It is as though all of the city/court encounters take place in one labyrinthine enclosure. At the end of the play the characters return to this interior space for the wedding, but by then it has been hung with polyurethane, part drapery, part dust cover, and has become a series of empty rooms.

Although Edzard has deliberately chosen to conform to certain theatrical limitations, there is nothing of a filmed play about this movie. Edzard's experience as a filmmaker is apparent by her skilled use of the camera's point of view as well as by editing. A series of quick cuts reposition scenes with a flexibility that would be difficult to achieve on stage, especially with characters doubling roles. For instance, in 1.1 when Charles, the Duke's wrestler, tells Oliver of the old Duke's banishment, the film cuts to the old Duke in the forest for his 71-line speech in 2.1, then returns to Oliver's office and resumes the ominous discussion of the wrestling match. The first act's action then continues on as written until the end of the second scene, when the fifth scene of act 2 is inserted so that we have the Jaques and Amiens "Greenwood" song sequence placed between Le Beau's dismissal of Orlando and Celia's attempt to comfort the tear-drenched Rosalind (1.3). The viewer has already met James Fox's elegantly rueful Jaques at the opening of the film in which he wandered through the Duke's mirrored halls reciting his Seven Ages of Man speech, in effect, establishing himself as our guide to this "society he both shuns and seeks."[8] The remaining scenes in act 2 follow: four, two, and three.

Sometimes it is the sequences within the scenes that are shifted, as when Orlando's recitation of his love verses, spray-painted graffiti on a wooden wall (3.2.1–10), segues into the duel of melancholies with Jaques (3.2.231–65). Corin and Touchstone's comic exchange on manners (3.2.11–87) follows. There are scene and speech transitions throughout the film, and they always work toward clarity while providing a sense of movement and variety achieved without overloading the film with intrusive visual images.

For the most part Edzard limits what appears on the screen to images directly connected to establishing and expanding the characters. This is why the use of food as props is so important in the film. Images connected to food and drink are used on screen as integral parts of the characters' actions in 9 of the play's 22 scenes,[9] starting in 1.2 with a spiritless Rosalind morosely nibbling an eclair, the self-pampering Le Beau licking a cream puff, and Celia rejecting food in favor of cigarettes. Food is used again on several levels in 3.4.1–40, here set inside the cabin instead of the forest. While Celia chides Rosalind by saying, "tears do not become a man," she herself is eliding socially constructed gender roles by enacting a scene generally reserved in movies for a man. As she speaks, Celia is inexpertly attempting to cook a soft-boiled egg, a classic male-in-the kitchen-for-the-first-time routine.[10] (The egg is casually dropped into boiling water, which, as anyone who cooks knows, will cause it to break.) Edzard works with the intimacy of the camera and the expanse of the movie screen, here and elsewhere, to allow actors to play more subtly than the stage usually permits. Only the slight, bemused lift of an eyebrow registers Celia's surprise as she scoops out the inept results without a break in her speech or a moment's loss of her air of amused sophistication. In this scene, the sight gag is amusing but discreet, allowing the focus to remain on the dialogue. The fact that Edzard knows how to take advantage of the screen's ability to establish characters quickly through subtle gestures also helps the success of the actors' doubling, a stage device that expands nicely on film and further emphasizes the play's use of mirror contrasts. Both dukes are played by the same actor, as are the brothers Orlando and Oliver. All of the inhabitants of Arden also appear in the court, if only as extras. (Edzard does not, however, fully exploit the power of film by using a split screen to show the actor in both roles, even in the final scene where actors appear both in their court and Arden personae or in 1.1 where Andrew Tiernan as Oliver pushes himself around as Orlando.)

Photographically the film is built around carefully framed close-ups with well-chosen backgrounds and shifting points of view that continually engage the viewer's eye. A series of deliberately rare long shots emphasize the exhilarating sense of freedom Rosalind experiences as Ganymede in the forest, away from the constrictions of court. There is a great sense of roominess in this industrial wasteland on the river that makes up the Forest of Arden, and there are open spaces for Rosalind and Orlando to do their tentative dance of mock-wooing. Many of the shots are framed to include great swatches of sky, and the camera makes the most of a wonderful variety of textures in the old wooden fences, stone walls, and piles of industrial rubble. There are even a few trees that turn some scenes into bucolic interludes. There is only one scene in the film that attempts to offer a concrete illustration identifying the play's language as metaphoric: Oliver's story of his rescue by Orlando (4.3). Through a flashback accompanying Oliver's story, we see a very human stalker attacking him in the dark in a robbery attempt, and Orlando battles with a thief instead of the lioness and the female snake specified by the text. It is a cinematic moment at odds with the rest of the film because it is the only time that something being described is shown in a flashback. It also works to neutralize the only images in the text where female figures are seen as threatening.[11] However, the menacing night setting introduces the feeling

of an encroaching darkness. This premonition that the open skies of freedom are closing in continues as swirls of nighttime fog in 5.2 shroud each
of the disembodied lovers whose faces appear on screen as they emerge from
the mist to declare their love. Rosalind realizes that she must leave behind
the empowerment of Ganymede's male body if she is to accept love in the
world as it exists. The remainder of the film (5.4) takes place back in the
now-deserted palace where a heavy golden haze, suggesting a different version of the fog, lights Rosalind's reemergence as woman, the reunion with
her father and the marriage. There is one last view of open sky, in the next
to last shot, as a solitary Jaques is seen outlined against the sky, crossing the
Rotherhithe embankment.

As I have noted, one of Edzard's most prevalent interests is the way in which
the stories from the past remain relevant to our own social and economic situation. This is not to say that she turns her films into polemics; rather these ideas
emerge in the movie as it unfolds on screen. Critics might argue that in *As You
Like It* this is achieved by making far too many changes: the action is shifted to
an abandoned dockyard; the time becomes the 1990s; the sense of poetry is lost
in the attempt to replicate modern speech patterns; and the introduction of
extra stage business for the women is distracting. Indeed, many of the critics
protested against this urban Arden with its background of traffic noises, refusing to accept the idea that "Arden is a metaphor, a symbolic landscape of the
imagination and not some slice of Warwickshire countryside."[12] Edzard's
empty docks may have made some viewers feel robbed of an anticipated pastoral experience and definitely seem to have left most critics nostalgically longing for a magic forest where reconciliations occur under leafy boughs. However,
one can argue that, in general, the references to trees and forest manage to work
well, sometimes literally, sometimes metaphorically, and frequently with telling
irony that seems quite in keeping with the text's ambivalence about a natural
world that is as menacing as it is beautiful. There may be sermons in stones in
Arden, but there are also snakes under those rocks. In Edzard's urban Arden,
Corin's single pet sheep on a leash ceases to seem absurd when you realize that
it is a poignant remnant of a lost agrarian world. The paving-over of countryside by expanding suburbs may be today's version of Elizabethan Enclosure
Laws. The use of the term "forest" is scarcely a problem when you remember
the grandiose names given to some of the more destructive building projects.
"Forest of Arden" could easily be the name of an industrial development.

Some critics went on to complain that Edzard took other enormous lib-
erties with the play—time, characterizations, line readings, and linguistic
emphasis—in order to achieve a film that has too much of a modern sensi-

bility, particularly in the way it overemphasizes the women's roles at the expense of the men's and turns this into a production where the minor characters (i.e., women) "bustle in and out . . . following instructions to work on their individual identities."[13] But it is these unique identities that give the roles a feminist reading as the film replaces clichés with comparatively real women. One of the most intriguing aspects of *As You Like It* is the way it provides a feminist interpretation of the play through its presentation of the women. There is true innovation in the film's realization of the roles of Rosalind, Celia, Phebe, and Audrey. Christine Edzard has brought about a remarkable transformation in the women's roles in *As You Like It* simply by casting strong actresses who give their parts specific characteristics and establish identifiable personalities that are well maintained. Even more important, Edzard ties the roles to the various agendas/categories that are used to judge and define women: class, economic status, age, and physical attributes. Miriam Margolyes's plump, thirtyish Audrey and Valerie Gogan's younger Phebe are working-class women in sharp contrast with the upper-class, slim, and educated Celia (Celia Bannerman) and Rosalind (Emma Croft), women of similar ages whose gender-identity has been differently defined by class. It is difficult, for instance, to imagine either Audrey or Phebe having the spirited independence of Rosalind. Edzard's direction makes it clear that Shakespeare has given the play women's parts that lead to questioning traditional gender roles: by setting Celia and Rosalind off on the path to independence, going "content / To liberty and not to banishment"(1.3.137–38); by giving Phebe agency to refuse Corin's "shepherd's passion"; even by allowing Audrey surprising autonomy over her own highly seducible body.

Two very interesting things happen in the film. Tropologically these "readings" of Rosalind, Celia, Phebe, and Audrey help to open up the theme of mutuality in the play to include ideals of mutuality between women as well as between women and men. Metaphorically the film makes visual the play's use of food imagery as the characters seem to be continually eating and cooking: pastries and wine at court, sandwiches and french fries on the dock, a simple boiled egg at the cottage. We see the men eat, and Orlando bursts in demanding food while Duke Senior's camp is at dinner (2.7). But mealtime there is a rough business that speaks of makeshift, shanty-town living where meat is cooked over oil-drum braziers, and crates of oranges stacked on the ground offer a silent comment on the mechanics of feeding a retinue in the "desert." Still, it is the women's relation to food that provides details about their lives and personalities, augmenting and sometimes even undercutting their speeches.

As a modern version of a marginally financially independent woman, Audrey now runs a snack van serving tea and sandwiches. It is a tidy place but tiny, barely large enough to hold the generous proportions of Audrey; it is indeed Touchstone's "great reckoning in a little room" (3.3.13). Throughout Touchstone's randy wooing, Audrey is industriously making ketchup sandwiches with Wonder Bread, as out of touch with gastronomy as she is with Touchstone's subtle language. However, though she may still be "knowledge ill-inhabited" (3.3.7), she is not a fool and is far removed from the usual interpretation of Audrey as an over-sexed "country wench," the original "farmer's daughter," an interpretation that would have opened the film to the inclusion of what Laura Mulvey has termed the camera's "male gaze."[14] Touchstone's hand may creep over to fondle Audrey's ample bosom, but the camera does not invite the viewer to leer at the action. Margolyes's Audrey means it when she says she is not a slut, and the camera does not compromise her statement. The final scene will not bring her on screen in the advanced state of pregnancy that seems to have become a standardized theatrical trope for the "country copulative."

The younger, black-leather-jacketed, long-haired Phebe is, one suspects, probably on the dole and possibly a dropout from the local poly-tech. From the moment the mobile-faced Gogan appears on the screen as Phebe (3.50), with the adoring Silvius at her heels, she is munching unconcernedly on french fries. She continues her placidly self-centered eating until Rosalind's Ganymede captures her attention. This authoritatively spoken young man, so full of assurance, is clearly the most interesting thing to appear on the horizon, and Phebe silently offers him a french fry. The presence of the greasy bag of fries goes a long way in defusing the question of play's transgressive sexual desire explored by Valerie Traub and Jean Howard.[15] Rosalind never gives any indication of desire for Phebe, although she continues to enjoy experiencing the sense of power Ganymede gives her. While Phebe's "arousal" is certainly "imbricated with power differences"[16] the degree of actual eroticism that comes through from Phebe is not strongly charged—there is little there to attract Rosalind/Ganymede's desire in return. When Rosalind rejects Phebe, she also denies the possibility of forming an expanded female community, a potential that is denied because of class barriers.[17] Phebe is genuinely enthusiastic, like a child who has seen a captivating new pet; she has also seen the possibility of a more interesting life. As she writes her love note on the french fries wrapper, the feminized damask of the cheek seems the least of Ganymede's attractions. A youthful desire for adventure, more than eroticism, seems to dominate Phebe's pursuit. The letter writing also turns her attention to the now-useful Silvius, and she shares her fries with him for the first time. Sheer youthfulness also seems to be a strong part of the Orlando/Ganymede friendship. Emma Croft, fresh out of acting school, presents her tomboy Rosalind to Orlando as a kind of very smart kid brother. It is her ability to talk and fantasize that fascinates the relatively unimaginative Orlando. There is no hint of the homoerotic in their early, playfully scuffling relationship; the shift comes with the embrace at the end of the mock wedding (3.3). Rosalind gives her kiss with sweet enthusiasm, and Orlando, surprised by it, wipes his lips dry with his index finger. But then he looks at Ganymede and puts the finger back in his mouth as if rechecking its pleasant taste. In this film, that is the moment when the erotic enters, and it is this awareness of adult sexuality that begins the loss of Arden's freedom. Edzard's placement of the marriages back in the Duke's palace (or city) underscores questions about the loss of personal freedom, even within the partnership of a union that acknowledges mutuality in marriage.

However, throughout most of the play the one relationship that demonstrates mutually affectionate equality is that of Celia and Rosalind, cousins whose bond is "dearer than the natural bond of sisters," as Le Beau says with a knowing simper (1.2.244). They have shared every moment of their lives: "slept together, / Rose at an instant, learned, played, eat together; / And wheresoe'er we went, like Juno's swans, / Still we went coupled and inseparable" (1.3.67–72). The two women seem to illustrate Erik Erikson's definition of mutuality as a "relationship in which partners depend on each other for the development of their respective strengths,"[18] particularly in their first scene, a cocktail party where the younger, less-experienced Rosalind's suggestion "let us devise sports . . . what think you of falling in love?" is countered by Celia's wry "love no man in good earnest" (1.2.20–21; 23). One critic, incidentally, complained that Bannerman, who appeared to be in her early thirties, was too old for the role of Celia.[19] He did not see the wonderful balance that a slightly older, wiser Celia provides and the way that balance can help to define her position in some of the more difficult scenes, such as her confrontation of Ganymede/Rosalind's attacks on women. The age difference allows the women's two personalities to be clearly drawn. Here they are not duplicates; one is a very well-heeled, sophisticated "princess," comfortable with her position as the only daughter at the center of her father's "court," and the other is her more naive, financially dependent cousin. Bannerman's Celia wears her wealth lightly, but it is always there, in her confident bantering tone or in an imperiously given order to a servant. Right down to her little black dress with the double row of matched pearls, she is rooted in her class. Rosalind, younger, less sure of herself, similarly well educated and of equal birth, seems tentative, as if detached, waiting, missing her father, aware of her lack of voice except in conversation with Celia. But none of this mars the tone of pure friendship between the women, a friendship based on shared expectations of what each will provide to the other.

They alternate strength and weakness: it is Celia who proposes their journey "to seek my uncle in the Forest of Arden," replacing one father with another, and who sensibly suggests taking their jewels (as though money is of use in a forest—which, of course, it actually is). In stage productions, Celia seems to lose her strength in the second half of the play, starting with her arrival in Arden footsore, weary, and able to "go no further." In this film, however, Arden liberates both women: Celia to control over her own time (her sense of contentment in simply rolling a cigarette is wonderful) and Rosalind to a tomboy's freedom. When Rosalind meets Orlando they are the ones who are, at least in appearance, Juno's twin swans, dressed in their matching blue jeans, baggy sweaters, and knit caps. Instead of playing mock macho this Ganymede/Rosalind explores her new freedom to talk as an equal with Orlando by skipping and moving about with big, joyful gestures among the puddles on the dock, much to Orlando's confusion and amusement over the actions of this "kid." He only begins to take Ganymede seriously when the offer is accepted to woo him as "Rosalind," with its delicate undertones of eroticism that are so necessary to the energy of the play.

The film makes it very clear that Rosalind's total absorption in Orlando makes the break in the happy continuity of her female friendship—a break that Celia, now truly feeling like Aliena, suffers silently, with tears in her eyes. (Their rapport will only be reestablished when Celia falls in love with Oliver, Orlando's previously oppressive brother.) Although Celia suffers this slight in silence, one of the reasons that she remains such a strong character in the film may have to do with the way the medium otherwise allows her to be present as an active participant, showing up primarily only when she is speaking. In contrast, stage productions tend to have her standing around for long chunks of time silently observing a hyperactive Rosalind.

Meanwhile Croft's Rosalind has been careening about this vast wasteland of a Forest of Arden, delighting not only in her blue-jeaned freedom (in some ways this is more about a freedom from pantyhose than from petticoats) but also in her liberation from the role-playing conventions of a young, moneyed-class woman to become someone whose ideas are now of interest to her fellow "men." Everyone seems to want to talk with her as a young male, even the solitary Jaques. So happy is she in this disguise that Croft's Rosalind seems genuinely disappointed at having to give up the role of Ganymede. Although she has reached her goal—Orlando is hers—it brings diminishment and banishment from a world she could not have imagined before. Her last moment of power—"I am a magician"—occurs in a misty fog (5.2).

At this point, perhaps not quite coincidentally, Edzard seems to lose interest in the play. All of the previous energy falls away as the film moves rapidly to conclusion. The lovers meet in the Duke's palace, now abandoned and hung with sheets of polyurethane. The plastic is both a reminder of the tents in Arden and, with its reflective surfaces sparkling in the lights, also a link to the mirrors in the palace. Furthermore, up until the final act almost no dialogue has been cut from the play, an unusual fact for a Shakespeare film making the number of omissions here surprising and significant. The deletions create a feeling of destabilization that undercuts the closure Shakespeare provides by tying up loose ends with marriages and conversions. In the film's truncated final scene, when there is no appearance of Hymen it is as though Rosalind's magic has actually failed. The clever polyurethane wedding dresses and veils link Celia and Rosalind to Arden, but Rosalind looks the way she did at the beginning of the film. The glowing beauty she developed in Arden seems to have disappeared, and everything about her seems weighed down. The heavy gold light that permeates the scene might be an allusion to a Hymen's supernatural light, but it is also a kind of dissembling fog. Rosalind's reconciliation speech has been shortened; Jaques's blessings paralleling Rosalind's lines have been dropped. In the triple-tiered final minutes of the film, we hear the description of Duke Frederick's conversion while the credits roll and the actors who have played dual roles mimic curtain calls and bow to their doubles in a nice final nod to the play's dense sets of doubling. Finally, Rosalind's epilogue is deleted, effectively silencing her with marriage. The penultimate shot to appear on screen is a silhouette of Jaques crossing the dockyard, an image that further undercuts the "happy" closure of the marriages and reminds us that weddings can also mean a loss of freedom and mobility. This ending, which requires Rosalind to renounce the male freedom she had appropriated, can be explained in terms of sixteenth-century expectations for women, but it is more difficult to justify it in a twentieth-century setting. By shifting the action back to the palace, Edzard links the final pairings to a reacceptance of patriarchal hierarchy, a move that subverts viewer expectations. The problems are solved and lessons have been learned. The eldest son is returned to power, the usurper converted, brothers reunited, lovers taught that women want mutuality and not the blazons of Petrarchan verse. At the play's conclusion, every "Jack has his Jill." However, although Edzard has given us a sweetly joyful *As You Like It,* she still leaves the viewer questioning just what it is that "Jill" actually has gained. Perhaps just as food in the film tied each of the women to class status as a formative element in gender identity, the ending encodes the pressures to stay within marriage (or the corporate city) as a means of economic survival. In other words, "a girl's got to eat," and if she strays too far, it may not be possible. Tellingly, as if to ask us how true this still is, the final image on screen is a mirrored, closed door.

### Notes

1. *As You Like It*, (1992, 117 min.). Director, Christine Edzard; photography, Robin Vidgeon; music, Michel Sanvoisin. Produced by Sands Film Production, U.K.; producers, George Reinhart and Richard Goodwin. With Cyril Cusack (Adam); James Fox (Jaques); Don Henderson (the Dukes); Miriam Margolyes (Audrey); Emma Croft (Rosalind); Celia Bannerman (Celia); Griff Rhys Jones (Touchstone); Andrew Tiernan (Orlando/Oliver); Ewen Bremmer (Silvius); Valerie Gogan (Phebe); Roger Hammond (LeBeau, Corin); and others.
   The other three directors are Liz White for *Othello* (1980), Jane Howell for her underrated BBC productions: *The Winter's Tale* (1980), *Henry VI, Richard III* (1981–82), and *Titus Andronicus* (1985), and Janet Suzman for *Othello* (1988). Line references for *As You Like It* are from Stephen Greenblatt et al., ed., *The Norton Shakespeare* (New York: W.W. Norton & Company, Inc., 1997).
2. Guy Phelps, "Victorian Values," *Sight and Sound* 57 (Spring 1988): 108.
3. Ibid., 109. Today the studio has a reputation for the creation of nineteenth-century costumes, many of them devised by Edzard, and has dressed the recent films of *Sense and Sensibility* and *Emma,* as well as Steven Spielberg's *Amistad,* and Oprah Winfrey's *Beloved.*
4. Hugh Thomson illustrated *Shakespeare's Comedy of* As You Like It (London: Hoddert Stoughton, 1910). Will H. Low illustrated *As You Like It: A Pleasant Comedy* (New York: Dodd, Mead and Company, 1899). The 1936 film of *As You Like It* was produced by Inter-Allied Film Producers; director, Paul Czinner; with Laurence Olivier and Elisabeth Bergner. Happily, Edzard's film's quality of gritty realism bears no resemblance to Cedric Messina's archly mannered version of the play in the BBC series.
5. Phelps, "Victorian Values," 109.
6. Unsigned review in *Plays and Players* (November 1992): 27.
7. Jane Howell's BBC films are listed in note 1. Elijah Moshinsky has directed the BBC series *All's Well That Ends Well, A Midsummer Night's Dream, Cymbeline, Coriolanus,* and *Love's Labour's Lost.*
8. Samuel Crowl, "*As You Like It,*" *Shakespeare Bulletin* 11, no. 3 (Summer 1993): 41.

9. In the film, visual images of food appear in 1.2, 1.3, 2.1, 2.5, 2.7, 3.3, 3.4, 3.5, and 5.2. There are textual references to food in nearly every scene of the play.

10. The rich girl who could not cook (i.e., fulfill her traditional gender role) has its screen origins in such Hollywood screwball comedies of the 1930s as *It Happened One Night.*

11. Jan Stirm, "'For solace a twinne-like sister': Teaching Themes of Sisterhood in *As You Like It* and Beyond," *Shakespeare Quarterly* 47 (Winter 1996): 375.

12. Crowl, *"As You Like It,"* 41. This review, on the same page, called it "a lovely, intelligent film." The other notably favorable review was by Ilona Halverstadt, *Sight and Sound* 61 (Fall, 1992): 45.

13. Lindsay Duguid, *Times Literary Supplement* 4671 (October 9, 1992): 19. The BBC version (1978) of *As You Like It* was unimaginatively filmed on location in the country and the verdant landscape proved to be highly intrusive and irritatingly ineffective.

14. Edzard works within the "alternative cinema" that Mulvey identifies as providing "a cinema which is radical in both a political and aesthetic sense and challenges the basic assumptions of the mainstream film." Laura Mulvey, *Visual and Other Pleasures* (Bloomington: Indiana University Press, 1989), 15.

15. Jean Howard, *The Stage and Social Struggle in Early Modern England* (London: Routledge, 1994); Valerie Traub, *Desire and Anxiety* (London: Routledge, 1992).

16. Traub, *Desire and Anxiety,* 104.

17. Stirm, "For Solace," 385.

18. Erik Erikson, quoted by Marianne Novy in *Love's Argument: Gender Relations in Shakespeare* (Chapel Hill: University of North Carolina Press, 1984): 4. Novy's chapter on *As You Like It* provides an expanded exploration of questions of mutuality.

19. Unsigned review, *Plays and Players,* 27.

*4*

## Saving Desdemona and/or Ourselves: Plays by Ann-Marie MacDonald and Paula Vogel

### Marianne Novy

Two very different recent plays take a new and transforming look at Shakespeare's Desdemona, in ways influenced by different feminist ideas. The transformation in Ann-Marie MacDonald's *Goodnight Desdemona (Good Morning Juliet)* can easily be connected to a feminist impulse to show female strength and authority, though the play shows limitations in its woman warrior.[1] By contrast, Paula Vogel's *Desdemona: A Play about a Handkerchief* contains no character anything like a role model for women. But, in its critical analysis of male power, the ideologies and structures that maintain it, and the exploitative possibilities in relationships between women of different classes, it shares concerns with feminists who focus on structures of oppression.[2] Both plays raise the question of whether women can escape tragedy, and in neither one does Desdemona seem like an obvious victim. However, in MacDonald's play, Desdemona is, arguably, a recognizable extrapolation of Shakespeare's character in a completely different plot, while Vogel's Desdemona is almost totally opposite to Shakespeare's in character but concludes the play about to suffer the same death.

The rewriting of Desdemona in *Goodnight Desdemona* is mediated for the audience by the views of Constance Ledbelly, an easily put-upon assistant professor at Queen's University in Canada, recently deserted by Claude Night, the colleague for whom she has been ghostwriting. In her rather old-fashioned doctoral thesis, still in progress, Constance has been speculating about the possibility of a lost—comic—original for *Othello* and *Romeo and Juliet*. In a magical time-warp the play moves Constance from late-twentieth-century Canada to Renaissance Cyprus, where she meets Othello, shows him the handkerchief in Iago's pocket, and efficiently ends his jealousy. When Constance meets Desdemona, however, she is overwhelmed, for this is where her real emotional connection to the play ignites. A feminist critic without an interpretive community, Constance tells Othello of her reading of his wife:[3]

> I've always thought she had a violent streak,
> and that she lived vicariously through you,
> but no one else sees eye to eye with me. (32)

When this play's Desdemona appears, she confirms Constance's speculations from her first speech: "O valiant general and most bloody lord!" (32). She introduces herself using some of Shakespeare's own lines, some that vary only slightly—as when she resolves the ambiguity of "that heaven had made her such a man"—and some completely new ones:[4]

> *That I love my lord to live with him.*
> *My downright violence and storm of fortunes*
> *may trumpet to the world.* My sole regret—
> that heaven had not made me such a man;
> but next in honour is to be his wife.[5]

A fair warrior indeed. Constance, gratified to find her interpretation validated, denounces the "sacred herd of Academe" (41) who have labeled her opinions crackpot: "Academe/ Believes that you're a doomed and helpless victim." Constance's view of Desdemona is actually very close to that of several more sophisticated feminist critics; for example, Mary Beth Rose says, "Openly and proudly acknowledging her love for her husband, Desdemona characterizes herself as a soldier-spouse," and Carol Thomas Neely calls her "strong" and full of "energizing power."[6] With such energizing power, Desdemona sees Constance too as an Amazon; eventually the example of Desdemona works on Constance as the example of the first player describing Hecuba works on Hamlet.

> O, what would Desdemona do to Claude,
> had she *the motive and the cue for passion*
> *that I have?* She would drown all Queen's with blood,
> and cleave Claude Night's two typing fingers from
> his guilty hands. (49)

Like Hamlet, Constance works herself up to exclaim, "O Vengeance!!!" (50).

But this Desdemona has not only physical courage, anger and pride like Othello's, she also has Othello's susceptibility to Iago's manipulations. Although Constance has saved Othello from suspecting Desdemona, Iago gets Desdemona to suspect Constance not only of adultery with Othello but also of witchcraft and spying.

As Desdemona starts to fall apart like Shakespeare's Othello, using some of the same words, and threatens Constance with her sword, the time-warp effects begin again, to pull Constance out of this danger and into the Verona of *Romeo and Juliet*. Constance gives them the information that saves them from killing themselves; then, Juliet falls for Constance, who is cross-dressing as Constantine. Juliet wants a double suicide for love; Desdemona reappears and calls Constance to return to Cyprus and kill Iago. As they repeat their conflicting commands—"Nay come! Nay Stay! Nay kill!! Nay die!!" (84)—Constance breaks out into prose for the first time since her time-warp and tells them off:

> I've had it with all the tragic tunnel vision around here. You have no idea what—life is a hell of a lot more complicated than you think! Life—real life— is a big mess. Thank goodness. And every answer spawns another question; and every question blossoms with a hundred different answers; and if you're lucky you'll always feel somewhat confused. . . . Desdemona, I thought you were different; I thought you were my friend, I worshipped you. But you're just like Othello—gullible and violent. (85)

Miraculously, having saved Desdemona and Juliet from being tragic victims, Constance convinces them to give up their tragic absolutism and instead, as Desdemona says, "to live by questions, not by their solution." In effect, this changes them into comic heroines instead of tragic heroines, and Constance concludes, "I was right about your plays. They were comedies after all, not tragedies." She recalls earlier having thought "only a Wise Fool could turn tragedy to comedy," and learns that she herself is both the Wise Fool and the Author (86). Magically, a scrolled manuscript appears which reads:

> For those who have the eyes to see:
> Take care—for what you see, just might be thee.
> Where two plus one adds up to one, not three.

In other words, Desdemona and Juliet in their extremes of anger and love are aspects of Constance that she has denied and can now accept without being limited by their simplifications. This is a Jungian message (though not an exclusively Jungian one) and MacDonald encourages relating the play to Jung. The Chorus refers to archetypes, the unconscious and alchemy. Constance is obsessed with a mysterious "Gustav manuscript" bearing C. G. Jung's middle name, and the published version includes an epigraph from Jung.

Paula Vogel's *Desdemona: A Play about a Handkerchief* is much darker. Vogel also imagines an adventurous Desdemona, but her adventurousness is channeled into sexuality, and while the play stops before Othello kills her, at the end we know he will. In this play there is no Constance to give the play a contemporary and comic frame—on the other hand its Desdemona has ceased to be a tragic or heroic icon and becomes an ordinary, if upper-class, woman who just wants some excitement.

Desdemona complains, "Women are clad in purdah, we decent, respectable matrons, from the cradle to the altar to the shroud, . . . bridled with linen, blinded with lace" (19). She goes to Bianca's brothel to escape this confinement:

> And the men come into that pitch-black room—men of different sizes and smells and shapes, with smooth skin—with rough skin, with scarred skin. And they spill their seed into me, Emilia—seed from a thousand lands, passed down through generations of ancestors, with genealogies that cover the surface of the globe. And I simply lie still there in the darkness, taking them all into me; I close my eyes and in the dark of my mind—oh, how I travel! (20)

As MacDonald's Desdemona could be said to exaggerate one aspect of Carol Neely's and Mary Beth Rose's, Vogel's could be said to exaggerate Shirley Garner's, who discusses Lodovico with Emilia in the willow scene because she finds him attractive.[7] Vogel's Desdemona has a long-term affair with her Ludovico, in both plays the ambassador from Venice, who seems to offer her the chance of an escape.

But the relationships this play scrutinizes are those between women. Ever since she was five, Vogel's Desdemona has been making messes for Emilia—in this version her scullery maid and laundress—to clean up. Now she keeps promising Emilia promotions, raises, and escapes, and then taking back the promises. Much of the interest in the play is in their changing relationship and in the question of how much they are going to confide each in other. Emilia's rival for Desdemona's interest is Bianca. For a while Desdemona idealizes Bianca as "a free woman—a new woman, who can make her own living in the world—who scorns marriage for the lie that it is"(20). But even before she discovers that this is a misreading of Bianca, it becomes obvious that Desdemona's interest in Bianca is really a condescending whim: "I never tire of hearing your stories. They're so lively, so very funny. What else have I got for amusement's sake"(37).

These two plays have had radically different fates. MacDonald's, first produced by Nightwood Theater in Toronto in 1988, toured Canada in a revised version in 1990 and that year won the Canadian Governor General's Award for Drama, and in August 1997 went into its eighth printing. While Vogel herself went on to win a Pulitzer Prize in 1998 for *How I Learned to Drive,* her *Desdemona* closed after very short runs at the Bay Street Theatre Festival (July 1993) and the Circle Repertory Company (October 25-December 5, 1993). One could postulate that part of the difference here results from a greater interest in Shakespearean intertextuality in Canada: Linda Hutcheon has speculated that "writers in places like Ireland and Canada, working as they do from both inside and outside a culturally different and dominant context," are especially drawn to parody, and, while there are many Shakespeare festivals in the United States, the Stratford Shakespeare Festival in Ontario, which MacDonald visited while writing the play—a passage on male nudity in Shakespeare productions has often been taken as commenting on it—probably looms larger as part of Canada's theater scene than any Shakespeare festival does as part of the U.S. scene.[8] On the other hand, MacDonald's play has had successful runs in the United States at such diverse locations as Pittsburgh, off-Broadway, Cambridge, Berkeley, and even Slippery Rock, Pennsylvania; as of 1997 it had had more than fifty productions worldwide.[9]

The difference in tone between the plays probably is more responsible for the difference in their popularity than the national contrast. Both plays are parodies, but MacDonald's is much more affectionate, and thus more likely to appeal to an audience drawn by the Shakespearean names in the title. MacDonald's is so playful about its parodic status that in one of her early scenes, her Desdemona says, "I hate a tripping, singing, licensed fool, / that makes a motley of the mighty, / And profanes the sacred with base parody" (48). In an interview, MacDonald says of her work in general, "I take something people identify with or revere, like Shakespeare, and say, 'Excuse me while I turn this upside down.'"[10] She, however, continues, "I would never lampoon something that I hated. It can only be something that fascinates me for some reason and if I'm fascinated by it then it means there is a deep attraction to it."

Vogel's play does not suggest the same kind of attraction to Shakespeare. At the beginning she says, in a "Note to Director," "*Desdemona* was written as a tribute (i.e., 'rip-off') to the infamous play, *Shakespeare the Sadist* by

Wolfgang Bauer" (4). The Bauer play (which in its original German has the title *Frauen und Film*) is about a group of slackers, one of whom acts out a role called Shakespeare in an onstage version of a porn film. Shakespeare's role here begins with such lines as "Stupid harlot, insolent woman, you don't seem to know who I am, you whore," and ends by sawing the woman's head off as he shouts "TO BE OR NOT TO BE!!!!" (The woman playing the victim reappears, live, a minute later.)[11] This play is obviously not a sophisticated critique of violence in Shakespeare's plays or in his life but rather a send-up in which his name is used for the shock value of profaning it. There is something of the same spirit in Vogel's attitude toward Desdemona.

Behind both of these Desdemona plays, however, is a fascination with two apparently polar opposites for women—adventurer and victim—and Shakespeare's Desdemona is each play's interest partly because, in his version, she begins as one and turns into the other. MacDonald's Desdemona loves Othello and is faithful to him (though by the end of the play she seems more interested in Constance), but she exaggerates the love of military heroism suggested in Shakespeare's play. Her Desdemona is not a victim and is instrumental in the transformation of Constance away from victimhood. The play gently mocks Constance's obsession with her own theories about Shakespeare but ultimately suggests that following her own obsessions—getting into the world of the characters that fascinate her—will teach her something about complexity and about herself, and also lead her to a new sense of her own agency inside and outside scholarship. MacDonald's use of Shakespeare's own language—assigned to different situations and sometimes to different characters—and her blend of it with her own writing in an iambic pentameter often rich in imagery and puns, is also indicative of her continued fascination with Shakespeare.

Vogel's play is parody of a different kind. Here the emphatically chaste Desdemona of Shakespeare's play is as wanton as Iago claims she is—with every man but Cassio. (Thus the play makes Othello, who never appears, seem even more foolish.) Onstage she learns from Bianca how prostitutes fake pain for a sadistic client, and she reminisces about youthful sexual activities—in church—with Ludovico. Emilia is given Shakespeare's Desdemona's belief in chastity, while Desdemona twice speaks something very close to one of the Shakespearean Emilia's lines: "The world's a huge thing for so small a vice" (19; cf. 32). "How large the world now for so small a vice, eh, Mealy?" and "The world's a huge thing. It is a great price for a small vice"—4.3.67–68. The language is mostly prosaic twentieth-century slang, with dialects indicated to place the characters: "Upper class. Very" for Desdemona, "Broad Irish Brogue" for Emilia, and "Stage Cockney" for

Bianca (4). Though the tone is ultimately different, the play has irreverence in common with the nineteenth-century burlesques of Othello discussed by Lawrence Levine.[12] But one thing remains constant: while Desdemona is now degraded, not just sexually but also in her exploitative attitude toward the other women in the play, she still is going to die at the end—she has not turned into a survivor.

Clearly the fact that so much of Shakespeare's plot remains when the character is so different is part of the point. The play asks, among other things: "Do we feel different about a husband killing a wife who really is unfaithful? Should we? In what ways do we feel the same? How is it that this Desdemona, who is so different from Shakespeare's, in many ways apparently so 'modern,' still is about to suffer the same fate?

In her book *The Currency of Eros,* Ann Rosalind Jones, drawing on Stuart Hall and Christine Gledhill, establishes three categories for women poets' responses to tradition in their own poetry: (1) "close repetition of a model"; (2) "negotiated"—accepting "the dominant ideology encoded into a text but particulariz[ing] and transform[ing] it in service of a different group"; and (3) "oppositional"—in which "the ideological message and force of the reigning code is . . . pulled out of its dominant frame of reference and subversively inserted into an 'alternative frame of reference.'"[13] Both these rewritings belong in the oppositional category, but, like some other plays discussed by Susan Bennett in *Performing Nostalgia,* they are not "so much concerned with the question 'what have we done to Shakespeare's play?' (although both [both Bennett's examples and both these] clearly work with the pleasure in recognition of connection to, yet difference from, the Shakespeare text) but with another which asks 'how can this material be useful to us?'"[14] Like many other twentieth-century women writers, these playwrights use Shakespeare to stress the limitations of his plays as well-known cultural myths about women's possibilities. They use Shakespeare because his cultural authority means that the received notion of female characters in his plays matters more than the received notion of, say, Ben Jonson's Celia. At the same time, they use Shakespeare because many of his female characters provide more material for interesting interpretations than those of most other playwrights.[15]

Both Vogel's play and MacDonald's stress the difference between their images of women and Shakespeare's, yet both playwrights still assume that the play's images of women, and the tradition of criticism surrounding them, are live enough issues to be contested, and MacDonald's play, or at least her protagonist, finds Shakespeare's women appealing in ways she claims the critical tradition has not recognized.[16] MacDonald's assertive

Desdemona is a critique of interpretations of Shakespeare's Desdemona as passive, and of views of women in general as naturally or ideally passive while Vogel's is more of a critique of Shakespeare's Desdemona's marital fidelity and of idealizations of this trait in women. Both plays also critique a tragic worldview. MacDonald imagines a Desdemona who carries a love of war and vengeance so far it becomes comic—for example, when she enthusiastically offers Constance the severed head she has picked up after a battle. Vogel critiques more bitterly, turning tragedy into melodrama mixed with satire, by removing from Desdemona, until the final moments when she is concerned for Emilia, any love of anyone.

Both plays use characters and plot elements from a play focused on a man (and secondarily on his relation to a woman and another man) to construct one focused on a woman and her relation to other women. While lesbianism is an overt part of MacDonald's play (and of MacDonald's and Vogel's own lives), I am not talking specifically about lesbianism here, though I will return to its relevance to both plays later. Constance is more excited about meeting Desdemona and Juliet than she is about meeting their husbands, and MacDonald is much more interested in Desdemona's and Juliet's relationships with Constance than in anyone's relationship with Othello or Romeo. The most important plot development in Vogel's play is the fact that Emilia finally trusts Desdemona enough to tell her about the handkerchief—as she never does in Shakespeare—and what she's observed of Othello's behavior. Critics have sometimes wondered how it is that Shakespeare's Emilia, having stolen the handkerchief, can watch Othello's growing jealousy and Desdemona's growing anxiety and not say anything until it is too late—and then transform herself into a martyr on behalf of Desdemona's chastity. Such a critic may postulate that the shock of Desdemona's death results in a moral growth for Emilia, but Vogel gives us another possibility: Emilia resents Desdemona's exploitation of her and loathes her morals, so her loyalty to Desdemona and her concern about Desdemona's fate are very limited until Emilia's total disillusionment with her husband close to the end.

Both of the plays return to Shakespeare's paradigmatic story of wife-murder to raise the question of why women are killed (or otherwise victimized) and what can prevent this. Both are concerned with the various cultural influences that contribute to women's victimization, though in different ways. Vogel imagines the narrowness of possibilities for Desdemona when Emilia recalls:

> At age 12 she was washin' the courtyard stones for penance, with us wiping up behind her. Then she was taken with horses, thank Jesus, and left sainthood be-

hind—and then in turn again, she thought she was dyin'—stopped eating, and moped, and talked all dreamy and a little balmy-like—until her father finally saw sense and sent her to the convent to be bred out of her boredom. (25)

Vogel underlines the various limiting assumptions that Desdemona and the other characters make: Desdemona thinks she needs Ludovico's help to escape and go back to her father's house—and finally, that she can escape being killed by Othello by pretending to be asleep. Emilia thinks that prayer is the best way to deal with unhappiness in marriage, that women can only rise through their husbands, that there's no friendship between women, and evidently—since she's so devastated by news that he has been at the brothel—that Iago is sexually faithful to her. Bianca thinks that Cassio is going to marry her—"'Coz a gen'l'men don't lie to a bird" (39)—and that, after she gives half her money to a priest so she can consider herself unstained on her wedding night, they will have a cottage by the sea and be happy. Economics, ideologies, and lack of solidarity combine to confine women in this play; it is significant that women make economic gains here either by working formally as prostitutes or, as Desdemona remembers from her youth, in taking expensive presents from men in exchange for sexual favors. Hiding out in Bianca's brothel until she can leave Cyprus would actually provide the best opportunity for Desdemona to survive, but she doesn't understand the need for this until too late, since Emilia doesn't give her enough information until after Bianca has left in a rage over Desdemona's supposed affair with Cassio.[17]

As the play disabuses Emilia and Bianca of their illusions about their men, it leads toward what might be considered in the strictest sense a radical feminist analysis.[18] Late in the play, having learned of her husband's visit to the brothel, Emilia remembers her married life:

Days could pass without a word between us—and he'd take his fill of me the same. I could have been the bed itself. . . . Women just don't figure in their heads—not the one who hangs the wash, not Bianca—and not even you, m'lady. That's the hard truth. Men only see each other in their eyes. Only each other. (*Beat.*) And that's why I'm ready to leave the whole pack of them behind and go with you and the Ambassador. (42–43)

Here Emilia moves away from her previous delusions past the disillusioned view of Shakespeare's Emilia (in her speech attacking the double standard) to an even bleaker view of men, permitting however an escape into a new world.

But at least two details in the play complicate this analysis. On the one hand, Desdemona's own treatment of Emilia is shown to be as much of an exploitation as any man makes of any woman during the play itself, and, furthermore, she is not—until the very last moment—willing to let Emilia go with her. On the other hand, if Desdemona didn't figure in Othello's head, he wouldn't be as preoccupied with her as he is—after this speech Emilia recalls seeing Othello standing outside Desdemona's room, and at other times smelling her sheets for evidence of a lover.

In this conversation Emilia and Desdemona both give up the illusion they have had about Othello's love of Desdemona, but at the end Desdemona still thinks "Surely he'll not . . . harm a sleeping woman" (45). The audience should remember, then, Othello's entrance in Shakespeare's version, seeing Desdemona sleeping, and his waking her up to kill her.

In MacDonald's play, two factors prevent Desdemona's murder. First, Constance appears in Cyprus at the right time and points out to Othello that Iago has the handkerchief. Second, MacDonald has rewritten Desdemona's character to make her more aggressive than in Shakespeare and to leave out the vulnerability that combines with assertiveness in his version. MacDonald also uses both Constance's intervention and a change in personality to redefine Juliet away from victimization: her Juliet, a melodramatic character who enjoys only star-crossed romance, is bored with Romeo after one night's marriage and ready to fall in love and kill herself for Constance.

But the play is even more concerned about the victimization of Constance herself and how it can be ended. At the beginning, in her uncritical devotion to a man who exploits her, Constance seems another version of the popular image of Desdemona. The play suggests that her interactions with Desdemona and Juliet, and the self-discovery they provoke, move Constance beyond victimhood. First, she recalls her bad treatment by Claude, as well as by others back to the bully girls of fifth grade (females are not all good in this play either); she learns to express her anger and to realize that she actually enjoys swordplay with Iago when she thinks she is defending Desdemona. Then, in Verona, she tells Juliet the story of her relationship with Claude, and, at Juliet's urging, is able to declaim, "I love that shit, Claude Night!" (71). After protesting "I'm not up on Sappho," Constance has a flashback to her loss of an erotically tinged friendship from the eighth grade—"I know I felt bereft" (77)—and is briefly ready to contemplate lovemaking with Juliet. Having tried out a bit of the behavior that she associates with Desdemona and Juliet, and seeing what it looks like in the extreme form that it takes in MacDonald's Cyprus and Verona,

Constance becomes assertive enough to tell off her former models and articulate a worldview that, unlike theirs, accepts complexity. Illusions are easier doffed in MacDonald's play than in Vogel's; the main illusions that her Constance needs to lose are her idealizations of Desdemona and Juliet, and spending a little stage time with them makes this simple.

Susan Bennett discusses rewritings of Shakespeare as, among other things, instances of nostalgia, a trait that could be thematized in a fairly strict sense in MacDonald's Constance.[19] She is fascinated not only with Shakespeare but also with an old manuscript, won the Dead Languages Award in college, writes with a pen (made from her dead parakeet) on foolscap, and keeps on her desk relics of her past—her Brownie Owl wings, her appendix. Her interest in Shakespeare's desiring women, Desdemona and Juliet, while she follows a self-sacrificing attachment to a man which involves mainly ghostwriting, could be seen to exemplify the "desire for desire" that Bennett, following Susan Stewart, associates with nostalgia.[20] During the play, however, Constance comes to understand more about her own desires. Moreover, she confronts not only her heroines' limitations as models but also some unattractive aspects of Shakespeare's time, such as belief in witches and enjoyment of public hangings.

Thus, while Constance is nostalgic, both MacDonald's and Vogel's plays unnostalgically rewrite the past mainly to make points about the present.[21] The ideologies that mislead Vogel's women are ideologies held, arguably, by many women today. Vogel may be suggesting that her play represents what Shakespeare's Desdemona, or other women of the time, were really like, contrary to the idealizing version in Shakespeare, but she is even more interested in suggesting that these issues are relevant today: the description on the back cover (presumably approved by Vogel) ends, "What were the roles women had to play then, and still have to play now?" This is one reason why Vogel puts more emphasis on ideological imprisonment than on economic imprisonment. Similarly, MacDonald is more interested in what Desdemona and Juliet mean to Constance, what it's like for her to experience life in an aggressive or more erotic mode, than in Desdemona and Juliet themselves, vivid as both of them are.

Desdemona has not been one of the most rewritten of Shakespeare's female characters, and her fictional and dramatic re-imaginers have usually paid attention to either race or gender but not to both. Frances Burney and George Eliot both wrote novels (*Camilla* and *Middlemarch*) about women and jealous men of the same race (white) with *Othello* allusions that underlined some similarities in restrictions on women in their own societies to those in Shakespeare.[22] In the twentieth century, until recently the best-known rewritings that clearly engaged with *Othello* were much more concerned with race than with gender, and their Desdemonas were of comparatively little interest. Jyotsna Singh has discussed two such rewritings from Africa: Murray Carlin's play *Not Now Sweet Desdemona* and Tayib Salih's novel *Season of Migration from the North,* both published in 1969.[23] Salman Rushdie's 1988 epic novel *The Satanic Verses* writes a version of *Othello* in which both Othello and Iago are Indians—Gibreel and Saladin—in love with white English women and their culture. In two recent novels, Nadine Gordimer's *My Son's Story* (1991) and Caryl Phillips's *The Nature of Blood* (1997), a reminder of the absent woman of color slighted in the interracial romance transforms the *Othello* story, a concern that does not enter the plays I am discussing,

Performed in an often self-consciously multicultural Canada and United States, MacDonald's and Vogel's plays remain in the tradition of pre-Gordimer women's rewritings of *Othello,* mostly concerned with women's gender issues—deliberately decentering the play to de-emphasize Othello himself—but racial issues emerge in both. Vogel's Desdemona explicitly says that part of Othello's original attraction was his blackness and his exoticism, but he disappointed her: "I thought—if I marry this strange dark man, I can leave this narrow little Venice with its whispering piazzas behind—I can escape and see other worlds. (*Pause.*) But under that exotic facade was a porcelain white Venetian" (20). Vogel's Emilia, more like Shakespeare's in this point than in many others, says, "he's as jealous as he's black"(25), though she also knows that her own husband is at least as jealous.

Something more complicated may be going on with regard to race in *Goodnight Desdemona,* but much of it depends on the casting and is not written into the script. Arguably the fact that Desdemona, in MacDonald's version, develops a jealousy like Othello's in Shakespeare's makes an anti-racist point. On the other hand, if Claude Night—who gets a full professorship and an Oxford job on the basis of ghostwritten publications—is played by a black man, as he was in the U.S. premiere in Pittsburgh, and as he often would be, if the actor playing his role doubles as Othello—does the play flirt with racism in its contemporary plot?[24] Still, MacDonald's Constance says, after meeting Othello, "He's not a Moor" (32). In the production in Cambridge, Massachusetts, the actor playing these roles was white.[25] The same actor also typically plays Juliet's Nurse—a role in which, in the version I saw, the actor's blackness fit with playing the role as a parody of a stereotype. He also played a very homophobic Tybalt who is last seen "ardently" carrying off Romeo dressed in Juliet's clothing. By the end, a white spectator, at least, is likely to find flirtation with racism dissolved in the kaleidoscopic reshuffling of many different kinds of stereotypes of race, gender, and sexuality, which alludes to and goes beyond the ambiguous eroticism of Shakespeare's cross-dressing plays.

The minority experience most represented in *Goodnight Desdemona* is lesbianism, though it is presented not as an identity so much as a possibility. When Juliet woos Constance, there is a surprising seriousness and even eloquence in some of her lines, and the emphasis on Juliet's finding beauty in Constance's older face (although she and Romeo have earlier taunted each other about the signs of aging in theirs) suggests that here as elsewhere in the play one of the key issues is Constance's own self-acceptance.[26]

> More beauty in thy testament of years,
> Than in the face of smooth and depthless youth,
> Nay, lovelier by far, now that I see
> the sculpting hand of time upon thy brow;
> O look on me with eyes that looked on life
> Before I e'er was born an infant blind . . . (78)

In an interview with Shannon Hengen, MacDonald says that she uses comedy to help audience members "enter an experience that they thought they had no sympathy for. And in the end they find themselves identifying with people who they thought were perverse or alien or deviant, and that's my credo if I have one."[27] Like Hengen, I find the interchange between Juliet and Constance here a radical moment in the play that recalls this credo.[28] A spectator who sympathizes with Constance and has been drawn into her odyssey in this play has by this point had to deal with her disappointment in Claude and Desdemona and the relatively crude advances of Romeo, who thinks she is a boy. In contrast to Romeo's pursuit in a skirt—and in contrast to Tybalt's attacks on Constance as "an Hellenic deviant"(63)—Juliet's love for Constance, which begins when Constance is disguised as Constantine, may well seem acceptable to spectators often uncomfortable with same-sex wooing. When her love continues after Constance is revealed as female, the disengagement that Shakespearean characters such as Olivia and Phebe experience at similar moments is also rewritten. This play thus rejects the "compulsory heterosexuality" of Shakespearean comedy as well as the equally compulsory death of Shakespearean tragedy.[29]

Vogel, by contrast, presents a world in which both compulsions are in full force, and one clearly leads to the other. Unlike MacDonald's play, *Desdemona* contains no moments of verbally acknowledged sexual attraction between women; yet trust between Emilia and Desdemona, the play keeps hinting, is a way that the two women could escape the deaths ordered for them by Shakespeare's plot. "There's no such thing as friendship between women"(26), says Emilia, and this belief is a large part of what dooms them both.[30]

Still, there are three points in the play of extended physical contact between women. In the first one, Bianca beats Desdemona at her request, reenacting the sadomasochism of interest to some of her clients, giving Desdemona instructions about how to moan. In the second, after Emilia learns that Iago was at the brothel and begins to cry, the stage directions state that "*Desdemona sits beside her, and tentatively puts her arms around Emilia. Then, Desdemona rocks her maid.*" In the third, at the very end of the play, in a transformation of Bianca's strokes, Emilia brushes Desdemona's hair. The play ends with three different segments of the 100 strokes Emilia has promised; the last stroke we see is the ninety-ninth. At the end of these strokes, we know, Desdemona will go to bed and will then be murdered.

The beating scene seems, at first glance, simply added for its shock value: further ritual desecration of the idol Desdemona. To add to the sense of shock and desecration, Emilia prays loudly during this beating. Perhaps the play is just out of control at this point, which is one of the scenes that make it very unlikely that this play would be frequently adapted for classroom use as a companion to *Othello*. On the other hand, one of the key concerns of this play, highlighted in the blurb, is with women's pretenses. Desdemona pretends to be innocent and girlish for her husband, even using fake blood to make herself appear virginal; Emilia pretends that she hasn't stolen the handkerchief. Bianca says that she is not hitting Desdemona very hard but encourages her to moan to make the pain appear worse. What prostitutes do in such beating scenarios, the play suggests, and what Desdemona is presumably doing, is just what performers do—including the performer who is now playing Desdemona. So if we as audience members are swept up into thinking that perhaps Bianca is hitting Desdemona harder than she says she is, this is another example of how the performers are pretending as the characters are. The fact that Vogel's apparatus specifically mentions the Bauer play, which also includes highly theatrical violence revealed as illusory, underlines this theme. At the same time, the audience is being asked to compare the violence that they see onstage here with the violent killing of Desdemona that they never see but know is looming in the background.

A lesbian reading may give even a fuller understanding of this scene, without making it any less transgressive. Perhaps part of the point of this beating is to underline an erotic charge in Desdemona's interest in Bianca—perhaps even to try arousing such a charge in the audience, to give at least a subliminal message that if lesbian eroticism is possible then it is even more perverse for Desdemona to stay with a murderous husband. But an additional suggestion of the lesbian reading is another dimension of the fact that Desdemona begins the play clearly preferring Bianca to Emilia and ends the play having broken up with Bianca and relying, if in a limited way and too late, on Emilia. It is after this beating that Desdemona decides not to go back to the brothel, which signals some distancing from Bianca. Though she claims to find it "smashing," Desdemona turns away from this sort of eroticism.[31] The hair-brushing scene at the end involves physical service that could well be taken as a gentler form of eroticism. Here, though under the threat of Othello's return, Desdemona momentarily finds respite and comfort, as she has given comfort to Emilia in the rocking scene. In the lens the play turns on cross-class relationships among women, it focuses on areas of special interest to lesbians but of importance to other women as well.

Women's rewritings of Shakespeare's tragedies often focus on the possibilities of new plots that will lead to at least survival and often greater freedom for the female characters: think, for instance, of Ginny in *A Thousand Acres* or of Melissa Murray's play *Ophelia,* written in 1979 for the feminist group Hormone Imbalance, in which Ophelia runs off with a maidservant.[32] The fact that Constance manages to save Desdemona's life, and do more with her own, exemplifies one impulse that drives many of these rewritings—though Constance's critique of the surviving Desdemona adds a level of complexity. Vogel, by contrast, in keeping the plot of the murder, rather than letting Desdemona survive, is using a rewriting style more like that of several of the male rewriters concerned with racial issues, such as Salih and Rushdie, rather than that of most of the female rewriters. Like the postcolonial authors, she finds the reasons for the cultural myth of cross-racial wife-murder deeply rooted and examines them.

MacDonald's play, as Richard Paul Knowles has discussed, can be performed and received with a radical edge but also can be domesticated to some extent.[33] Perhaps one of the reasons for its eight printings is that it can be used as a text in a course dealing with Women and Shakespeare, or Rewritings of Shakespeare, and many students will enjoy it while few if any complain about its subversive laughter. Vogel's play is harder to domesticate and riskier to assign. But it is well worth scrutiny for its theatricality and its probing questions about why women are victimized and how women victimize each other.[34]

## Notes

1. Ann-Marie MacDonald, *Goodnight Desdemona (Good Morning Juliet)* (Toronto: Coach House, 1990). Page references will be included in the text.

2. Paula Vogel, *Desdemona: A Play About a Handkerchief* (New York: Dramatists Play Service, 1994). Page references will be included in the text.

3. On feminist interpretive communities, see Annette Kolodny, "Dancing Through the Minefield: Some Observations on the Theory, Practice, and Politics of a Feminist Literary Criticism," *Feminist Studies* 6 (1980): 1–25, and Patrocinio P. Schweickart, "Reading Ourselves: Toward a Feminist Theory of Reading," in *Gender and Reading,* ed. Elizabeth A. Flynn and Patrocinio P. Schweickart (Baltimore, MD: Johns Hopkins University Press, 1986), 31–62.

4. Shakespearean lines quoted outside MacDonald's text are taken from Stephen Greenblatt, ed., *The Norton Shakespeare,* (New York: W. W. Norton, 1997). The lines quoted are from *Othello,* 1.3.162. Subsequent references will be included in the text.

5. Lines taken from Shakespeare are italicized in MacDonald's texts. Often they are used by characters other than those that speak them in Shakespeare.

6. Mary Beth Rose, *The Expense of Spirit: Love and Sexuality in Renaissance Drama* (Ithaca, NY: Cornell University Press, 1988), 137; Carol T. Neely, *Broken Nuptials in Shakespeare's Plays* (New Haven: Yale University Press, 1985), 115, 126; see also Marianne Novy, *Love's Argument: Gender Relations in Shakespeare* (Chapel Hill: University of North Carolina Press, 1984), 148, on how Desdemona identifies with Othello's military abilities.

7. S. N. Garner, "Shakespeare's Desdemona," *Shakespeare Studies* 9 (1976): 233–52. A view of Desdemona even closer to Vogel's has been developed by a few non-feminist critics, such as W. H. Auden, *The Dyer's Hand and Other Essays* (New York: Vintage, 1968), 269 ("Given a few more years of Othello and of Emilia's influence and she might well, one feels, have taken a lover.") Since Auden, like Vogel, uses the unusual form "Ludovico," rather than "Lodovico," his essay may have been one of the inspirations for her play. Garner cites Auden's comments, more cynical than her view, from their earlier publication in "The Alienated City: Reflections on 'Othello,'" *Encounter* 17 (1961): 13. As Garner notes, most critics before her, except for Auden, simply ignored Desdemona's lines about Lodovico.

8. Linda Hutcheon, *A Poetics of Postmodernism: History, Theory, Fiction* (New York: Routledge, 1988), 39. In *The Canadian Postmodern: A Study of Contemporary English-Canadian Fiction* (Toronto: Oxford University Press, 1988), Hutcheon notes, "Parody and irony, then, become major forms of both formal and ideological critique in feminist and Canadian fiction alike"(7).

9. This figure appears in the author's description at the beginning of Ann-Marie MacDonald, *Fall on Your Knees* (London: Vintage, 1997), a novel that won the 1997 Commonwealth Writers Prize for Best First Book.

10. Judith Rudakoff and Rita Much, *Fair Play: Twelve Women Speak: Conversations with Canadian Playwrights* (Toronto: Simon & Pierre, 1990), 136.

11. Wolfgang Bauer, *Shakespeare the Sadist,* trans. Renata and Martin Esslin (London: Eyre Methuen, 1977), 18, 21.

12. Lawrence Levine, *Highbrow/Lowbrow: The Emergence of Cultural Hierarchy in America* (Cambridge, MA: Harvard University Press, 1988).

13. Ann Rosalind Jones, *The Currency of Eros: Women's Love Lyric in Europe, 1540–1620* (Bloomington: Indiana University Press, 1990), 4–6. Jones is building on Christine Gledhill, "Pleasurable Negotiations," in *Female Spectators: Looking at Film and Television,* ed. Deirdre Pribram (London: Verso, 1988), and Stuart Hall, "Encoding/Decoding," in *Culture, Media, Language,* ed. Stuart Hall et al. (London: Hutchinson, 1980), 128–48.

14. Susan Bennett, *Performing Nostalgia: Shifting Shakespeare and the Contemporary Past* (New York: Routledge, 1996), 56.

15. I discuss these issues further in my book *Engaging with Shakespeare: Responses of George Eliot and Other Women Novelists* (Athens: University of Georgia Press, 1994). See also Martha Tuck Rozett, *Talking Back to Shakespeare* (Newark: University of Delaware Press, 1994), esp. 6, for her discussion of transformations and their relation not just to one previous text but also to its social or reception history. Her discussion of *Goodnight Desdemona* compares Constance to her own students (163); Rozett has also written a review of *Desdemona* that emphasizes its connection with Thomas Rymer's complaint about the handkerchief in *A Short View of Tragedy* (1693). Rozett, "*Desdemona: A Play About a Handkerchief,*" *Shakespeare Bulletin* 12, no. 3 (Summer 1994): 17.

16. There is a surprisingly long history of women's protest against popular views of Desdemona. See Elizabeth Griffith, "From *The Morality of Shakespeare's Drama Illustrated*" (1775), rpt. in *Women Critics 1660–1820,* ed. Folger Collective on Early Women Critics (Bloomington: Indiana University Press, 1995), 122, who says, "She speaks little, but whatever she says is sensible, pure, and chaste," and, for a view more like Constance's, see Helena Faucit, writing in 1880 of Desdemona as "courageous," and protesting against a usual view of her as "a merely amiable, simple, yielding creature," *Women Reading Shakespeare 1660–1900: An Anthology of Criticism,* ed. Ann Thompson and Sasha Roberts (New York: Manchester University Press, 1997), 191.

17. The prefatory information in the text, which presumably would appear in the program, refers to "Desdemona's last day on Cyprus," which might well lead to the hope that she might survive.

18. Emilia's speech uses some imagery close to that of the radical feminist philosopher Marilyn Frye in her essay "To See and Be Seen: The Politics of

Reality," in *The Politics of Reality: Essays in Feminist Theory* (Trumansburg, NY: The Crossing Press, 1983): "Women's existence is a background against which phallocratic reality is a foreground. . . . The background is unseen by the eye which is focused on foreground figures" (167).

19. Bennett, *Performing Nostalgia,* 7. On 6–7 Bennett emphasizes the pervasiveness of nostalgia across ideology and other categories.

20. Ibid., 6, quoting Susan Stewart, *On Longing: Narratives of the Miniature, the Gigantic, the Souvenir, The Collection* (Baltimore, MD: Johns Hopkins University Press, 1984), 23.

21. The plays themselves have affinity with Linda Hutcheon's "postmodernist ironic rethinking of history . . . definitely not nostalgic . . . [which] critically confronts the past with the present, and vice versa." Hutcheon, *Poetics of Postmodernism,* 39.

22. For Burney, see Margaret Doody, *Frances Burney* (New Brunswick, NJ: Rutgers University, 1988), 224–25. For Eliot, see Novy, *Engaging with Shakespeare,* 104–5.

23. Jyotsna Singh, "Othello's Identity, Postcolonial Theory, and Contemporary African Rewritings of *Othello,*" in *Women. "Race," and Writing in the Early Modern Period* (New York: Routledge, 1994), 287–99.

24. According to the photo, he seems also to have been played by an actor of color in the Toronto production discussed by Mark Fortier in "Shakespeare with a Difference: Genderbending and Genrebending in *Goodnight Desdemona,*" *Canadian Theatre Review* 59 (Summer 1989): 47–51. Fortier says, on page 51, that the play elides the issue of race. Possibly, because of Canada's different history with regard to slavery, and greater consciousness of French and Indian minorities, Night's blackness would look different than it would in the United States.

25. Personal communication, Carolyn Swift.

26. Earlier in the play, Constance has asked Juliet, "Are you afraid of growing old?" (65). The praise for the beauty of middle age, in the context of both homoeroticism and rewriting Shakespeare, rewrites the association of aging with losing beauty in many of Shakespeare's sonnets.

27. Shannon Hengen, "Towards a Feminist Comedy," *Modern Drama* 38 (Fall 1995): 103.

28. Ibid., 107.

29. See Adrienne Rich, "Compulsory Heterosexuality and Lesbian Existence," in *Blood, Bread, and Poetry: Selected Prose 1979–1985* (New York: Norton, 1986), 23–75. Rich's emphasis in this essay on a "system of heterosexual propaganda" (71) suggests an analysis in some ways similar to Vogel's underlining of how Bianca, Emilia, and Desdemona all hold beliefs about men that, at best, confine them, and, at worst, kill them.

30. It is a sign of this play's bad luck with its critical reception that the *New York Times* critic took "There's no such thing as friendship between women" to

be "a typical billboard declaration"—i.e., the play's message. See Ben Brant-ley, "Review," *New York Times,* November 12, 1993, C: 20. Like the acade-mics about whom Constance complains, he also referred to Desdemona as "one of Shakespeare's most passive and virtuous heroines."

31. For a review and analysis of lesbian debates about sadomasochism, see Shane Phelan, *Getting Specific: Postmodern Lesbian Politics* (Minneapolis: University of Minnesota Press, 1994).

32. This play is discussed by Elaine Showalter, in "Representing Ophelia: Women, Madness, and the Responsibilities of Feminist Criticism," in *Shake-speare and the Question of Theory,* ed. Patricia Parker and Geoffrey Hartman (New York: Methuen, 1985), 77–94.

33. Richard Paul Knowles, "Reading Material: Transfers, Remounts, and the Production of Meaning in Contemporary Toronto Drama and Theatre," *Es-says on Canadian Writing* 51–2 (Winter-Spring): 258–295; see esp. 279.

34. I would like to thank Attilio Favorini for giving me a copy of the script used in the Three Rivers Shakespeare Festival production of *Goodnight Desde-mona,* Nona Fienberg for persuading me to look again at *Desdemona,* Bob Sawyer for inviting me to speak at his 1997 SAMLA special session, "The Appropriation of Shakespeare," and Jyotsna Singh for her comments on an earlier version of this paper in her role as respondent for that panel.

# 5

# Rita Dove's Shakespeares

## Peter Erickson

> every song he sings
> is by Shakespeare
> and his mother-in-law.
>
> —"Shakespeare Say"
>
> .
>
> Fig newtons
> and *King Lear,* bitter lemon as well
> for Othello, that desolate
> conspicuous soul.
> But Macbeth demanded dry bread,
> crumbs brushed from a lap
> as I staggered off the cushions
> contrite, having read far past
> my mother's calling.
>
> —"In the Old Neighborhood"

Black writers' approaches to Shakespeare have never been monolithic. Two of the most memorable passages on Shakespeare in twentieth-century African-American letters define the opposite ends of a very broad spectrum. In the paragraph that concludes chapter VI of *The Souls of Black Folk* (1903), W. E. B. Du Bois declares: "I sit with Shakespeare and he winces not."[1] Fifty years later Du Bois's mood of serene mutuality is sharply undercut by the angry sense of exclusion articulated in James Baldwin's 1953 essay "Stranger in the Village": "The most illiterate among them [white Europeans] is related, in a way that I am not, to Dante, Shakespeare, Michelangelo, Aeschylus, Da Vinci, Rembrandt, and Racine; the cathedral at Chartres says something to them which it cannot say to me"[2]

Du Bois's triumphant placement of "not" as the positive final word in the sentence—"he winces not"—is reversed by the insistent negative force of Baldwin's stress on "not"—"in a way that I am not," "which it cannot say to me." Baldwin thus explicitly questions and denies Du Bois's central image of harmonious communication—"Across the color line I move arm in arm"—in an idealized cultural realm where "wed with Truth, I dwell above the veil."

"Shakespeare Say" in *Museum* (1983) and "In the Old Neighborhood" in *Selected Poems* (1993),[3] two poems in which Rita Dove presents different images of Shakespeare, need to be read in this larger context of the history of African-American responses to Shakespeare. The purpose of the plural Shakespeares in my title is to suggest not only that Dove inherits a tradition with multiple versions of Shakespeare but also that she actively intervenes in this tradition by ranging across its spectrum, playing with her own combinations and freely creating new variations.

The present essay is organized in two parts. The first consists of the full transcript of Rita Dove's comments in response to a set of questions concerning Shakespeare, while the second part presents my commentary on her two poems involving Shakespeare. I am extremely grateful to Rita Dove for her participation in this project and for her permission both to print the interview and to quote from her poetry.

## I. Shakespeare Questions

PE: As background, I am working with two of the greatest Shakespearean touchstones in African-American letters: W. E. B. Du Bois's "I sit with Shakespeare and he winces not" in *The Souls of Black Folk* and James Baldwin's "The most illiterate of them is related, in a way that I am not, to Dante, Shakespeare" in "Stranger in the Village," the final essay in *Notes of a Native Son.* I am interested in any observations you may have about these two passages.

I am also wondering whether you encountered either of these when you were growing up. If so, what do you recall about the specific moment and the specific meaning of the encounter?

RD: The difference between W. E. B. Du Bois's comment in *The Souls of Black Folk*—"I sit with Shakespeare and he winces not"—and my first encounter with Shakespeare is rather radical. I encountered Shakespeare as an innocent—that is, I was not "introduced" to Shakespeare but rather stumbled upon him, much as one would bump into a stranger at a party and discover that one had a lot in common to talk about. Shakespeare was on the bookshelves in my parents' home, and though I knew he was a Famous Writer, at the age of 10 or 11 I did not truly comprehend just what that meant. I began reading Shakespeare as a challenge to myself, not a challenge set up by an Authority Figure, and I believe that has made all the difference in the world regarding my entry into literature, for I found Shakespeare a kindred soul. My discovery of James Baldwin, on the other hand, is a different story. My first contact with him was the startling encounter with his portrait on the back of his essay collection *Notes of a Native Son.* My parents had bought the book, and I remember my mother taking it along to read while I had my private cello lessons at the Akron Conservatory of Music. In a way, Baldwin might have been amused by the irony of such a situation, since the essay you mention, "Stranger in the Village," discusses this very question of legacy.

PE: I assume that "Shakespeare Say" may have originated in your seeing an actual live performance by Champion Jack Dupree. If so, could you comment on the circumstances and on your reactions at the time? How would you characterize the relation between the event and the poem? Do you see the poem at all as a reflection or reconsideration (though not necessarily as an emotion recollected in tranquillity!)?

Also, do you have any feelings about the European context of the poem? Does it make a difference that the setting is Munich rather than somewhere in the U.S.?

RD: I did experience a live performance by Champion Jack Dupree. It occurred not in Munich, as the poem claims, but in the city of Bielefeld, where I spent ten weeks as part of a group of international writers and critics in the fall of 1980. How I relate the event, however, is pretty much true to the way it happened. Champion Jack Dupree did use "Shakespeare Say" as a running joke throughout his banter; the audience was enamoured by his "exoticism"—and completely unaware of their own ignorance. Of course, I imagined the thoughts that Champion Jack entertains while playing his sets. I think it does make a difference that the setting is Germany rather than somewhere in the United States, for the very same reasons that James Baldwin's reflections on the White Man's Privilege [were] sparked by his experiences in Europe. Sometimes one needs to get away to see clearly the conflicting circumstances from which one has arisen.

PE: Concerning "In the Old Neighborhood," I continue to be struck by your use of the 1970 epigraph from Adrienne Rich's emotionally explosive *The Will to Change*. Could you comment on how you discovered and responded to Rich's work?

RD: It's difficult for me to comment on Adrienne Rich, except to say that she has always been an example to me—not only for the quality of her work, which I admire, but also for the paradigm of her life. Here is a poet who was willing to jettison all of the easy trappings of fame—after all, her first book was chosen by Auden for the Yale Younger Poets Prize—in order to discover what kind of language would be capable of bearing witness to the life she was experiencing.

PE: How did the two "wine-red" "bouillon cubes" enter your family library? Were the Shakespeare volumes associated with a particular family member? Did you discuss your reading?

With regard to "Othello, that desolate / conspicuous soul," can you recall your experience on first looking into this play and where, in the overall sequence of reading Shakespeare's works, did you read *Othello?* Did you see it as an equal part of the great tragic sweep of *Hamlet, Othello, Lear, Macbeth,* or did you experience it as set apart, different? Finally, have you witnessed any performances of *Othello* that had a powerful impact?

RD: I never discussed my early reading of Shakespeare with anyone. And I do not know exactly how the Shakespeare volumes appeared in my family library. My father has always read voraciously; when my older brother and I were not quite in our teens, my father ordered the entire Great Books of the Western World, as much for his own pleasure as for our education. I can only imagine that the two "wine-red" volumes of Shakespeare were part of his hunger to understand as much about the umbrella culture under which he was born as possible. I cannot recall exactly when I read *Othello,* except to say that I know I read it before I turned thirteen. The very first Shakespeare play I read was *Macbeth,* mainly because I heard my mother reciting from it at length; it was rapidly followed by *Romeo and Juliet, Julius Caesar,* and *A Midsummer Night's Dream.* I started *Lear* but didn't finish it (nor did I read *Hamlet*) until years later, in school. *Othello* must have happened sometime around *Romeo and Juliet* (I read all of these in one summer!), and I did read *Othello* because I was intrigued by the fact that this British Elizabethan had such a large mind that he was able to imagine a black man as a prince in Italy! It was certainly not the kind of imagination that I saw bearing any fruit in the more contemporary literature I had come across up to then. Interestingly enough, I have never seen a live performance of *Othello.*

PE: I need to ask you about the way stanzas 10 to 12 in "In the Old Neighborhood" are bracketed in parentheses because these seem to mark a separate zone that disrupts the temporal counterpoint between 1993, the present moment when the poet returns home for a family reunion occasioned by her younger sister's wedding, and 1973, "twenty years before," the moment when the poet at 21 with a new B. A. perhaps first left the home within which she had lived so completely up to that point. But when I reach the section in parentheses, I don't know where I am! The verbs don't allow me easily to identify the timeframe. The tone and mood of "I'll ask" make me imagine the final Lear-Cordelia encounter—no doubt the result of my excessively Shakespeare-steeped intellect! In any event, the transition from *"All weeds"* to *"Chink. Chink."* is so excitingly abrupt that I hardly know how to talk about it. I would welcome your comments here.

RD: Actually, the present in the poem is closer to 1982, when the poet is 30, and the "twenty years before" refers to about 1962, an "innocent" age of 10 when the child was taught to read the newspaper "correctly"—maybe so she would begin to understand what was going on in our country at that time of social and racial upheaval. But back to the gist of your question: These parenthetical stanzas in the poem "In the Old Neighborhood" are a dream sequence interrupting the collage of memory and present activity in the poem at large. In a way, these stanzas are like an invocation to memory—an attempt, through incantatory language, to summon up a kind of psychic landscape through which the speaker can travel and discover the subconscious significance of familial relationships. The speaker asks to go back to "the white rock on the black lawn." There is actually a huge white rock in the front yard of my parents' house; and on this rock they have painted the house number in black paint. I did not expect the casual reader to figure this out through the poem; instead, I think that in these stanzas the house looms as the "white rock" "moored in moonlight." The speaker, therefore, is in this dream landscape, one in which the house appears as an impenetrable brightness and the speaker is walking along the dark grass, in effect almost sinking into the darkness. Everything around her is quieted and sealed away from her understanding—even the pansies have been placed behind bars of the picket fence. When the speaker dares to address the father directly, ostensibly to ask him a gardener's question, all the father can offer is another image of failure. We discover, however, that the father is not out in this psychic landscape with the speaker; rather, he "intuits" her presence outside the house—the house she dare not/cannot enter—he mutters from his pillow that all of these plants that he has tried to nourish are not presentable but are "All weeds."

The first words after these parenthetical stanzas represent a sound, because sounds are often what will snatch us out of a deep reverie. *Chink* could be the sound of a hoe hitting rock; it also suggests, rather disconcertingly, an unsavory racial epithet. But just as the reader is confused, fascinated and a little bit repulsed by the sound, the speaker of the poem struggles to make sense of it—and finds in the true reason an even more horrifying event.

PE: Could you please comment on whether you ever met the novelist Leon Forrest? I realize this may seem an odd, off-the-wall question but as I am rereading *Divine Days,* I'm struck by two connections between his work and yours. You both explicitly address the limitations of the Black Aesthetic and you both engage Shakespeare. If you did meet Forrest, was there any discussion of these themes?

RD: I met Leon Forrest only once—and very briefly—in the spring of 1995. I was in Chicago for the American Booksellers Association's annual fair, and after my reading he approached me and gave me a copy of *Divine Days.* Unfortunately, I never had the opportunity to meet him again. We had no time to discuss our affinities, but I have always felt him to be a kindred spirit.

## II. Poetic Transformations

My approach in this section is twofold. First, I aim to establish the multiplicity of Rita Dove's invocation of Shakespeare's name by suggesting that as an initial step we think of "Shakespeare Say" as her Baldwin poem and "In the Old Neighborhood" as her Du Bois poem. Though I shall subsequently explore connections between the two poems, I want first to bring out their differences in order to emphasize the extraordinary range that Dove encompasses and, in particular, her capacity to embrace both sides of the Baldwin-Du Bois opposition. Second, I hope to demonstrate that Dove does not merely reproduce two received images of Shakespeare but also plays with them to create new effects and novel outcomes. My strategy for this part of the argument will be to show how convergences between Baldwin and Du Bois may be seen as providing a flexible basis on which Dove can conduct her mobile experiments in poetic transformation.

The contrasting tones of "Shakespeare Say" and "In the Old Neighborhood" stem from the divergent status of their speaking voices: in the former, Dove speaks through, and is partly hidden behind, the black blues singer Champion Jack Dupree, whereas in the latter she speaks directly in her own voice. The ease with which Dove herself claims access and connection to Shakespeare in "In the Old Neighborhood" follows from his location within

the family home: "I've read every book in this house, " and the second line
of the poem indicates that the family has reunited for her sister's wedding,
an event that signifies family renewal and continuity. The poem builds the
family constellation by introducing each member in turn—sister, mother,
father, self, brother—and celebrates their unity in a summary italicized line:
"*whole again whole again now.*" In keeping with this spirit, Shakespeare is so
congenial as to be almost part of the family. The affirmation of familial harmony is matched by her harmonious initiation as a reader of Shakespeare,
an activity portrayed as natural as the specific images of eating associated
with each play. Like Du Bois, the Dove of this poem can positively imply
that Shakespeare "winces not."

As we might expect, Champion Jack Dupree in "Shakespeare Say" seeks
oral satisfaction of a rawer sort. The image of Champion Jack wielding "the
bourbon in his hand" as he readies himself for the third set is both raucous
and strangely subdued. Alcohol signals release—the license to transcend
codes of politeness and to speak without constraint. Yet, at the same time,
the singer's mirroring of the audience's "stinking on beer" testifies to his
need for emotional numbness in the face of underlying sadness and pain.
As early as lines 10 and 11, the expansive, genial, affectionate portrayal of
Champion Jack is cross-cut with a disturbingly harsh note that pulls us up
short: "with sand / in a mouthful of mush." Like the Baldwin of "Stranger
in the Village," Champion Jack is an artist in European exile and a figure
of alienation.

His alienation is double-edged. As an outsider, he mocks and rejects the
Western tradition epitomized by Shakespeare's dominant canonical position.
Shakespeare is the most quotable of authors: Champion Jack parodies this
cultural reflex by violating the sacred status of Shakespeare's actual words
and using Shakespeare's name as an ironic all-purpose endorsement for
whatever the Champion improvises on the spot. This is an effective way of
making Baldwin's point that Shakespeare does not speak to or for everyone.
But the other side of this subversive public performance is the unredeemable
loss he expresses in his private voice—"so no one hears"—at the poem's culmination: "*my home's in Louisiana, / my voice is wrong.*"

The "near-tragic" depth of this final self-negation may be understood
in terms of Ralph Ellison's definition of the blues: "The blues is an impulse to keep the painful details and episodes of a brutal experience alive
in one's aching consciousness, to finger its jagged grain, and to transcend
it, not by the consolation of philosophy but by squeezing from it a near-
tragic, near-comic lyricism."[4] Yet despite the aptness of Ellison's eloquent
statement to Champion Jack's situation, the enormity of the pain this

poem evokes can perhaps be fully measured only by reference to June Jordan's ringing counterassertion in "Poem about My Rights": "*I am not wrong: Wrong is not my name.*"[5] This is a response of which we feel Champion Jack's entrapment makes him incapable. Of course Dove herself cannot be identified with the poem's main character in this regard. Although she allows him to retain a basic dignity and even an endearing flair, she is also unsentimentally clear-eyed about his self-pity, his limited view of women, and his musical deficiencies—the word "mistakes" in "even the mistakes / sound like jazz" has a sting that is not entirely forgiving.

Having established the counterpoint between Champion Jack cut off from home in "Shakespeare Say" and Rita Dove ensconced in family environment in "In the Old Neighborhood," I now want to explore the possibility of a more comprehensive perspective from which, without canceling the contrast, we might begin to see points of overlap that could lead to a larger synthesis.[6] My starting point is a reconsideration of the Baldwin–Du Bois tension. While the perception of tension remains valid, we can also discern elements of convergence that qualify the idea of absolute diametrical opposition.

On Baldwin's side, the total rejection of Shakespeare registered in "Stranger in the Village" is substantially modified when he reverts to Shakespeare and Chartres twenty years later in *No Name in the Street.* Baldwin now envisions a two-step process in which "throwing out" Shakespeare is followed by a second move: "Later, of course, one may welcome them back, but on one's own terms."[7] On Du Bois's side, the "I sit with Shakespeare" declaration is frequently distorted because it is excerpted in a decontextualized manner.[8] Du Bois's homage to Shakespeare is in fact counterbalanced in the immediately preceding paragraph by an equally strong assertion of the power of American blacks to make an innovative cultural contribution: "Herein the longing of black men must have respect: the rich and bitter depth of their experience, the unknown treasures of their inner life, the strange rendings of nature they have seen, may give the world new points of view and make their loving, living, and doing precious to all human hearts." Although the contrasting emphases are indeed present in their key passages on Shakespeare, Baldwin's subsequent shift to "on one's own terms" and Du Bois's commitment to "new points of view" nonetheless bring the two authors closer together in a shared conceptual arena. Similarly, while the contrast between "Shakespeare Say" and "In the Old Neighborhood" still stands, at another level points of connection emerge when we take a second look at the latter poem.

"In the Old Neighborhood" is easy to underestimate because of the way its amiable surface tone is carried by a flood of genuine family affection. Yet there is an underlying complexity that pulls back away from this emotional tide and moves the poem in another direction: a meditation on reading and, by extension, on the writing career into which the poet has been led by this childhood habit.

After portraying her parents' respective styles of imaginative profusion and extravagance, Dove turns to herself in the poem's fourth stanza, where she intimates a slight tension between two versions of reading:

> I am indoors, pretending
> to read today's paper
> as I had been taught
> twenty years before:
> headlines first,
> lead story (continued on A-14),
> followed by editorials and
> local coverage. Even then
> I never finished, snared
> between datelines—*Santiago,*
> *Paris, Dakar*—names as
> unreal as the future
> even now.

The first version, defined by the phrase "as I had been taught," portrays the act of reading as an orderly process of gleaning factual information. The resistance to this mode is quietly pursued through the ongoing motif of the newspaper: "I skip to the daily horoscope," "I fold the crossword away." The horoscope and the crossword puzzle are not, one is made to feel, part of the authorized agenda. The poem's concluding lines involving the newspaper's obliteration in recycling pick up and linger over the telltale phrase—"properly, / as I had been taught to do"—as though definitively to set it aside by repeating it with an ironic twist.

The alternative version of reading is harder to define since its pleasure is portrayed in part as the evasion of regulation: "as I staggered off the cushions / contrite, having read far past / my mother's calling." A hint is given in the way the child is drawn by the single words of the cities in the datelines into a global expanse that entices the imagination far beyond the domestic household. The goal, however, is not merely escape or adventure but also a worldview in a deeper sense. It is no coincidence that Dakar appears as the decisive final term in the list, for it points to Africa and to the history of race. This motif is subtle but recurrent: we hear it again in the reference to Othello as "that desolate / conspicuous soul." Compressed as this notation is, it introduces a moment of troubled questioning that counteracts the easygoing appreciation of Shakespeare. Othello is the only character who is accorded adjectives, and the two adjectives attract attention because their apposition lacks a comma and is split over two lines. Othello is not only conspicuous because he is desolate; his desolation has its mainspring in his conspicuousness, his visibility as a black man in a white culture. The child reader is tacitly shown stumbling on discoveries, though these are presented with a restraint that avoids intruding on the overall upbeat atmosphere.

The poem's characteristic deftness is displayed in the understated quality of the epigraph citing Adrienne Rich: "*To pull yourself up by your own roots; / to eat the last meal in your own neighborhood.*" Without counterpoising Rich and Shakespeare in direct confrontation, Dove nevertheless implicitly indicates alternatives to Shakespeare for authoritative reading experiences.[9] In contrast to the generally pleasurable mix of eating and reading associated with Shakespeare, Rich presents a sterner image of food involving renunciation of comfort and security in favor of change and the development of new identity. The positioning of Rich's lines as the epigraph casts the entire poem in a retrospective frame: the Dove who is writing the poem is no longer the Dove described within the poem. She has already grown up and moved on. If she returns now, it is only to confirm her departure by symbolically "eating the last meal." The Rich quotation also subtly provides "In the Old Neighborhood" with a literary genealogy of far more explosive intensity than we might at first glance realize. Dove's identification with Rich's lines has larger ramifications because they are the very last two lines in *The Will to Change: Poems, 1968–1970* and hence poised on the cusp of the dramatic transition to *Diving into the Wreck: Poems, 1971–1972.*[10]

In order to test the thesis that "In the Old Neighborhood" is structured by means of a strategy of deceptive understatement, I turn to the question of the poem's pattern of color imagery. "Color" in relation to Dove's father's roses is an announced theme. But there is a distinct strand that has specifically racial significance whose impact depends on the cumulative power of slight effects to convey a larger metaphorical resonance.

The first instance, the raccoons' "black-gloved paws" with which the opening stanza ends, is so slight that it passes by unnoticed. Like "Shakespeare Say" ("He drums the piano wood, / crowing"), "In the Old Neighborhood" begins with an energetic, colloquial tone turned up full volume. But the heightened mood concentrates our attention on the single arresting word "faggy." Our uncertainty thus engaged elsewhere, the detail of the "black-gloved paws" strikes us as vivid but innocent. Surely, we conclude, no subliminal allusion to "coon" as a racial slur can be intended here.

The references to Dakar and Othello put us sufficiently on alert to hear the potential for something more than a race-neutral night scene: "(Let me go back to the white rock / on the black lawn, the number / stenciled in negative light. / Let me return to the shadow / of a house moored in moonlight." The eeriness of Dove's chiaroscuro has its playful, teasing aspect even as it seems haunted, driven. To apply Dove's word for Othello, the color scheme is "conspicuous": it stands out, calls out, suggestively. We are forced to consider the possibility that racial reverberations are metaphorically present in this overdetermined language of white and black. Her father's spectacular success with mutant roses—"this sudden teacup / blazing empty, its rim / a drunken red smear"—is now unaccountably turned to failure.[11] The "negative light" makes his flowers seem worthless: "*Weeds,* my father mutters / from his pillow. *All weeds.*" Only the fragile wedding corsage at the end pulls back from this image of despair—a precarious recovery.

The final drama of the destruction of the starling by the attic fan's blades reads like such an outlandish parody of the caged bird in Paul Laurence Dunbar's "Sympathy" that it at first appears more like comedy than "the first tragedy of the season." Yet how do we interpret the seemingly offhand dismissal in the rhetorically loaded question: "Who could guess it would be / a bird with no song, / no plumage worth stopping for?" If we are willing to see an analogy between the weeping girl trapped in the tent and the bird, then the latter's destruction expresses in hyperbolic form a danger faced by the former. The fear of a black poet's failure is registered in the bird's triple negative: the starling has "no plumage worth stopping for" because it is black; the "bird with no song" signifies poetic inability; the bird's annihilation, concluded by the unceremonious disposal with the fan's reverse switch, condemns it to anonymity. Dove's own poetic splendors are proof against this fate, but her cruelly macabre farce of the starling's demise ruefully acknowledges the lingering force of the stereotype that she has had to overcome.

Closer examination reveals that, contrary to the initial impression of pure congeniality, "In the Old Neighborhood" has an attitude as questioning as that of "Shakespeare Say." In both poems the allusion to Shakespeare prompts not an occasion for simple celebration but rather an exploration of a problematic inheritance.

### III. Coda

I began by placing Rita Dove's poems in relation to an African-American literary tradition; I conclude by situating them in a wider American context.

Far from being mutually exclusive, the terms African-American and American are mutually constitutive. Perhaps the single most important feature of Dove's work as a whole is the remarkable sense of freedom conveyed by her verbal exuberance, dexterity, and audacity. A central challenge is how to describe the culturally specific American implications of this freedom.

Helen Vendler, the dominant shaper of Dove studies to date, is right to emphasize Dove's freedom from separatist formulas of racial identity and hence from rigidly circumscribed expectations of what it means "to make a poet black, and bid him sing."[12] However, valuable as Vendler's critical perspective is, it is ultimately limited and one-sided because she does not devote equal attention and sophistication to the critique of universalism, even though she is aware of the problem of "false 'universality.'"[13] In order to perceive the full scope of the freedom Dove asserts with regard to race, it is necessary to present a balanced analysis of the simplifications of universalism as well as of separatism. For the freedom Dove enacts in her poetry is not just freedom from race but also freedom to address racial issues by rejecting both separatist and universalist constructions of them.

With a view to reopening and expanding the racial significance of Dove's work, I turn to the nineteenth-century American phenomenon of minstrelsy, of which Champion Jack Dupree can be seen as a distant descendant. Two of the most potent signifiers for exploring a distinctive American identity are Shakespeare and race; this potency is intensified by their conjunction in instances of Shakespeare burlesque involving blackface.[14] In one paradigm the intersection of representations of Shakespeare and representations of blackness leads to a double satire in which one stone kills two birds by licensing the display of both anti-Shakespeare and anti-black feeling.[15] Mockery of Shakespeare that signals American cultural independence is thus fundamentally compromised at the outset because such self-definition is simultaneously tied to a racist outlook.

This particular formation is tantalizingly suggested as a central motif in Mark Twain's *Adventures of Huckleberry Finn*. Jim's characterization draws in part on blackface minstrelsy,[16] while the King and the Duke perform Shakespeare burlesque. But although the two elements are placed in proximity, they are not joined, with the result that the problem of race is incompletely probed and therefore left unresolved.[17]

This is the sensitive cultural zone in which Dove's poems intervene to perform their liberating work. Dove does not sidestep but rather works with the given materials of Shakespeare and of blackness so as innovatively to recast them. Using her own vigorous poetic presence to reconstitute these basic categories, Dove develops new possibilities for American self-fashioning. The consequence is a transformative poetic space that frees us from the endlessly problematic monopoly that *Othello* and *Huckleberry Finn* seemed to hold over our literary discourse on race. As black poet, Dove empowers us to think in new ways about the significance of blackness and hence to reenter the central crux of American national identity.

## Notes

1. W. E. B. Dubois, *The Souls of Black Folk* (New York: Bantam, 1989), 76.
2. James Baldwin, "Stranger in the Village," *Notes of a Native Son* (New York: Dial Press, 1955), 148.
3. Rita Dove, *Museum* (Pittsburgh, PA: Carnegie-Mellon University Press, 1983); *Selected Poems* (New York: Pantheon, 1993).
4. Ralph Ellison, "Richard Wright's Blues" (1945), in *Shadow and Act* (New York: Random House, 1964), 90.
5. June Jordan, "Poem about My Rights," *Passion: New Poems, 1977–1980* (Boston: Beacon Press, 1980), 89.
6. In "On Voice," in *Dwelling in Possibility: Women Poets and Critics on Poetry,* ed. Yopie Prins and Maeera Shreiber (Ithaca, NY: Cornell University Press, 1997), 111–15, Dove describes Europe and home as two points in her own overall trajectory: "In *Museum* (1983) I was very concerned with presenting a type of antimuseum, a collection of totems that would not be considered 'essential' to the canon of Western culture—and to that end I adopted a voice that was distanced, cool, ironic; of all my books, this is the most 'European.' After *Museum* I felt I had gone away from home and was now able to return, like a prodigal daughter"(111).
7. James Baldwin, *No Name in the Street* (New York: Dial Press, 1972), 47–48. In a short piece chronologically midway between "Stranger in the Village" and *No Name in the Street*—"'This Nettle, Danger'" (1964), in *James Baldwin: Collected Essays* (New York: Library of America, 1998), 687–91—Baldwin defined the terms that enabled his return to Shakespeare: "Every man writes about his own Shakespeare—and his Shakespeare changes as he himself changes, grows as he grows—and the Shakespeare that I am reading at this stage of my life testifies, for me, to this effort" (688). However, Baldwin's new acceptance goes so far as to remove Shylock and Othello from critical scrutiny; in my view, this reaction goes too far in the other direction.
8. For further discussion of this decontextualization, see the section on Du Bois in Peter Erickson, "The Two Renaissances and Shakespeare's Canonical Position," *Kenyon Review,* n.s., 14, no. 2 (Spring 1992): 58–60.
9. An extended account of Rich's work is given in my essays: "Adrienne Rich's Re-Vision of Shakespeare," in *Rewriting Shakespeare, Rewriting Ourselves*

(Berkeley: University of California Press, 1991), 146–66; "Singing America: From Walt Whitman to Adrienne Rich," *Kenyon Review,* n.s., 17, no. 1 (Winter 1995): 103–19; and "Start Misquoting Him Now: The Difference a Word Makes in Adrienne Rich's 'Inscriptions,'" *Shakespeare and the Classroom* 5, no. 1 (Spring 1997): 55–56.

10. The Rich quotation that Dove chooses belongs to the same moment as Rich's critical shift in "When We Dead Awaken: Writing as Re-Vision" (1971) in *On Lies, Secrets, and Silence* (New York: Norton, 1979), 33–49. Rich's concept of "re-vision" inspired the three-volume project edited by Marianne Novy: *Women's Re-Visions of Shakespeare* (Urbana: University of Illinois Press, 1990), *Cross-Cultural Performances: Differences in Women's Re-Visions of Shakespeare* (Urbana: University of Illinois Press, 1993), and the present collection. A full picture of black writers' responses to Shakespeare can be completed only when male authors are taken into account; in addition to Du Bois and Baldwin discussed here, examples can be found in my essays: "Contextualizing *Othello* in Reed and Phillips," *The Upstart Crow: A Shakespeare Journal* 17 (1997): 101–107, and a work in progress on Leon Forrest's Shakespeare-saturated texts.

11. In the final "Autobiography" section of *The Poet's World* (Washington, D.C.: Library of Congress, 1995), Dove locates a source for the father's despair in the racial discrimination that thwarted his career, despite his university degree (75–76), while, in poignant contrast, the recording of her own career landmarks demonstrates the expanded possibilities for black Americans in the very next generation. The encounter with her father at the poem's center negotiates the emotional terrain of this generational shift.

12. Vendler's work on Dove consists of six items: "Louise Glück, Stephen Dunn, Brad Leithauser, Rita Dove," in *The Music of What Happens* (Cambridge, MA: Harvard University Press, 1988), 437–54; "An Interview with Rita Dove," in *Reading Black, Reading Feminist,* ed. Henry Louis Gates, Jr. (New York: Meridian, 1990), 481–91; "A Dissonant Triad: Henri Cole, Rita Dove, and August Kleinzahler" and "The Black Dove: Rita Dove, Poet Laureate," in *Soul Says* (Cambridge, MA: Harvard University Press, 1995), 141–55 and 156–66; "Rita Dove: Identity Markers," in *The Given and the Made: Strategies of Poetic Redefinition* (Cambridge, MA: Harvard University Press, 1995), 59–88; and "Twentieth-Century Demeter," *The New Yorker,* May 15, 1995, 90–92.

Dove herself provides ample testimony to her rejection of a purist Black Aesthetic mode in favor of a stance open to multiple, hybrid influences. See especially her extraordinary comprehensive historical survey of black poetry co-authored with Marilyn Nelson Waniek: "A Black Rainbow: Modern Afro-American Poetry," in *Poetry After Modernism,* ed. Robert McDowell (Brownsville, OR: Story Line Press, 1991), 217–75, as well as her revealing commentaries on two individual poets in "Telling It Like It I-S *IS:* Narrative

Techniques in Melvin Tolson's *Harlem Gallery*," *New England Review* 8
(1985): 109–17, and "'Either I'm Nobody, or I'm a Nation,'" *Parnassus* 14,
no. 1 (1987): 49–76. On the other hand, we must also note Dove's equally
strong dismissal of the traditionalist posturing represented by Harold Bloom
in "Screaming Fire," *Boston Review* 23, nos. 3–4 (Summer 1998): 31.

13. Vendler, *The Given and the Made,* 80.
14. The brilliant recent work on blackface—the chapter on "Blackface Minstrelsy" in Alexander Saxton's *The Rise and Fall of the White Republic* (London: Verso, 1990), the chapter on "Black Skins, White Masks: Minstrelsy
and White Working Class Formations before the Civil War" in David Roedi-
ger's *The Wages of Whiteness* (London: Verso, 1991), and Eric Lott's *Love and
Theft: Blackface Minstrelsy and the American Working Class* (New York: Oxford University Press, 1993)—pays virtually no attention to Shakespeare.
The extremely important exception is Joyce Green MacDonald's "Acting
Black: *Othello, Othello* Burlesques, and the Performance of Blackness," *Theatre Journal* 46 (1994): 231–49.
15. In "William Shakespeare in America," in *Highbrow / Lowbrow: The Emergence of Cultural Hierarchy in America* (Cambridge, MA: Harvard University
Press, 1988), Lawrence W. Levine emphasizes the continuity between Shakespeare's plays and Shakespeare burlesques: "It is difficult to take familiarities
with that which is not already familiar; one cannot parody that which is not
well known" (15–16). However, burlesque transformations frequently have
a parodic bite that pays no respect to the original; hence Levine underesti-
mates the extent to which familiarity with Shakespeare is employed to register a characteristically American form of contempt.
16. Jim's partial derivation from blackface roles is noted both by Ralph Ellison,
*The Collected Essays of Ralph Ellison,* ed. John F. Callahan (New York: Modern Library, 1995), 731, "Jim is flawed by his relationship to the minstrel
tradition," and by Toni Morrison, Introduction to *Adventures of Huckleberry
Finn* (New York: Oxford University Press, 1996), xxxv ("the over-the-top
minstrelization of Jim").
17. Anthony J. Berret is unconvincing when he argues in *Mark Twain and
Shakespeare* (Lanham, MD: University Press of America, 1993) that "it is
probable that Twain thought of *Othello* while composing" *Huckleberry Finn*
(176). The link to *Othello* represents a critical fantasy of what we would like
to have happened in Twain's novel but does not in fact occur. The connection between Shakespeare burlesque and blackface minstrelsy that could
have been illuminating is never actually made. The novel's lack of resolution
has produced an ongoing debate exemplified by Jane Smiley's "Say It Ain't
So, Huck," *Harper's Magazine,* January 1996, 61–67.

# 6

## Cleopatra as Diva: African-American Women and Shakespearean Tactics

### Francesca T. Royster

Appropriation is neither dispassionate nor disinterested.

—Jean Marsden[1]

She makes hungry where most she satisfies.

—Shakespeare, *Antony and Cleopatra* (2.3.238–239)[2]

In *Notorious Identity*, her recent study of fame and Shakespeare, Linda Charnes includes Cleopatra in the menagerie of Shakespeare's legendary figures "who mean—and mean intensely" for both past and present cultures.[3] Shakespeare not only reproduces Cleopatra's already established legendary mythology, Charnes argues, but also makes use of Cleopatra's signification as stranger queen and decadent lover to add to Cleopatra's meaning by staging the very process of legend-making. From Shakespeare's opening scene onward, Cleopatra is the topic of the gossip of the "common liar"; she is an object of fantasy, and the nature of her appeal is dissected and debated by those who know her intimately and by those who know her only by rumor. In addition, Cleopatra herself reflects on her experience as a famous object of desire. She tests out different roles and worries about her future stagings: "I shall see / Some squeaking Cleopatra boy my greatness/

I' the posture of a whore" (5.2.218–20). This self-consciousness about role-playing becomes a part of the tradition of playing Cleopatra. In what will henceforth shape the uses of Cleopatra, *Antony and Cleopatra* explores reiteration from the point of view of an already infamous Cleopatra. If, as Gilles Deleuze and Felix Guattari have written in *A Thousand Plateaus,* "the proper name is not the subject of a tense but the agent of an infinitive,"[4] "to cleopatra" might mean "to become infamous" and with this, "to be available"—sexually and as an icon citable in many different cultural locations. After Shakespeare, I would add, Cleopatra becomes a role about performing the role of infamous "other."

Through parody, ventriloquism and other forms of revision, African-American performers have commandeered the Cleopatra image, using it to stage, among other things, the precarious conditions of performing blackness. Despite or perhaps exacerbated by the lack of opportunity for black actors to play Shakespeare's Cleopatra in mainstream productions, Cleopatra has become an iconographic staple in African-American arts. In the black action film *Cleopatra Jones* (1973), for example, Cleopatra has been seized to anatomize, critique, and perhaps also reconstruct the "other" as a performative.

Scholarship over the past 25 years has seen a renaissance of feminist and post-colonial readings of *Antony and Cleopatra;*[5] of New Historicist approaches to *Antony and Cleopatra* and early modern England's imperialist projects;[6] and of studies of early modern England's nascent racial identity.[7] Many of these projects consider Cleopatra's significance as an archetypal barbarian and stranger—the necessary scapegoat for early modern England's cultural past.[8] Others consider Cleopatra's significance for England's cultural present—for example, Cleopatra as a warning against the dangers of travel and imaginary wandering,[9] or as an orientalized figure of excess for James I's court.[10] While most of these critics are concerned with Shakespeare's use of past texts to reconstruct his particular version of Cleopatra, there has been little focus of these concerns on the staging of Cleopatra *after* the Shakespearean moment. Critics who discuss post-Shakespearean Cleopatras—Linda Charnes, Mary Hamer, and Lucy Hughes-Hallett—do not extend their analyses to consider race in an extended way.[11] In her book *Signs of Cleopatra: History, Politics, Representation* (1993), Hamer acknowledges that the question of [Cleopatra's] non-European ethnicity is rarely foregrounded. . . . The dynamic of ethnicity as it interacts with gender in the representation of Cleopatra and its work in maintaining Eurocentrism deserves a book of its own."[12] Taking Hamer's cue, this essay will consider the impact of race on the Cleopatra icon as it travels in the twentieth century.

I see these failures to take race into account as, in part, an indication of the relative newness of race in Shakespeare and early modern studies in general. The first major anthology on race and the early modern period, *Women, "Race," and Writing in the Early Modern Period,* was published by Routledge only in 1994. As recently as 1993, Kim Hall could describe the enterprise of Black Studies in Early Modern England as "Reading What Isn't There." Hall's essay title reminds us that in the recent past, critics of Shakespeare as well as racial theorists of other historical periods have argued that race-based analyses of Shakespeare are historically anachronistic, because they considered race a nineteenth-century construction. It has been the burden of this recent group of theorists to establish the relevance of race to the sixteenth and seventeenth centuries, and many have done so by grounding their claims in early modern texts and performances rather than by extending their historical reach to include the continuing cultural impact of these texts.

The continued value of the Cleopatra figure for African-American popular culture in the twentieth century is an important aspect of contemporary Shakespearean practice, as I define it. I differ somewhat from recent studies on Shakespeare and popular culture pursued by Lawrence Levine, Derek Longhurst and others.[13] Levine's highly influential work *Highbrow/Lowbrow: The Emergence of Cultural Hierarchy in America* (1988)[14] argues that the overall "bifurcation" of American culture into two class levels by the turn of the twentieth century has changed the availability of Shakespeare, his characters, and his references. Instead of appealing to a popular audience, Shakespeare has become the property of cultural elites—a highbrow entertainment, Levine argues. My study shows how the conditions of Shakespeare's availability differ within historically marginalized cultures such as the African-American community. In this example of African-American appropriation, Shakespeare becomes a way of addressing and performing social and cultural marginality, strategies that, as Levine notes, resemble the way nineteenth-century American immigrants used Shakespeare.

I

At first glance, *Cleopatra Jones* would seem to bear little resemblance to Shakespeare's *Antony and Cleopatra.* This film, set primarily in Los Angeles, is historically and geographically distanced from both Shakespeare's England and Cleopatra's Egypt. Indeed, one of the film's selling points is its contemporaneity: car chases down gritty urban alleyways; funky Afros, leather jackets and other clothing that scream "late twentieth century," and allusions to historical events specific to the late 1960s through early 1970s: the Watts uprising, the Black Panthers, COINTELPRO, the feminist movement, and the development of the "blaxploitation" film genre of which the film itself is a part.

While *Cleopatra Jones* is an action film, with a liberal number of karate scenes, chases, and shoot-outs, most of *Antony and Cleopatra*'s "action" is in the highly charged banter between the lovers. Much of the play's political negotiations take place behind the scenes or via civil-seeming gestures such as the trade between Octavius and Antony of Octavia in marriage. *Antony and Cleopatra*'s battles are confined to the last third of the play, and even the deaths of its heroes are relatively quiet, witnessed by one or two onstage characters. *Cleopatra Jones*'s character development and dialogue, moreover, are hardly on par with Shakespeare's. The film quotes no lines from Shakespeare's play, though it does transform one of *Antony and Cleopatra*'s key tableaus: Enobarbus's description of Cleopatra's arrival on her barge. But this event is never made part of the action of Shakespeare's play.

So what is it that makes *Cleopatra Jones* a revision of Shakespeare? *Cleopatra Jones*'s Cleo shares with Shakespeare's Cleopatra the capacity to serve as an agent—the ability to stimulate the desires of competing camps and to instigate change through these desires. Tamara Dobson's Cleopatra is a lost African queen, dripping in furs and silk robes. She is a hybrid of an exotic queen from the past, a homegirl who knows her way around her old neighborhood of Watts, and a special agent for the CIA. In the film, we see a double act of appropriation made possible by the ambiguity of the Cleopatra icon. The film uses Cleopatra to advance an ideal of the authentic black woman based on the rhetoric of contemporary black cultural nationalism. At the same time, the film represents Cleopatra Jones as universally desirable—she is a heroine for all time, and all men (and women) want her. This desire ultimately unifies the vying powers of Los Angeles. If in Shakespeare's play Cleopatra distracts Antony from his political responsibilities to Rome, CIA agent Jones protects Los Angeles from the brink of riot.

Like *Antony and Cleopatra*, *Cleopatra Jones* is about the protection of territorial borders and with it, the protection of cultural integrity. In Shakespeare's play, Antony's meanderings with Cleopatra in Egypt threaten his interests in Rome and its holdings. Likewise, in *Cleopatra Jones*, the police suspect that Watts is the point of entry for a Middle Eastern heroin ring attempting to infiltrate the rest of Los Angeles. Watts and the underground movement that has formed there is *Cleopatra Jones*'s Egypt, while Rome is represented by the Los Angeles government—particularly by the police. In *Cleopatra Jones*, the Los Angeles Police Department is as much of a threat to Watts—and the ways of the officers as foreign—as Watts is threatening to greater Los Angeles. This is where *Cleopatra Jones* departs from Shakespeare's play and its bias toward Rome as a civilized culture. We watch a corrupt Los Angeles Police Department invade Watts homes without warrants and brutalize their inhabitants. The officers befriend and then double-cross Cleopatra Jones and the people of the neighborhood. As the story unfolds from the Watts point of view, we see that the fear of the "other" is mutual. As Cleopatra moves between these worlds, she is used by Rome (the police department) to protect Rome. But the people of Watts fear her loss. Her "universal" sexual appeal allows her to move between these worlds, but both groups also want her for their own. The film ends with the haunting question of whether Cleopatra is being "used up" by her employers, and we sense resistance by the black men as they watch her leave. If both *Antony and Cleopatra* and *Cleopatra Jones* portray the invasion of strangers, *Cleopatra Jones* privileges the perspective of what a mainstream film might figure as the "other," Watts.

*Cleopatra Jones* borrows, improvises, and repeats one of Shakespeare's most important scenes for establishing Cleopatra's control over Antony and her audience: Enobarbus's description of her arrival at Cydnus (2.2). The film takes what Shakespeare stages as report and transforms it into several structurally significant action scenes, each time highlighting the film's African-American visual aesthetic. Tamara Dobson has several arrival and departure scenes where she performs the pageantry of Shakespeare's queen, but here she performs them as an action hero. With each costume change Cleopatra's "cloth-of-gold of tissue" is replaced by fur, kente cloth, or red leather. Cleopatra's barge is replaced by an airplane, a Corvette, a luggage belt, an escalator, a motor bike—indeed, whatever form of transportation is most readily available for the action at hand. If her onlookers are lulled by her beauty at first, they must pay immediately for their passivity. In one early scene, Cleopatra Jones sneaks into a crowded airport lobby on a luggage conveyor belt, and chops, karate kicks, and shoots her unsuspecting enemies, all the while maintaining the jaunty tilt of her African-beaded cap. These transformations of Cleopatra's arrival at Cydnus demonstrate this action film's ability to take one of Shakespeare's most quoted scenes and perform it to meet the specific generic and aesthetic demands of the blaxploitation film. In this way, the film implicitly counters Shakespeare's institutional power.

Ultimately, *Cleopatra Jones* is a film that attempts to be a representational corrective—to replace with African-American heroines and heroes the mainstream images that have previously been represented as white as a matter of course. As I'll discuss further, the recasting of Cleopatra as a black crime fighter is all the more politically charged given the absence of black actresses in the Cleopatra role on the Shakespearean stage or in other popular images of Cleopatra. This representative imperative is one that is basic to the blaxploitation film genre. Along with some other films of the blaxploitation genre such as *Blacula* (1973) and *Black Caesar* (1973), *Cleopatra Jones* specifically addresses white literary culture. Significantly, however, *Cleopatra Jones* goes further than to represent Cleopatra in blackface. The film attempts to demonstrate the significance of the Cleopatra legend to a particular moment in African-American culture and transforms its Cleopatra to suit the generic demands of the blaxploitation film and the perceived tastes of a primarily African-American audience. In this way, *Cleopatra Jones* is "re-visionary."[15]

## II

Black actors and actresses have traditionally been left out of *Antony and Cleopatra* stage productions and films. In his comprehensive study of black Shakespearean actors, *Shakespeare in Sable* (1984), Errol Hill points out that although the opportunities for black actors on mainstream stages increased with the Federal Theatre Project and in "color-blind" casting productions such as those of the New York Shakespeare Festival, "Cleopatra is seldom portrayed as a black woman even in contemporary productions."[16] Michael Neill seconds Hill's findings in his introduction to the 1994 Oxford edition of the play:

> it is a telling paradox of the play's stage history that, despite Shakespeare's clearly envisaging Cleopatra as a North African queen whose skin is either "tawny" or "black," there is no history of black Cleopatras as there has been, since the triumphs of Ira Aldridge in the mid-nineteenth century, a series of striking black Othellos.[17]

Until recently, black actors have been used in mainstream productions as "local color"—nameless servants and dancers—or in slightly juicier roles, as members of Cleopatra's inner circle of servants. This convention of using blacks as "local color" has roots in the eighteenth century. Mary Hamer points out that eighteenth-century artists such as Tiepolo typically figured Cleopatra as a blond Venus waited on by a retinue of dandily dressed blacks.[18] Anita Bush, an actor in the Lafayette Players (1917–1932), one of the first major professional black dramatic companies in the United States, got her start as a serving maid in an otherwise all-white production of *Antony and Cleopatra* at the Park Theater in New York. Earle Hyman, Ellen Holly, and Nichelle Nichols[19] have all played Cleopatra's servants in major Shakespeare festivals. Black actors are also either servants or extras in most

Hollywood-made films about Cleopatra and Egypt. A retinue of black servants surround Edith Storey in the film *The Dust of Egypt* (1915) and Claudette Colbert in *Cleopatra* (1934). The most notorious example of this strategy might be seen in Joseph Mankiewicz's 1963 *Cleopatra,* starring Elizabeth Taylor and Richard Burton, where black servants and dancers provide local color, especially in the Cecil B. DeMille-inspired production numbers. Lucy Hughes-Hallett vividly captures the importance of black extras in the depiction of Julius Caesar's coronation in the Mankiewicz film:

> Trumpeters, mounted twelve abreast on white horses, gallop through a triumphal arch into the forum. . . . Brown-skinned archers let loose volleys of arrows. . . . A hollow pyramid opens up to release hundreds of white doves . . . black dancers stamp and gyrate in tiny beaded bikinis . . . Drums roll, cymbals clash, trumpets sound. Three hundred straining slaves appear, tugging behind them a mobile stone Sphinx as high as the Senate House. And there, between its paws, dressed in pleated gold lamé, sits the twentieth century's most celebrated Cleopatra, Elizabeth Taylor. A silence falls as the extraordinary edifice crosses the square. . . . Steps are lowered, a red carpet rolls out, Cleopatra, still enthroned, is carried down the monumental steps by black slaves. . . . The camera stays on Elizabeth Taylor's face, made up in fashionable early sixties style with heavy eyeliner, false lashes and pale lipstick. And, as she catches Caesar's eye, Cleopatra winks.[20]

Peopled by a retinue of black attendants, this scene represents Taylor's coronation as a white cultural icon. The wink is her mark of ownership of the Cleopatra role, a slippage of the mask that reminds us of the actor underneath even while it makes the role her own, establishing Taylor's distance from Egypt and from what is black. Taylor, our guide to enjoying Egyptian exoticism, figures herself as a consumer of Egyptalia by reminding us that she is, in fact, in costume. In the film, Cleopatra tells Antony that she has "a little bit of Egypt in her," but she is always marked as different from her Egyptian household, the key members of which are Asian and black.[21]

   The absence of black Cleopatras is not for lack of effort. Black actors have been vying for Cleopatra roles since the nineteenth century. As early as 1860, African-American actor Henrietta Vinton Davis performed public readings from Shakespeare's *Antony and Cleopatra* to great acclaim, even sharing the stage with Frederick Douglass at one performance in Washington D.C. A critic with the *Buffalo Sunday Truth* wrote:

> Miss Davis is a singularly beautiful woman, little more than a brunette, certainly no darker than a Spanish or Italian lady in hue, with illustriously

expressive eyes and a mouth molded upon Adelaide Nielson's. . . . her use
of the English language is not only excellent but exemplary. . . . We could
not help thinking what a magnificent Cleopatra she would make to a com-
petent Antony.[22]

Significantly, this review reveals the prevailing taste for a Cleopatra who
does not necessarily register as Negro—even in venues that made clear that
she was an African-American actor and even in forums where Davis is reading solo, rather than performing with an entire cast. Davis never had success in securing a role as Cleopatra in a fully staged production of
Shakespeare's play. The heart of the problem was not simply the difficulty
of locating a good actor who could play Antony, as the *Buffalo Sunday Truth*
review suggests, but the more weighty decision of whether or not to stage
*Antony and Cleopatra* as an interracial romance. While Ira Aldridge had already broken the barrier with his Othello, it is worth noting that he did so
on the European stage. Hounded by racial boycotts, Henrietta Davis was
prohibited from joining a professional company. Eventually, Davis abandoned her dramatic career, going on to be a very successful political organizer for Marcus Garvey.[23]

   In this century, there have been only three major theatrical productions
of *Antony and Cleopatra* featuring black actors as Cleopatra: Rosalind Cash
in the Los Angeles Theater Center's 1987 production, Francelle Stuart Dorn
as Cleopatra in the Folger Shakespeare Theatre's 1988 production, and
Dona Croll's Cleopatra in a 1991 all-black production of *Antony and Cleopatra* co-produced by London's Tawala and Bloomsbury theaters. Significantly,
all three of these productions also seem to be haunted by a problem in dealing with *Antony and Cleopatra* as an explicitly racialized romance. But rather
than being criticized as being *too* sexual (which the history of representations
of black sexuality might lead us to expect), these performances have been
criticized as sexually repressed, lacking the passion necessary for us to take
Antony and Cleopatra seriously as lovers. In his review of the 1991 Tawala
Theatre/ Bloomsbury Theatre production, Michael Billington wrote that it
is "a bit lacking in sexual heat," though "stirringly spoken."[24] Martin Hoyle
wrote more strongly of the same production that "the play has been pruned,
characters amalgamated and even unsexed."[25] In his review of the 1988 Folger Shakespeare Theatre production of the play, David Richard wrote that
"the very scenes that allow actors to explore the succulent pleasures and bitter poisons of that relationship are among the flattest at the Folger."[26] While
Dorn, he said, "has never looked so ravishing or exercised such exotic appeal" as Cleopatra, her pairing with Kenneth Daugh's (white) Antony, who

"seems to be nurturing a hangover, rather than a grand passion,"[27] seemed dramatically "out of kilter." Similarly, the 1987 production of *Antony and Cleopatra* starring Rosalind Cash "goes through the motions, but its life signs are nil."[28] The play's director, Dan Sullivan complained, "hasn't found a way to put his two stars in the same play."[29]

These reviews persuasively suggest that even in the 1980s and 1990s, the idea of a black woman performing Cleopatra still makes critics uncomfortable. These productions all seem to share a prophylactic quality, as though any less restrained a performance would threaten the minimum requirement of propriety necessary for the serious Shakespearean stage. Notably, when Dorothy Dandridge failed to win the role of Cleopatra eventually filled by Elizabeth Taylor in the 1963 film version of *Cleopatra,* Dandridge told her manager, "It would take too much guts to use a Negro in the part."[30] Leslie Uggams auditioned but also did not get the Cleopatra part in the Mankiewicz film. Uggams *was* cast, however, as Cleopatra in a Broadway comic spoof of Shaw's *Caesar and Cleopatra, Her Favorite Roman* (1968), declaring to *The Philadelphia Afro-American:* "I'm a better Cleo than Liz."[31] The acceptability of Uggams as a parodic Cleopatra, as well as the acceptability of Dorothy Dandridge as Bizet's Carmen in the campy all-black musical *Carmen Jones* (1954), suggests that in the 1950s and 1960s at least, black actors were allowed in such "high brow" territory only as kitsch.

Perhaps for these reasons, black Cleopatras are often deterritorialized, taken out of Cleopatra's original historical and literary contexts, fragmented, hybridized, or put into new contexts. Jack Starrett's *Cleopatra Jones* hybridizes the exotic and literary associations evoked by the name "Cleopatra" as it works as a Shakespearean property with the "street" sense of "jones" as both a common American last name and the slang for a drug craving—the local and the legendary are equally important to the film. Cleopatra Jones demonstrates aspects of desirability inherently tied to the cultural availability of Shakespeare's character. This, I would argue, is more than a coincidence: it is a tactic, a maneuver "within the enemy's field of vision." "The space of the tactic is the space of the other," says Michel De Certeau in *The Practice of Everyday Life.* "It must vigilantly make use of the cracks that particular conjunctions open in the surveillance of the proprietary powers. It poaches in them. It creates surprises in them. It can be where it is least expected. It is a guileful ruse."[32] As a tactic, *Cleopatra Jones* uses Shakespeare's cultural authority for its own purposes. It is a sneak attack in that in the act of sampling mainstream culture the film seeks to revise mainstream culture.

## III

Critic Mike Phillips offers a potentially utopian vision of the form and function of the blaxploitation film:

> The characters talked like street people, they dressed the way you could see people dressed any Saturday night, they hung out in recognizable black streets, restaurants and clubs, they moved to a soundtrack of black music. There was a realism that seemed to offer a new value to black manners and issues.[33]

In contrast to past successful black film heroes such as Sidney Poitier, Harry Belafonte, and Bill Cosby, Phillips argues, the heroes of the first wave of blaxploitation films in the 1970s, such as *Shaft* and *Superfly,* were part of a "new civil rights move" that included "a black cultural aesthetic which privileged the style, language and landscape of the black ghetto."[34] In the black press as well as in white press sources, there was an exhilaration about this black film movement. Black neighborhood newspapers such as the *Chicago Defender* praised the growth of interest in black films for providing work for black film crews, actors, and directors. Legendary among these was *Superfly,* whose very completion depended on the taste and finances of the black underground. According to the *Chicago Defender, Superfly* was saved from the Warner Brothers trash bin with the financial help of "pimps, madams and drug dealers" as well as black businessmen, dentists and financiers.[35]

*Cleopatra Jones*'s 1973 arrival was late in the development of the blaxploitation film genre. In the same season as *Cleopatra Jones*'s release, *Shaft* saw its second sequel, *Shaft in Africa.* While *Shaft* was considered a breakthrough film by mainstream critics and critics in the black community alike, *Shaft in Africa* was dismissed as "less daring, less ethnically sophisticated, more antiseptic, more comfortably middle class" than its predecessors.[36] At this point we see not only the waning of the freshness of the blaxploitation genre but also a frustration by some activists with what they saw as the aestheticization of black nationalism and its emptying of content. *Shaft in Africa* was released in the wake of boycotts by the Hollywood branch of the NAACP and the Congress on Racial Equality of blaxploitation films' sexualized violence and limited range of black heroes.[37] The *Chicago Defender,* whose entertainment pages frequently featured blaxploitation-related reviews, interviews, and ads, began increasingly to position itself against these films. In a May-June 1972 review of the black action film *Top of the Heap, Defender* film critic Sharon Scott wrote, "I feel that black people are paying for and supporting the short end of the stick. I am afraid that as soon as these 'money-makers' are obsolete, not one positive or truthful three-dimensional film will have been made about the black experience or black people in this country."[38] In letters to the editor published in the *Defender* in the summer of 1972, community citizens fingered the films for spawning a rise in heroin and cocaine use in black neighborhoods and for encouraging copycat crime sprees, such as a Chicago robbery and kidnapping said to be inspired by a scene from *Shaft's Big Score.*

Nevertheless, *Cleopatra Jones* grossed over $3.25 million in its commercial release, and the soundtrack album sold more than a half a million copies, according to Edward Guerrero.[39] If by 1973, the blaxploitation film had already crested in terms of its popularity and its image as a transformative art, it at least arrived with an audience ready made and in a market that had perfected a number of distribution strategies, including double features, dollar days, midnight shows, and drive-in shows.

As a late entry in the blaxploitation genre, *Cleopatra Jones* has commonly been read as "black bubble gum stuff" (in the words of critic Leonard Maltin).[40] Critics saw it as derivative, commercial, and lacking in the political bite of *Shaft, Superfly* or Pam Grier's "superwomen" films, such as *Coffy* and *Foxy Brown.* Even Darius James, whose book *That's Blaxploitation!* praises the film for its efficient use of action-film formula, writes that *Cleopatra Jones* contains "comic book theatrics" and "the clumsiest martial-arts action I've ever had to sit through."[41] Nevertheless, the film's negative portrayal of the Los Angeles Police Department, its gleeful portrait of underground systems of rebellion within the black community and its anti-authoritarian ending (fists, upheld and clenched) lend it some critical power and argue for interests beyond commercial appeal.

It is hard to ignore Jack Starrett's choice of Watts as the film's main setting. Watts was in fact the cultural birthplace of the blaxploitation genre. The Watts uprising spurred a local version of the Black Arts movement, with its geographic center being Watts's Inter-City Cultural Center, founded in 1966 by Bernard Jackson and J. Alfred Cannon. Out of this movement came blaxploitation film's founder: Melvin Van Peebles, whose first film, *Sweet Sweetback's Baadasssss Song,* demonstrates what Mike Davis calls "a distinctive Watts idiom."[42]

The 1965 uprising in Watts left scars still visible in 1973. Neighborhoods were riddled with gaping holes where homes and business once had been. Many local business owners, if financially capable, established themselves elsewhere. The burned-out quality of post-uprising Watts is captured by *Cleopatra Jones's* darkened doorways and swirling trash, but the film also conveys Watts as a neighborhood with activity just below the surface.

Preoccupied with negotiating the politics of community, *Cleopatra Jones* taps into two sets of preoccupations of the Watts rebellion: the policing of neighborhood borders and the protection of black women. Although these struggles came to a dramatic head in 1965, they continued to be a part of the cultural moment of 1973, in particular black distrust of the police and white backlash. For Gerald Horne in *The Fire This Time,* the Watts rebellion marked

> the rise of black nationalism as blacks revolted against police brutality. But what began as a black revolt against the police quickly became a police revolt against blacks. This latter revolt was a milestone too, one marking the onset of a "white backlash" that would propel Ronald Reagan into the governor's mansion in Sacramento and then the White House. White backlash proved to be more potent than what had given it impetus, black nationalism.[43]

*Cleopatra Jones* is a complicated marker of this transition. Like many blaxploitation films, its loyalties seem mixed. On the one hand, the film exposes the police brutality that was still taking place on Watts streets in the 1970s. It conveys the aesthetic and some of the ideological vocabulary of black nationalism, especially in its struggles with black emasculation and the protection of black womanhood. On the other hand, *Cleopatra Jones* conveys a solution that still upholds the authority of an otherwise faceless CIA, in the historical context of the CIA's dedicated campaign of violence against black nationalist movements such as the Black Panther Party.

## IV

The opening of *Cleopatra Jones* is a bit confusing. In the first moments the camera pans over an expanse of desert, dotted with camels. We hear the first *waca wacas* of a rhythm guitar and then hear Joe Simon's craggy soul tenor singing the film's theme, "Cleopatra, All I See is Your Face." Next, we hear a helicopter, and our confusion ends. Like Cleopatra from her barge, Cleopatra Jones, dripping in furs, emerges from the helicopter. On the authority of the CIA, Agent Jones is on a mission to destroy this Turkish field of opium poppies and, by long-distance magic, clear the streets of Los Angeles's Watts of the "shit" (heroin) that plagues it. Through a series of fantastic firebomb explosions, commanded by the word and pointed finger of Cleopatra herself, she demonstrates her power to control the activities of one nation from the distance of another. At one point, Cleopatra proclaims: "My jurisdiction extends from Ankara, Turkey, to Watts Tower, baby."

In her black Corvette with U.S. government plates, Agent Jones effectively brings the world of Watts within the global grasp of the CIA. She returns to Watts to investigate a drug ring and to clear the good name of Reuben, her boyfriend and organizer of a Black Pantheresque drug rehabilitation halfway house. There, she uses the strengths of her contacts in her old neighborhood. She gets the "word on the street" from Esther Rolle, proprietor of a soul food restaurant and mother of two karate instructors, both of whom also come to her aid. She locates and roughs up the neighborhood drug pusher, a diminutive and down-on-his-luck Shaft look-alike. Next, she reports in to the Los Angeles Police Department, sharing her new information and guiding their ineffective strategies.

Cleopatra Jones moves between these worlds but is never quite of either. She doesn't have an office or desk in the police station; instead she meets in restaurants with the smitten police commissioner or communicates by phone from her lush and harem-like apartment. She is always only passing through when she returns to Watts, her old neighborhood, as well. The film features many scenes of either her backside or the tail end of her car, motorbike, or plane, with others watching her leave, in wonder. These departure scenes provide the film's best examples of Hollywood-style black dialect: "What kind of mammer jammer was that?" exclaims one man. "Right on, sweet sister!" yell two kids, watching her car speed away. "Boy, I sure would like to get me some of that," says another man.

It is particularly in her function as an agent that Cleopatra Jones resembles Shakespeare's Cleopatra. An agent moves between worlds that are often seen to be embattled. Her mode of transmission—the way that she links one shore to its "opposite"—is to complete a circuit of desires or need. ("She makes hungry where most she satisfies." 2.3.238–39) While on one level, Shakespeare's Cleopatra satisfies the need for escape from Roman responsibilities, Cleopatra ultimately completes and therefore enables the circuit of Roman virtue in bonds between men. As Coppélia Kahn has argued in *Roman Shakespeare: Warriors, Wounds and Women,* the competition between Antony and Cleopatra's romance and Antony's military duties creates a Girardian triangle of desire between Antony, Cleopatra, and Octavius Caesar. Calling on Eve Kosofsky Sedgwick's formulation of homosocial desire, Kahn argues, "Despite the obvious contrasts of character that distinguish Antony and Caesar, they mirror each other in a blinding desire for *imperium* . . . 'the affective or social force, the glue' that binds them."[44] At the same time, though, we must account for the fact that Cleopatra is never sidelined in the men's pursuit of *imperium.* For each member of the triumvirate, Cleopatra energizes the exercise of these virtues, whether in spite of her or because of her. From supposedly opposite ends, both Octavius Caesar and Antony fear that Cleopatra will use her power to bring on the fall of Rome. Antony fears his personal fall—the sapping of his physical strength and his ability to make good decisions in war. Cleopatra has knowledge of Antony at his most compromised (drunken, feasting, naked, or even worse, in women's dress). Octavius and Enobarbus fear that through her persuasion, Antony's loyalty and power will be lent to Egypt and the selected kingdoms of her choosing: "He hath given his empire / Up to a whore, who now are levying/ The kings o' the earth for war" (3.6.66–68). Cleopatra helps Enobarbus and Octavius Caesar to formulate the stakes of Antony's complicity in the triumvirate. And in threatening to unman Antony, she whets his appetite to be included in the Roman circle: "I am Antony yet" (3.13.92). Although the agent may appear to have competing loyalties in both worlds, she enables a line of desire that connects both sides.

In *Cleopatra Jones,* Cleopatra's structural and symbolic role as agent of desire also has important meaning given the film's interest in drug trafficking. The circulation of heroin throughout the film places *Cleopatra Jones* "smack" in the middle of the contemporary context of the rising war on drugs in both Los Angeles and internationally, especially in Vietnam, during this era. William Parker, Los Angeles police chief during the Watts uprising, was especially concerned that the South Central and East L.A. neighborhoods such as Watts were acting as hubs from which narcotics exported from Colombia and Mexico could be distributed to the surrounding white neighborhoods in the rest of Los Angeles. Parker alleged that this was all sped along by an international communist plot to instigate the moral degeneration of America.[45] This background gives Cleopatra Jones's quality as an agent a contemporary connection.

While she is assigned to police routes of drug entry from Turkey to Watts and from Watts outward, Cleopatra's mobility and ability to affect the officers and to take their minds off their work attest to the permeability of the borders between Watts and the LAPD. Cleopatra herself is a narcotic, satisfying the Cleopatra "jones" felt both by the police office in the film and by the men of her neighborhood. Consider, for example, this phone conversation between the film's police chief and Agent Jones, following an altercation with crime boss Mommy's men:

> Police Chief: Are you O.K.?
> Cleopatra: My body's O.K.
> Police Chief: It's magnificent.

As long as her ability to affect the police is contained, Cleopatra is the ideal crime fighter because she can move around in "enemy" territory, keeping the police in touch with the black world without forcing the officers to share space with her. Best admired from a distance, Cleopatra works by herself; she is not—she cannot be—absorbed into the community of the all-white police station, where the officers can refer to blacks as "niggers" without them overhearing. This is a pre-affirmative action dream where the workplace is still maintained for white males.

Cleopatra's mobility requires a variety of settings in which the action takes place. The Watts neighborhood is represented as a labyrinth: Esther Rolle's soul food restaurant, advertised with misspelled signs of dishes served, has no evidence of food and is strangely empty of customers. In reality, it houses a back-room craps game and a basement karate studio. The halfway house, the other Watts site, also promises to have much happening behind its walls—on the other side of its suburban, stucco, tract-house facade are posters of Malcolm X and Che Guevara. In one bedroom, decorated in a way that suggests it might belong to a child, a junkie shivers over his addiction. We see two young Black Panther prototypes preparing weapons around a large dining room table. The scene is a nightmare of the takeover of the suburban Los Angeles space; this space, already corrupted from within, is also penetrable from without. Not only are the police in the film able to conduct a raid without a warrant, but one officer secretly plants heroin on one of its most vulnerable junkies. In addition to the Watts neighborhood and the police station, the film spends some time on the Los Angeles freeway, which acts as a kind of transition between communities. One of its most excitingly directed scenes is a car chase that moves from the freeway to a skidrow neighborhood of abandoned warehouses and empty lots. This zone is conveyed quite differently from Watts, the police station or Cleopatra Jones's apartment. Inhabited mostly by a few zombied wanderers and by cans of industrial waste, the film makes skid row its playland. Eight-track tape fired up, Cleopatra Jones moves between cars, under viaducts and overpasses. A wandering hobo barely misses being sideswiped by Cleopatra's Corvette. The villains are dumped in a vat of waste.

In its interests in police surveillance and new technologies of penetration into black neighborhoods, *Cleopatra Jones* addresses and engages with the tensions between the Los Angeles Police Department and Watts that led up to and followed the Watts uprising. As both human and larger than life, Cleopatra Jones brings together the old "flat-foot" techniques of policing a neighborhood with new technologies contemporary with Police Chief Parker's tenure. As Mike Davis notes, "Under Parker, ever alert to spin-offs from military technology, the LAPD introduced the first police helicopters for systematic aerial surveillance. After the Watts Rebellion of

1965 this airborne effort became the cornerstone of a policing strategy for the entire inner city."[46] Technologies used to quell the Watts rebellion included the "telecoptor," a helicopter that transmitted television images of the streets below. In a joint effort between the media and the police, ABC-TV turned over their telecoptor-produced film to Chief Parker during the riots. Parker also ordered the use of voice-printing of the film of a CBS interview to identify a shrouded looter who confessed on camera, under conditions of anonymity, about participation in firebombings. But the people of the Watts community matched the LAPD's innovations with their own tactics. They used low-technology tactics such as stone-throwing, disguising as store clerks to fool the police when looting, using hand signals to identify comrades from certain neighborhoods and zip codes (one finger meant Watts, two fingers meant Compton, and three meant that one was from Willowbrook, according to Robert Richardson, a *Los Angeles Times* reporter), as well as high-technology methods including the interruption of police radios and the erasure of credit records at local department stores.[47]

As she moves between her allegiances to the black underground and her role as government agent and LAPD informant, Cleopatra Jones shows a facility with both high- and low-tech maneuvers. Like Shakespeare's Cleopatra, Jones "wander[s] through the streets and note[s]/ The qualities of people" (1.1.52–53). Born in Watts, Cleopatra Jones is even closer to the citizenry of her "Egypt" than Cleopatra was. She shows her loyalty to Watts and to the black underground movement that stems from it. When her lover Reuben (played by former L.A. Ram Bernie Casey) is injured by police gunfire during the raid of his halfway house, Jones helps nurse him back to health by baking cookies and playing him slow love songs. Her place among the black underground is also signaled by her costumes, which echo Angela Davis's large Afro and other Afrocentric stylings, including beaded jewelry and dashikis. Integrated with these contemporary black "revolutionary" outfits are the flashier costumes that seem to have borrowed bits from the black musical counterculture, including a futuristic silver vinyl outfit worthy of Parliament Funkadelic and platform boots and feathers favored by Sly and the Family Stone. No doubt these styles were important in keeping the attention of her black urban audience.

Nevertheless, Cleopatra Jones's government plates and her CIA identification card (usually flashed after a good buttkicking) do other important work to signal her competing loyalties. In spite of the costume of the counterculture, the identification card shows us that Jones is "on the grid"—in the computerized bank of the CIA headquarters—and thus that her actions are authorized by the government. The karate fighting, brandishing of deadly looking ammunition and speeding down the freeway (all acts also committed by the "bad guys") are confirmed as "official" every time she flashes her identification card or her "Cleo" U.S. government license plates.

Importantly, the CIA remains otherwise faceless in the film. In fact, the only face that we see directly associated with the CIA is Cleopatra's own—more specifically, the photo on her identification card. By the end of the film, the film's theme song takes on even more important meaning. When Joe Simon sings "Cleopatra, all I see is your face," he speaks not only of the obsessive and nostalgic desire of the men that Cleopatra has left behind but also of the reconfiguration of the CIA itself. In this era of increasing public awareness of the CIA's underground tactics in the black power movement, the CIA spook is here, finally, given the face of black womanhood: Cleopatra Jones/Tamara Dobson.

The soundtrack has played an important role in the salability of the blaxploitation film. While extending the market potential of the films, the soundtracks sometimes complicate the political messages of the film—perhaps even contradicting them. Consider, for example, the function of Curtis Mayfield's best-selling song "Pusherman" in Gordon Park, Jr.'s *Superfly,* a song that criticizes the lifestyle and glamour of drug culture glorified in the film ("I'm your mama, I'm your daddy, I'm that nigger in the alley. I'm the Pusherman"). The sequence in which the song appears is separated from the rest of the film by a montage of photographic stills depicting more realistic and dark images of ghetto life: junkies shooting up, dark hallways, and empty lots. In *Cleopatra Jones,* then, "Cleopatra, all I see is your face" could be interpreted either as a love song for the woman who helps and then is gone or a critique of the co-optation of Cleopatra's face and body by the CIA. Read critically, the song could be asking, "What force lurks behind Cleopatra's face that we don't see?"

The action of the film is driven primarily by the exposure of the hidden corruption of the Los Angeles Police Department, made possible by the movements of Cleopatra between sites. *Cleopatra Jones* includes two clearly recognizable villains: Mommy, the broadly drawn lesbian crime boss played by Shelley Winters, and Officer Perdy, a comic caricature of the redneck in charge. The inclusion of Perdy's clear acts of injustice—he slams around his suspects and uses phrases like "don't crowd me, boy"—fully acknowledges the everyday presence of racism within the LAPD. But when Cleopatra's efforts reveal that the source of the planted heroin is not the obviously racist Perdy but the chief's partner, a "good cop" who speaks to Cleopatra and the Panther members with respect, the political message of the film grows more complex. As Cleopatra prepares to leave Watts for her next assignment, one of the members of the halfway house mocks the slogan painted on the side of all of the LAPD's squad cars: "To protect and serve? Shit!" The film ends with the shot of the humbled police chief, Lou, surrounded by Cleo and the members of the halfway house and raising his fist in a Black Power salute. The conversion of Police Chief Lou, while catalyzed by the exposure of corruption within his department, derives its passion from his contact with and lessons taught by Cleopatra Jones.

The tall (6 feet, 8 inches) and karate-chopping Dobson, a former high-school basketball player as well as a model, cuts a formidable figure. Her costumes in the film are always striking and aggressive—even amazonian—but they always signal her femininity. Most of her costumes include a lot of cleavage and very high heels. Dobson's speaking voice is quietly commanding; she is a woman of few words. The film advances the myth of the black superwoman, with the black men of the film remaining relatively marginal. Cleopatra's lover Reuben is wounded early in the film by a policeman's bullet, and Doodlebug (Antonio Fargas), an effeminate Watts homeboy who is lured into Mommy's gang, is brutally shot in an extended sequence. The film plays it both ways: Cleopatra Jones is more powerful than her men, while still extremely feminine and loving—the good mother. She is a feminine superpower who supports both black and white men.

The film uses the Mommy character played by Shelley Winters to further delineate good and bad feminine power. In contrast to Cleopatra Jones's positive maternal model, Winters's Mommy character leads a perverse gang that is both harem and family, made up of criminals of several white ethnic groups (cartoonishly marked as Irish and Italian). Her monstrous Mommyhood endangers Cleopatra Jones's good black womanhood. In one scene, set in a Skid Row junkyard, Cleo Jones and Doodlebug's girlfriend (played by Brenda Sykes) dangle trapped in the hull of a car, while Mommy, dressed in black leather Gestapo coat and brandishing a whip, yells sexualized taunts from above. In the black/white catfight dynamic that is even more fully exercised in women's prison films such as *Black Mama/White Mama* (1972) and then parodied in Jonathan Demme's *Caged Heat* (1974), *Cleopatra Jones* relishes Winters's incestuous plantation mother come-ons even while it encodes them as perverse. In fact, the specter of Winters possibly capturing and perhaps abusing Cleopatra sets up the perfect situation for her rescue by the two black karate instructors—the only black men in the film who have not been wounded or weakened. Through the Mommy/Cleopatra Jones dynamic, the film further elevates black womanhood by scapegoating white womanhood as monstrous and perverse.

The protection of a black woman may well have been the spark of the Watts uprising. On August 11, 1965, the police twisted the arm of a mother who was protecting her son after his arrest for inebriation.[48] The Watts uprising was fueled by outrage at the police's penetration of neighborhood space, the perception of arbitrary violence against black women, and, in a bigger sense, "the patriarchal, though comprehensible, complaint emerging from slavery that black men could not protect their families and 'their' black women."[49]

By depicting the LAPD's and CIA's proprietary relationship to Agent Jones's body and her beauty, as well as their exploitation of her community knowledge, the film taps into these issues of white male authority over black women. In some ways, the contest of loyalties of Cleopatra parallels the controversies of the blaxploitation film itself. Blaxploitation film was and is still a contested site of ownership. On the one hand, as Mike Phillips has argued, blaxploitation can be said to "belong" to the community because it reflects a black aesthetic, taking on the conflicts plaguing its communities and casting black people as its central actors. On the other hand, *Cleopatra Jones* was produced by Warner Brothers. As Jesse Algernon Rhines argues in *Black Film/White Money* (1996),

> of the hundred or so films featuring significant numbers of African American characters and/or an African American-derived storyline and produced during the blaxploitation period, roughly 1970 through 1974, fewer than one-fifth were under African American control. Even fewer came from Black-owned production houses, and fewer still were financed and/or distributed by African Americans.[50]

Given these conditions of white control over the production of most blaxploitation films, Rhines concludes that "the blaxploitation period was not an example of African American filmmaking."[51] Does *Cleopatra Jones,* then, "belong" to the black community—a reflection of its tastes, its lifestyle, and even of the black underground's financial power? Or was it an opportunistic project of Warner Brothers and other major film studios—a manipulation of social tensions and a thirst for images to drum up a dying cinema interest? It is in some ways fitting that the figure of Cleopatra is poised in the middle of this controversy of ownership.

## V

If "to Cleopatra" were a verb, it would suggest the process of legend making. Its qualities could include resiliency, recyclability, infamy, and mobility—in short, availability. Catherine Belsey has written that Shakespeare's Cleopatra "is shown as an exploiter of the lack which causes desire."[52] But we can also see the desire that Cleopatra inspires not as the perpetual state of lack but as the perpetual state of becoming satisfied. If, as Enobarbus says, Cleopatra "makes hungry where most she satisfies," the desire that Cleopatra inspires becomes all the more conscious of the nature of its hunger. More than lack, Cleopatra inspires in her fans a kind of awareness of the state of receiving satisfaction. In the true nature of addiction, the one who desires is altered by the process of desiring.

If we rethink this process of desire we then must also rethink Cleopatra's desire. To be Cleopatra is to also be infinitely adaptable. We can view this state as a process of evolution instead of an absence requiring a new presence. It is no wonder, then, that Cleopatra has been an alluring fantasy for African-American women, a group whose bodies have been historically constructed as a source of nourishment for others, from Mammy to Aunt Jemima.[53] Shakespeare exposes not just the hunger produced by Cleopatra but also the hunger produced by becoming the Cleopatra role. She too has desire—the desire to participate, to remain famous, to stay in the public imagination.

## Notes

1. Jean I. Marsden, ed., *The Appropriation of Shakespeare: Post-Renaissance Reconstructions of the Works and the Myth* (New York: Harvester Wheatsheaf, 1991), 1.
2. All line numbers and other references to Shakespeare's *Antony and Cleopatra* in this essay will refer to *Antony and Cleopatra,* ed. Michael Neill (Oxford: Clarendon Press, 1994).
3. Linda Charnes, *Notorious Identity: Materializing the Subject in Shakespeare* (Cambridge, MA: Harvard University Press, 1993).
4. Gilles Deleuze and Felix Guattari, "1730: Becoming Intense, Becoming Animal, Becoming Imperceptible" in *A Thousand Plateaus: Capitalism and Schizophrenia,* trans. and foreword by Brian Massumi (Minneapolis: University of Minnesota Press, 1987), 264.
5. See, for example, Janet Adelman, *The Common Liar: An Essay on* Antony and Cleopatra (New Haven, CT: Yale University Press, 1973); Phyllis Rackin, "Shakespeare's Boy Cleopatra, the Decorum of Nature and the Golden World of Poetry" in *New Casebooks:* Antony and Cleopatra, ed. John Drakakis (New York: St. Martin's Press, 1994), 78–100; L.T. Fitz (Woodbridge), "Egyptian Queens and Male Reviewers: Sexist Attitudes in *Antony and Cleopatra* Criticism," in Drakakis, *New Casebooks:* Antony and Cleopa-

tra, 182–211; Jyotsna Singh, "Renaissance Anti-theatricality, Anti-feminism, and Shakespeare's *Antony and Cleopatra*," in Drakakis, *New Casebooks: Antony and Cleopatra*, 308–29; and Joyce Green MacDonald, "Sex, Race and Empire in Shakespeare's *Antony and Cleopatra*," *Literature and History* 5, no. 5 (Spring 1996): 60–77.

6. See, for example, Barbara Bono, *Literary Transvaluation: From Vergilian Epic to Shakespearean Tragicomedy* (Berkeley: University of California Press, 1984); John Gillies, *Shakespeare and the Geography of Difference* (Cambridge: Cambridge University Press, 1994); Kim F. Hall, *Things of Darkness: The Economies of Race and Gender in Early Modern England* (Ithaca, NY: Cornell University Press, 1995).

7. See, for example, Margo Hendricks and Patricia Parker, eds., *Women, "Race," and Writing in Early Modern England* (London: Routledge, 1994); Kim Hall, "Reading What Isn't There: 'Black' Studies in Early Modern England," *Stanford Humanities Review* 3 (1993): 23–33; *Things of Darkness;* Ania Loomba, *Gender, Race, Renaissance Drama* (New Delhi: Oxford University Press, 1992); and Joyce Green MacDonald, ed. *Race, Ethnicity and Power in the Renaissance* (Madison, NJ: Fairleigh Dickinson University Press, 1997).

8. See Adelman, *The Common Liar,* and MacDonald, "Sex, Race and Empire," in particular.

9. Ania Loomba, "'Traveling Thoughts': Theatre and the Space of the Other," in Drakakis, *New Casebooks:* Antony and Cleopatra, 279–307.

10. See Hall, *Things of Darkness,* ch. 3–4.

11. Charnes, *Notorious Identity*; Mary Hamer, *Signs of Cleopatra: History, Politics, Representation* (London: Routledge, 1993); and Lucy Hughes-Hallett, *Cleopatra: Histories, Dreams and Distortions* (New York: Harper and Row, 1990).

12. Hamer, *Signs of Cleopatra,* xviii-xix.

13. Derek Longhurst, "'Thou Base Football Player!': Shakespeare in contemporary Popular Culture," in Graham Holderness, ed., *The Shakespeare Myth* (Manchester: Manchester University Press, 1988), 59–73.

14. Lawrence Levine, *Highbrow/Lowbrow: The Emergence of Cultural Hierarchy in America* (Cambridge, MA: Harvard University Press, 1988). See especially 56–81.

15. See Marianne Novy, ed., *Women's Re-Visions of Shakespeare: On Responses of Dickinson, Woolf, Rich, H. D., George Eliot, and Others* (Urbana: University of Illinois Press, 1990).

16. Errol Hill, *Shakespeare in Sable: A History of Black Shakespearean Actors* (Amherst: University of Massachusetts Press, 1984), 7.

17. Michael Neill, ed. *Antony and Cleopatra* (London: Oxford University Press, 1994), 65.

18. Hamer, *Signs of Cleopatra,* xviii-xix.

19. Nichols is noteworthy as the first black actress to kiss a white actor on television as Uhura in the November 1968 episode of *Star Trek*. In the "Plato's Step-Children" episode, which ran during *Star Trek*'s last season, Captain Kirk and Uhura are tortured and forced to kiss by a leader of a eugenically near-perfect race. In her memoir, *Beyond Uhura: Star Trek and Other Memories* (New York: G.P. Putnam and Sons, 1994), Nichols includes a photo of herself on the set for the ground-breaking episode. She is posed in a costume and in make-up reminiscent of Elizabeth Taylor's Cleopatra, including kohled eyes, jeweled evening gown, and a fur throw. Indeed, the caption for the photo reads "Cleopatra, eat your heart out!" These same racial barriers between actors had not yet been crossed in productions of *Antony and Cleopatra* or in Cleopatra films.

20. Hughes-Hallett, *Cleopatra,* 266.

21. Indeed, Mankiewicz's *Cleopatra* further perpetuates racial stereotypes by pitting the servants against one another. Iras, played by a tall blonde white actress, is Cleopatra's most vocal and trusted servant. It is Iras who discovers that Lily, played by an Asian actress, has been poisoning Cleopatra's food. Charmian, played by a light-skinned black actress, speaks only a few words and mostly is sent to fetch things.

22. See Hill, *Shakespeare in Sable,* 70–71.

23. Ibid., 64.

24. Michael Billington, "Theatre Choice," *Guardian,* June 1, 1991, 4.

25. Martin Hoyle, "Theatre: Antony and Cleopatra, Bloomsbury," *The Times,* (London) May 18, 1991, 21C.

26. David Richard, "*Antony and Cleopatra* Sans Lust," *Washington Post,* September 28, 1988, C1.

27. Ibid., C13.

28. Dan Sullivan, "'Antony and Cleopatra': WWII Desert Campaign," *Los Angeles Times,* July 6, 1987, 5.

29. Ibid., 5.

30. Earl Mills, *Dorothy Dandridge* (Los Angeles, CA: Holloway House Publishing, 1970), 221.

31. Anonymous, "Leslie Uggams Says She's Better Cleopatra than Liz," The *Afro-American* (Philadelphia ed.), August 31, 1968, 2.

32. Michel De Certeau, *The Practice of Everyday Life,* trans. Steven Rendall (Berkeley: University of California Press, 1984), 37.

33. Mike Phillips, "Chic and Beyond," *Sight and Sound* 25 (June 1996): 26.

34. Ibid., 25–26.

35. "Black $ Brings 'Super Fly' to Screens," *Chicago Defender,* July 29-August 4, 1972, 22.

36. *New York Times,* July 1, 1973, sect. 2, p. 7.

37. See Edward Guerrero's *Framing Blackness: The African American Image in Film* (Philadelphia: Temple University Press, 1993), especially pages 69–113.

38. Sharon Scott, "'Top of the Heap' is a Mediocre Black Movie," *Chicago Defender,* May-June 1972, 21.

39. Guerrero, *Framing Blackness,* 98.

40. Leonard Maltin, ed., *Movie and Video Guide* (New York: Signet, 1994), 228.

41. Darius James, *That's Blaxploitation!: Roots of the Baadasssss 'Tude (Rated X by an All-whyte Jury)* (New York : Griffin, 1995), 62.

42. Mike Davis, *City of Quartz* (London: Verso, 1990), 67–68.

43. Gerald Horne, *Fire This Time: The Watts Uprising and the 1960's* (Charlottesville: University Press of Virginia, 1995), 16.

44. Coppélia Kahn, *Roman Shakespeare: Warriors, Wounds and Women* (London: Routledge, 1997), 113.

45. Davis, *City of Quartz,* 294.

46. Ibid., 252.

47. Horne, *Fire This Time,* 66–67.

48. According to the California Highway Patrol accounts, however, Mrs. Frye entered the scene not to protect her sons from the police but to berate her sons for drinking. It was Mrs. Frye, not the police officers, who threw the first punch, the woman hitting one officer in the groin and pinching another's nose. Witnesses' reports are given in ibid., 55–56.

49. Horne, *Fire This Time,* 55.

50. Jesse Algernon Rhines, *Black Film, White Money* (New Brunswick, NJ: Rutgers University Press, 1966), 45.

51. Ibid., 45.

52. Catherine Belsey, "Cleopatra's Seduction," in Terence Hawkes, ed., *Alternative Shakespeares,* vol. 2 (London: Routledge, 1996), 42.

53. See Doris Witt, "What (N)ever Happened to Aunt Jemima: Eating Disorders, Fetal Rights, and Black Female Appetite in Contemporary American Culture," *Discourse,* 17 (Winter 1994–1995): 98–121.

# 7

# The Polluted Quarry: Nature and Body in *A Thousand Acres*

*Barbara Mathieson*

> The recognition of nature's shaping influence on human identity is a fundamental recognition, one that is shared by many non-Western cultures. Severing or denying human dependency on our relationship with nature is necessary only to the construction of the master identity, which lies at the center of the alienation of Western culture. . . .
>
> —Greta Gaard[1]

"Different views on Nature," writes John Danby, "are not differences of opinion only. They are felt as so many stubborn holds that reality has on us and we on it. They are such meanings as can become concrete people."[2] Noting the more than 40 uses of "nature" and derivative words in Shakespeare's *King Lear,* Danby argues that *Lear* can be understood as "a play dramatizing the meanings of the single word 'Nature.'"[3] In Jane Smiley's novel *A Thousand Acres,* a contemporary adaptation of *King Lear,* the natural world of elemental forms and forces similarly provides the tapestry into which human choices and acts are woven. The epigraph from Meridel Le Sueur with which Smiley prefaces the novel insists upon the interconnections between the human organism and its physical environment: "The body repeats the landscape. They are the source of each other and create each other." Smiley's landscape not only creates a backdrop for her narrator

Ginny's changing sense of her own organic life but, like the great storm that parallels Lear's tempest in the mind, suffers a violation analogous to that visited upon Ginny's body.

The nature of Nature, however—its imagery, power, scale, and relationship to human life—differs vastly in the two works. Indeed, just as the shifting meanings of the term "nature" within Shakespeare's play have been explored by critics such as Danby and Robert Heilman as one key to *King Lear,* so, too, the developing pattern of the natural landscape in Smiley's novel unfolds a narrative of loss, alienation, and exploitation. An early signal occurs in Smiley's title, in which the land itself displaces the eponymous human protagonist of Shakespeare's play as the focal figure. The "thousand acres" of land and all that it represents in terms of power, status, place, and spirit is arguably the site of tragedy and loss in the modern novel and the true claimant for our compassionate pity and respect. The early modern tragedy of a great individual thus gives way in the late twentieth century to a tragedy of the natural world and of the interconnected lives that Nature supports.

Smiley dramatically revises *King Lear*'s father-daughter story by using Ginny, her Goneril character, as the narrator. She retells the Lear story with characters recognizably similar to Shakespeare's beneath their modern dress and contemporary Iowa farm setting. This cast of characters participates in a critique of social and political assumptions familiar to us from *King Lear,* the dominant order of their lives disintegrating as the polite lies of family love and interpersonal relationship are unmasked, and a profound sense of vulnerability emerging as comfortable myths are sandblasted away. In Smiley's most daring act of revision, she draws on suggestions made earlier by Coppélia Kahn[4] and Lynda Boose[5] to shape the novel around an incest story, thus creating a domestic history for the violent breach between Lear and his two oldest daughters. Though the bulk of critical attention has focused on intertextual matters and, like the recent movie version, on the impact of incest, Smiley is equally radical in linking the social, political, and personal problems of patriarchy inherent in Shakespeare's play with a twentieth-century awareness of the physical domination and economic exploitation of the natural world by industrialized human cultures.

It is on this arena of the natural realm and our human relationship to it that I want to focus, for Smiley's treatment of Nature exploited and poisoned reveals a uniquely twentieth-century tragic view. Just as Lear represents "all societies where there is a tradition of privilege" and the blind spots inherent to them,[6] so the concerns underlying Smiley's popular, Pulitzer Prize-winning novel speak immediately to readers in this century of ecological crisis. In examining the novel and its real differences from Shakespeare's earlier vision, I will make ample use of the rich analytic tool chest offered by the burgeoning philosophical and political position known as ecofeminism. Ecofeminist writers echo Smiley's concerns both for a loss of connection between the human and natural realms and for the interrelated exploitations of women and of our natural world. If we examine the novel through the lens of current ecofeminist analysis of our cultural and ecological situation, the parallel between incest and natural abuse becomes clear. The implied future Smiley depicts is, if anything, more bleak and less hopeful than the ending of *King Lear*.

Uniting the approaches of feminism and ecology, ecofeminism explores the connections between anthropocentrism and patriarchy. Both Nature and women have shared a common history of objectification in the Greco-Roman intellectual tradition. Justifications for the exploitation of the natural world rest upon a conceptual hierarchy of dualisms similar to those underlying the domination of women by men. The question posed by Sherry Ortner's groundbreaking 1974 essay, "Is Female to Male as Nature Is to Culture?"[7] brought out of the shadows the conflation implicit in the philosophical tradition of the West. In the pairings of putatively opposed terms made familiar by 30 years of feminist commentary, the first in each pair traditionally represents a possibility construed as superior: man/woman, culture/nature, spirit/body, reason/emotion, master/slave.[8] To this listing, ecofeminists add and highlight an additional pairing, human/animal, which has connected the logic of patriarchy to the broader arena of human egocentrism at least since the advent of our mission to "subdue" the earth and to hold "dominion over the fish of the sea, and over the fowl of the air, and over every living thing that moveth upon the earth."[9] In *Feminism and the Mastery of Nature,* Australian philosopher Val Plumwood interrogates the term "nature" to reveal

> a field of multiple exclusion and control, not only of non-humans, but of various groups of humans and aspects of human life which are cast as nature. Thus racism, colonialism and sexism have drawn their conceptual strength from casting sexual, racial and ethnic difference as closer to the animal and the body construed as a sphere of inferiority, as a lesser form of humanity lacking the full measure of rationality or culture.[10]

In response to concern that the parallels scrutinized by ecofeminists reinstate the woman-nature identification used for centuries to devalue women's qualities, Plumwood observes that merely "to say that there are connections, for instance, between phallocentrism and anthropocentrism, is not to say anything at all about women in general being 'close to nature.'"[11]

A number of ecofeminists have attempted to discover a common origin for the devaluations of women and Nature. In *The Death of Nature,* Carolyn Merchant suggests that until the Renaissance, "the root metaphor binding together the self, society, and the cosmos was that of an organism."[12] With increasing commercialism and industrialization, however, "new ideas, those of mechanism and of the domination and mastery of nature, became core concepts of the modern world."[13] Her argument, allied with John Danby's interpretation of the competing versions of nature in *King Lear,* discovers in the Scientific Revolution and the rise of industrial society a rupturing of the traditional vision of a vital nurturing force connecting the human and natural realms. In the current period of ecological crisis, Merchant continues, "Western society is once more beginning to appreciate the environmental values of the premechanical 'world we have lost,'" with its faith in the non-hierarchical interdependency of all elements of life: male and female; human, mineral, plant, and animal.[14]

Just as many members of the African-American, gay, and feminist communities have long predicted that the historic oppression each group has separately experienced will be addressed effectively only by a united front, so, argue ecofeminists such as Rosemary Radford Ruether, women can never achieve fully equal status with men until the rest of the devalued terms in the pairings are also "liberated" from our hierarchical thinking. Ruether envisions a future in which "mutual interdependency replaces the hierarchies of domination as the model of relationship between men and women, between human groups, and between humans and other beings."[15] The rifts generated during long centuries of inequality and alienation between sexes, classes, and ethnic groups, and between humans and the natural world, suggests Ruether, can only be healed holistically: the alienation must be eliminated simultaneously in all classes, including human and nonhuman. From this point of view, Smiley's incorporation of the incest theme and her treatment of the natural world, with its myriad abused forms of land, water, and plant and animal life, are actually two sides of a single coin.

Contrasting a pair of images from Shakespeare's play with one from the novel reveals the extremely different manner in which each work invites the audience to view Nature and to visualize the human form within its context. In Shakespeare's *King Lear,* Edgar's creatively conceived perspective from the cliffs of Dover where he has led his father offers a dizzying image of vast natural spaces that dwarf human occupants of the scene:

Come on, sir, here's the place. Stand still. How fearful
And dizzy 'tis to cast one's eyes so low.
The crows and choughs that wing the midway air
Show scarce so gross as beetles. Half-way down
Hangs one that gathers samphire, dreadful trade!
Methinks he seems no bigger than his head.
The fishermen that walk upon the beach
Appear like mice, and yon tall anchoring barque
Diminished to her cock. . . . [16]

Although this fantasized view invented for his father's benefit is not objectively "true," Edgar nonetheless speaks truly of the perspective generated by the looming presence of the natural world. Captured visually in the endless spaces suggested by Peter Brook's film version, Shakespeare provides a vast context that envelops individual lives within a complex continuum of meanings beyond the human and social. That context determines our human perspective; within the presence of the natural world, we human actors are able to view and assess each instance of life. Nature, as Edgar's speech reveals, is the central point of reference from which human experience acquires its relative scale. Against the immensity of Dover's cliffs, birds and fisherman diminish visibly.

Similarly, only within the context of heath and unrelenting storm does Lear's own experience acquire the meaning that we accord it. Awesome, potentially violent, and outside of human control, the great storm of Act III offers a reference point against which Lear's own drama must be measured and correctly comprehended. Initially contending with the storm, shaken by thunder and drenched in the deluge of rain, Lear finally understands the fragility of authority and power, the community of all "poor naked wretches," the essence of the human as a "poor, bare, forked animal." Only from within this elemental environment can Lear attain a true perspective and a genuine comprehension of his own position. Though the daughters for their transgressions are labeled "unnatural hags," implying that to be natural would be more kind, Shakespeare's Nature is both benevolent and violent. Lear begs the raging storm essentially to destroy the world: "Strike flat the thick rotundity o'th' world,/ Crack nature's moulds, all germens spill at once."[17] As Marilyn French notes, "Natural imagery is used to express the entire gamut of human experience. It describes human feelings, vices, and situations. Nature oppresses humans and animals, and sustains them."[18] In this multifaceted vision, whether Nature is bountiful or terrible, its presence provides a pervasive and powerful presence.

John Danby argues that Shakespeare's nature imagery reveals the Renaissance contention over the essential nature of Nature. Danby locates the assumptions and speeches of Gloucester, Edgar, Albany, and Lear himself in the orthodox Elizabethan view of a rational, orderly, and benevolent Nature, arranged and supported by divine will. In stark contrast stands the pre-Hobbesian view of Edmund, Goneril, and Regan, for whom the natural world is a "dead mechanism," divorced from divine meaning and susceptible to individual, rationalist manipulation and control. Thus, the unresolved question as to the degree of consciousness and creative power inhering in Nature creates an intellectual and spiritual controversy that underlies the narrative of *King Lear.* Nature herself, however, clearly marked by the feminine gender, is invoked by both sides as a goddess, a great and transcendent force in human life.[19] Can any conceivable force negate the power and endurance of the storm and the cliff, of the goddess herself? At the end of *King Lear,* the raging natural elements are quiet again but have never been disarmed; similarly, human bonds, both personal and political, are reforged after enormous pain and loss. The regeneration implies a temporary victory, a cyclical reemergence from the realm of upheaval and tragic suffering that doubtless will recur innumerable times. Although the intellectual controversy remains unresolved, Nature's power remains unchanged.

In contrast to Shakespeare's natural point of reference for the human figure, Smiley's narrator, Ginny, opens the novel with her childhood remembrance of the world as seen from the rise near her farm, apparently flattened and dominated by the human presence:

> From that bump, the earth was unquestionably flat, the sky unquestionably domed, and it seemed to me when I was a child in school, learning about Columbus, that in spite of what my teacher said, ancient cultures might have been onto something. No globe or map fully convinced me that Zebulon County was not the center of the universe.[20]

The self and the human construction of farm, home, and work provide the center to the characters in *A Thousand Acres,* the reference point for their perspectives, the high point of a flat world that has been successfully mapped, demarcated with roads, and rendered functional for human use.

Use of the verb "seemed" in the above passage, indicating an illusion in the past tense, allows Ginny to repudiate this naive perspective from her more mature position. Although the scale of the novel's flat landscape differs entirely from *King Lear*'s cliffs, the narrator unlearns her misperception of human centrality in the course of the novel and gains a core of new knowl-

edge not unlike that which Lear achieves: human power to possess and par-
cel out land is as fragile and easily reversed as the stability of social and familial bonds. Ginny comes to realize the self-serving falsity of the vision that
"what is, is, and what is, is fine."[21] Faith in human control over the physical
world is part of the "right order" invoked with irony throughout the novel,
a false confirmation of the value and inevitability of human life that is cher-
ished for the comfort of the listeners but ultimately must be abandoned as
an illusory perspective.

Greta Gaard comments upon the "shortsighted" perspective endemic to
modern Western cultures that absorption in the close, the human, and the
man-made carries with it:

> It is a physical and metaphoric fact that most inhabitants of Western culture
> are shortsighted. Whether engaged in factory work or a desk job, detasseling
> corn or driving on a highway, the eyes of Western culture are focused on the
> immediate task at hand. We are more accustomed to looking for parking
> spaces or concealed weapons than purple finch or elk. . . . The visual shift to
> a wilderness orientation is nowhere so evident as it is upon return to the sights
> of Western culture. There, a kind of figure/ground shift often occurs: where
> one had focused only on the artifacts of culture, those artifacts become back-
> ground to the figure of nature.[22]

Like Smiley's narrator, Gaard argues, we have lost the long view, the broader
perspective that can locate the human figure clearly within nature's context,
as occurs in wilderness. Unfortunately signaling the absence of new insight
for Smiley's "shortsighted" characters, however, no powerful, compensatory
image from the natural landscape, such as Edgar's cliffs, emerges during the
course of *A Thousand Acres* to replace the discredited vision of a flattened
world or of human centrality within it.

Within this shrinkage of the natural world, the great storm of *King Lear,*
though still the background for a cataclysmic disintegration of family, becomes in itself merely a minor inconvenience in *A Thousand Acres:* television
is disrupted; the electricity is temporarily lost. Smiley does not allow the
reader to enter the elemental force of the storm, to feel its power or its violence firsthand. Using the background of the storm to set off Rose's revela-
tions of childhood sexual violation, Smiley shifts the psychological analogy
to the storm from Lear/Larry's inner turmoil to the daughters'. The power
and dislocation of that inner emotional storm displaces the terror of the
physical storm outside; the outer storm is experienced only from within the
relative safety of a house that neutralizes its awesome violence.

Visualizations of the natural world in images of breathtaking beauty do proliferate in the early pages of the novel, although Smiley repeatedly presents them as a lost pastoral vision. "Nature" as a transcendent force, as a structuring element of the cosmos, as the "goddess" that various characters in *King Lear* apostrophize, in contrast, seems absent from the vocabulary and consciousness of Ginny, the narrator. In fact, the natural world seems powerless simply to sustain itself, and the human actors are increasingly distanced from the reference points that a powerful natural environment might provide. In *A Thousand Acres,* the continued vitality of the natural world itself becomes a question.

In the opening pages, Ginny walks along the Zebulon River in a stretch obscured from normal view, where the river has "made its pretty course a valley below the level of the surrounding farmlands" that is not visible from her farm and the Cabot Road junction.[23] As she delights in the blue water and "limpid sunlight of mid-spring," messengers from the past—a small flock of pelicans—surprise her:

> And there was a flock of pelicans, maybe twenty-five birds, cloud white against the shine of the water. Ninety years ago, when my great-grandparents settled in Zebulon County and the whole county was wet, marshy, glistening like this, hundreds of thousands of pelicans nested in the cattails, but I hadn't seen even one since the early sixties. I watched them. The view along the Scenic, I thought, taught me a lesson about what is below the level of the visible.[24]

The pattern established here recurs through the novel: images of the natural world, a landscape of uncurbed beauty and pleasure, emerge as lost pleasures, lost delights, a primitive pastoral vision replaced "since the early sixties" by human control and limit. The natural world still telegraphs to Ginny a crucial conceptual lesson—the truths of life are "below the level of the visible"—yet the teacher itself, Nature, clearly is fading in immediacy and potency.

Though not labeled as female like *King Lear*'s goddess Nature, the natural elements in *A Thousand Acres* share with women's bodies the promise and then the destruction of fertility. Ginny celebrates that fertility as she considers the natural and human history of the farm:

> For millennia, water lay over the land. Untold generations of water plants, birds, animals, insects, lived, shed bits of themselves, and died. I used to like to imagine how it all drifted down . . . and became, itself, soil. I used to like

to imagine the millions of birds darkening the sunset, settling the sloughs for
a night, or a breeding season. . . . And the sloughs would be teeming with fish:
shiners, suckers, pumpkinseeds, sunfish, minnows, nothing special, but millions or billions of them. I liked to imagine them because they were the soil,
and the soil was the treasure, thicker, richer, more alive with a past and future
abundance of life than any soil anywhere.[25]

Once again, Smiley casts this passage in the past tense: "I used to like to
imagine." Now this fertile land and water have been subdued and purchased
for several generations. The purpose of human activity in Zebulon County
has been to shape Nature to its own use, to transform technologically the
natural world for the sake of efficiency and function. The original marshland
of the county has been steadily drained over the decades and diverted into
tile channels (now PVC) laid by three generations of men beneath the surface of the land. The cost has been the loss of such fertility as is not immediately useful to the human enterprise.

The novel repeatedly parallels the technological invasion of the landscape
with the mastery and abuse of the female characters. Ginny first connects
the land with the female presence on it in the memory of her silent (or silenced) grandmother Edith, married at sixteen to her father's 33-year-old
partner, John Cook, a marriage that not only united bodies but "consoli-
dated Sam's hundred and sixty acres with John's eighty"[26] and produced
Larry, Ginny's father. Smiley insistently pursues the connection throughout
the novel. Chemical poisoning of farmland for agricultural power not only
causes but echoes the poisoning of the women's bodies in the novel, leading
to cancer and a plague of miscarriages. In parallel terms, ecofeminist Lin
Nelson surveys current research about contemporary biological hazards and
their impact on both general and reproductive health and writes of "the
damaged woman in the damaged environment."[27] Nelson quotes a 1984
*Conservation Foundation Letter,* "The womb is more sump than sanctuary."[28]

The connection Smiley draws between incest and abuse of the land has
implications far beyond the history of a single Iowa family. In her final confrontation with Ty, Ginny extends the connection between the control of
women's bodies and control of the land to implicate American society as a
whole:

"Do I think Daddy came up with beating and fucking us on his own?" Ty
winced. "No. I think he had lessons, and those lessons were part of the pack-
age, along with the land and the lust to run things exactly the way he
wanted to no matter what, poisoning the water and destroying the topsoil

and buying bigger and bigger machinery, and then feeling certain that all of it was 'right,' as you say."[29]

In addition to providing motivation for the distance between Cook and his daughters, violation of the older daughters mirrors the system's exploitation and rape of the land and water.

Far more than exploring "women's issues," however, as Roger Ebert derisively described the film adaptation in his widely published newspaper review, Smiley's novel recounts a universal human tragedy with implications for every being on the planet.[30] The images of human and natural interaction in *A Thousand Acres,* in contrast to the battering and enormous storm of Lear, cry the destruction of a helpless primeval world by human agents. The Cooks' neighbor Harold deliberately mowing down a fawn in his tractor's path provides the starkest example,[31] though most of the instances are unconscious and unplanned. Simply as the consequences of rapacious agricultural practices, the marshes have been drained, the pelicans driven away, the pond habitat plowed under, and the water table poisoned by fertilizers and pesticides; few in the society seem awake to the reality or disposed to mourn the destruction.

Water imagery in the novel offers a crucial index of loss in nature and in the characters' consciousness. Set in contrast to the remembered vitality of the river is the sterile Pike swimming pool, where Ginny and her nieces seek relief from the oppressive summer heat. The crowded concrete pool triggers memories for Ginny of an earlier summer in a farm pond in which she and Rose spent languorous hours as young girls "soaking up the coolness of the water and living in the blue of the sky."[32] When intimacy with Jess reawakens forgotten yearnings in her heart, Ginny returns to search for that old refuge but cannot "find even the telltale dampness of an old pothole."[33] Natural sources of water in the life of the farm community are disappearing with the thronging pelicans in the Midwestern landscape.

In the first half of the novel at least, Ginny registers very little anger that "Daddy drained the pond and took out the trees and stumps around it so he could work that field more efficiently,"[34] yet the reader clearly senses that something of value has been destroyed that occupies a different niche in the human psyche than a concrete city pool. L. Teal Willoughby writes of the archetypal resonance of water in its natural forms "as a primary element of life on earth, water as common component of both ocean and body, water as a flowing liquid element that moves and absorbs other things, water that has unknown depths and unknown origins."[35] Willoughby cites the warnings of Carl Jung that our modern world has disempowered such natural experiences that formerly enriched our psychic lives: "We have stripped all things of their mystery and numinosity; nothing is holy any longer."[36] The sense of freedom and peace, of connection with water and blue sky, the sensual experience of floating alone and unseen that Ginny's brief memory conveys, is not an experience Ginny and her nieces are able to duplicate in the city swimming pool. Dating the pond's draining as "not long before the death of our mother,"[37] Smiley heightens the emotional power and, in Jung's terms, the numinous value of that small body of water so casually destroyed.

The old quarry, which Ginny later pursues for a swim that will soothe her soul when "only water, only total, refreshing immersion, could clear my mind," embodies the fusion of natural and man-made.[38] Existing in memory as blue and sparkling, Ginny finds the quarry now "brown and murky."[39] Memory clearly has been unreliable, however, for Ginny also remembers "how we had always pulled rusty objects out of the water with guileless curiosity—hubcaps, tin cans, bashed-in oil drums. Now I saw the place with a new darkened vision."[40] Thus, the pollution and poisoning has been a long event, although Ginny's early sense of "right order" protected her from the reality. That pollution becomes reality for her when the old order is shattered and unveiled by the family's disruption, contact with Jess's questions and challenges, and her evolving understanding of the farm chemicals' effects on her own and Rose's bodies, with their resultant miscarriages and cancer.

In quite a different manner, *King Lear* incorporates numerous references to the "ruined piece of nature," the "great decay," and the apocalyptic "promised end," yet Shakespeare's referents are human. The ruin of nature always points symbolically toward Lear himself, the kingly masterpiece of nature, or the decaying familial and social structure. In *A Thousand Acres,* the decay attacks the natural world itself. Like the pond of Ginny's childhood, the marshes and pelicans have been erased by progress and human intrusion. Ginny herself, numbed by the status quo, registers but barely responds to the loss.

Instead of the storm forces of nature revealing the equality, shared corruption, and mutual compassion of humankind, the leveler in *A Thousand Acres* is the poison of human agriculture and activity. Though the novel shares with *King Lear* the poison motif as a metaphor for human greed and destruction, in *A Thousand Acres* the poisons are literal products—pesticides and fertilizers—potentially touching all human and natural existence. Apart from Ginny's deliberate attack on Rose with poisoned sausages, the intended target is nature itself and the regulation of its processes. The resulting costs for the human agents are visible and painful: Rose's and her dead mother's cancers, Ginny's miscarriages, Pete's drowning in the quarry. Yet the natural elements themselves do not take direct revenge on the human perpetrators and apparently have no force to do so. Although it may be argued that nature will bounce back—that it has always done so—Smiley and her narrator do not offer this assurance. Ginny becomes conscious of the "loop of poison we drank from,"[41] yet she finds no vision of purification; she simply abandons the vast, tainted water table for the sterilized comfort of water from a spigot in her apartment.

The nonhuman animals with whom we share the planet provide a major source of metaphor in both play and novel. Thus, Lear's humbling but authentic moment of insight as he takes refuge from the storm recognizes kinship with the nonhuman: "Unaccommodated man is no more but such a poor, bare, forked animal."[42] At the same time, this kinship clearly presents a "reduced" vision of human nature.[43] Poor Tom's animal images, on the other hand, offer purely accusatory visions of human nature, disturbing reminders of inharmonious and untamed traits: "hog in sloth, fox in stealth, wolf in greediness, dog in madness, lion in prey."[44] In both speeches, paradoxically, human nature is like animal nature and therefore "other" than we had supposed. This mistrust of animals, rooted in their embodied natures, mirrors the play's treatment of women. To Goneril and Regan accrue a host of bestial analogies linking them to undesirable behaviors: serpent, kite, and vulture. In his "wise" madness, Lear generalizes about all women:

> The fitchew nor the soiled horse goes to't
> With a more riotous appetite.
> Down from the waist they're centaurs,
> Though women all above.[45]

Shakespeare's intent throughout the series of metaphors seems to be to humble Lear, demean Goneril and Regan, and chasten the audience through acknowledgment of the animal within us. The vehicles for such chastisement are female and animal.

In *A Thousand Acres,* a different set of metaphors emerges: images of domesticated animals controlled and rendered powerless. Though still providing a humbling recognition to human egoism, Smiley's animal metaphors generate a sense of a plight shared with nonhuman animals that demands our broader compassion. The day before her first sexual encounter with Jess, for example, Ginny helps her husband castrate newborn pigs. That night she dreams she is a sow and experiences her most exciting intercourse with her husband: "my back came to seem about as long and humped as a sow's, running in a smooth arc from my rooting, low-slung head to my little stumpy tail."[46] This erotic fantasy brings momentary pleasure to Ginny's sterile sex life, yet the parallel between her body and the thousand "breeders" being prepared for Ty's hog venture provide a disturbing undertone. After the storm and the breach with her father, Ginny discovers a new animal within herself, "a horse haltered in a tight stall, throwing its head and beating its feet against the floor, but the beams and the bars and the halter rope hold firm, and the horse wears itself out, and accepts the restraint that moments before had been an unendurable goad."[47] Here Ginny's self-association with farm animals clearly emerges in her subconscious as an image of broken will and failed energy, the possibility offered to her as a daughter or wife. "Although we often regard nonhuman animals as pure representatives of nature," comments Greta Gaard, "most if not all the animals (human and nonhuman) living in the context of Western culture have been alienated from nature and from wilderness."[48]

Like the two visions of nature at conflict in *King Lear,* however, two visions of nature and farming contend in Zebulon County. Most of the inhabitants apparently subscribe to the "bigger is better" school of thought, and expect human effort to yield continual progress in farming output. Documenting the long-standing Western dismissal of nature and natural workings as "unproductive," Vandana Shiva analyzes the biases of modern farm methods toward technological intervention, chemical fertilizers and pesticides, and accelerating productivity:

> The assumptions are obvious. Nature is unproductive. Organic agriculture based on nature's cycles of renewability is unproductive. Women and tribal and peasant societies embedded in nature are also unproductive. Not because it has been demonstrated that in cooperation they produce fewer goods and services for needs, but because it is assumed that production only takes place when it is mediated by technologies for commodity production, even when such technologies destroy life. A stable and clean river is not a productive resource in this view. It needs to be "developed" with dams to become productive.[49]

Thus, Larry plows up the old swimming hole to improve bean production and satisfies, in Ginny's words, a "lust for every new method designed to swell productivity";[50] Harold's new, improved, and bigger tractor draws the envious attention of all the neighboring farmers; Ty borrows himself into bankruptcy in an effort to multiply his commodity production with a huge hog operation. A joyful family like the Ericsons, content with life, enjoying their menagerie of dogs, ponies, and other "unproductive" animal companions and indifferent to competition, is doomed to extinction.[51]

Only Jess's alternative vision of organic farming, of a nonintrusive human presence working in harmony with Nature, provides a hope of Paradise regained. Describing an organic farmer he has visited, Jess revels in the vision he discovered there:

> He's seventy-two years old and looks fifty. They've got dairy cattle and horses and chickens for eggs, but his wife only cooks vegetarian meals. They get great yields! Just with green manures and animal manure. The vegetable garden is like a museum of nonhybrid varieties. . . . I mean it was like meeting Buddha.[52]

Here the ideal balance between human and natural envisioned by ecofeminists seems to be realized. To reject such an organic vision, Jess insists, would be "like looking paradise in the face and turning away from it,"[53] yet that is precisely what the characters do. The established farmers continue their chemically intensive methods, Jess himself proves unable to bring the vision to fruition with Rose on her land and abandons the quest, and Ginny ends the novel in a thoroughly urban environment, removed from the last pelicans, soothing summer swims, and indeed from any natural elements whatsoever.

At the end of the novel, nature is vanquished on both the farm and in Ginny's life. The conglomerate Heartland Corporation owns the thousand acres, having expanded the hog operations and razed the dwellings so that now "the fields make no room for houses or barnyards or people."[54] Even the previously uneasy proximity of nature and humankind has ended, with both emerging as victims of the corporate process itself. Ginny continues to cling to the safety of human order. Her chosen new life extinguishes the natural world: in her apartment beside the freeway as in her waitress job, seasons no longer exist,[55] concrete and a contained swimming pool replace the vistas and abundant water table,[56] and she sinks into a welcome urban routine. Linda, one of the substitute daughters she has raised with love if not much guidance, is headed, in a final touch of irony, for a business career in the vertical food conglomerates for which landscape is merely a business opportunity. In the final lines of the novel proper, Ginny grinds up the poisoned sausages she had prepared for Rose in her apartment's garbage disposal and flushes them down the drain, relying on the city's unseen sewage treatment plant and the anonymity of urban technology, and feels a burden lift.

Students in my literature classes commonly treat the novel's ending as a relative victory for Ginny. After all, she has understood a great deal about the cultural and gendered forces that have worked upon her, she has found some empowerment in regaining her memory of incest and in saying "no" to her life as a farm wife and daughter, and she has a modicum of independence in her new life in the city. We need some caution, however, in embracing such resolutions in which a person appears to grow and become more fully "human" by ruthlessly distancing the natural world. Such a resolution

> assumes that the task for both women and men is now that of becoming simply, unproblematically and fully *human*. But this takes as unproblematic what is not unproblematic, the concept of the human itself, which has in turn been constructed in the framework of exclusion, denial and denigration of the feminine sphere, the natural sphere and the sphere associated with subsistence. The question of what is human is itself now problematised, and one of the areas in which it is most problematic is in the relation of humans to nature.[57]

Ginny has attained some independence from the human relationships that have shaped and constrained her life to this point, yet her already tenuous relationship to the visceral experience of the natural world—the world of sensuously floating in a farm pond, of thrilling to the birds in the river's cut, the world of seasons—is severed completely by the end of the novel.

Thus, although the novel aligns with the concerns of ecofeminist analysis, Ginny's own trajectory evades the goal and intention of ecofeminist consciousness, which is "to heal . . . the artificial separation of Western culture and nature."[58] Ginny acquires a great deal of valuable insight and manages to survive the novel, but she does so only as a fragmented, urbanized, isolated individual cut off from all connection with the natural world. Lear's lament, "Thou'lt come no more,/ Never, never, never, never, never," might be resurrected by Smiley to lament the loss of deep human relationship with the natural world. Such loss is integral to Smiley's rethinking of the price that human delusion and greed exact upon our world.

The novel's disturbing image of a polluted quarry does offer a true perspective, in any case: though dug out by human labor, within it is "the one place where the sea within the earth lay open to sight."[59] Smiley reminds us several times that the water persists, though now successfully hidden and contained except at the quarry: "The sea is still beneath our feet," comments Ginny, "and we walk on it."[60] Despite the assurance of success and "right order," the farm culture enjoys solid ground only through unrelenting will and effort, by controlling and uprooting the natural, and Ginny discovers vividly the instability of the land and the society built upon water. The polluted quarry reveals the natural element persisting but poisoned, its glories—the pelicans, fish, and children swimming—all lost. Though the water "beneath our feet" still threatens to evade human control, the water's positive fertile power has been destroyed with no apparent promise of regeneration.

Thus, any hopeful signs in the novel's end for a renewed and meaningful life for Ginny and her nieces seems drastically undercut by the abandonment and waste of the natural world. Perhaps the same ambiguous hope can be offered for Ginny's body as for the polluted quarry: it is still there; the sea of life is still visible through it, though polluted, poisoned, and rendered infertile. Can the quarry and the body regenerate themselves? Smiley offers no affirmation beyond the tenacious clinging to existence that both exhibit. Ginny herself remains childless. And as for the quarry, the fertile waters, and the land itself, now firmly under the control of food conglomerates with no memory of lost fertility or former beauty, the outlook is grim indeed.

## Notes

1. Greta Gaard, "Ecofeminism and Wilderness," *Environmental Ethics* 19 (Spring 1997): 16.
2. John F. Danby, *Shakespeare's Doctrine of Nature: A Study of* King Lear (London: Faber & Faber, 1949), 16. See also Robert Heilman, *This Great Stage* (Seattle: University of Washington Press, 1963).
3. Ibid., 15.
4. Coppélia Kahn, "The Absent Mother in *King Lear,*" in *Rewriting the Renaissance,* ed. Margaret W. Ferguson, Maureen Quilligan, and Nancy J. Vickers (Chicago: University of Chicago Press, 1986), 33–49.
5. Lynda Boose, "The Father and the Bride in Shakespeare," *PMLA* 97 (1982): 325–47.
6. Marilyn French, *Shakespeare's Division of Experience* (New York: Summit, 1981), 225.
7. Sherry B. Ortner, "Is Female to Male as Nature Is to Culture?" in *Women, Culture, and Society,* ed. Michelle Zimbalist Rosaldo and Louise Lamphere (Palo Alto, CA: Stanford University Press, 1974), 67–87.
8. Val Plumwood, *Feminism and the Mastery of Nature* (New York: Routledge, 1993), 42–43.
9. Gen. 1:28.
10. Plumwood, *Feminism and the Mastery of Nature,* 4.
11. Ibid., 10.
12. Carolyn Merchant, *The Death of Nature: Women, Ecology, and the Scientific Revolution* (New York: Harper & Row, 1980), 1.
13. Ibid., 2.

14. Ibid., 99.
15. Rosemary Radford Ruether, "Ecofeminism: Symbolic and Social Connections of the Oppression of Women and the Domination of Nature," in *Ecofeminism and the Sacred,* ed. Carol J. Adams (New York: Continuum, 1993), 21.
16. William Shakespeare, *The Tragedy of King Lear,* ed. Jay L. Halio (Cambridge: Cambridge University Press, 1992), 4.6.11–19.
17. Ibid., 3.2.7–8.
18. French, *Shakespeare's Division,* 229.
19. *King Lear,* 1.2.1; 1.4.230.
20. Jane Smiley, *A Thousand Acres* (New York: Ballantine, 1991), 3.
21. Ibid., 136.
22. Gaard, "Ecofeminism and Wilderness," 18–19.
23. Smiley, *A Thousand Acres,* 4.
24. Ibid., 9.
25. Ibid., 131–32.
26. Ibid., 132.
27. Lin Nelson, "The Place of Women in Polluted Places," in *Reweaving the World: The Emergence of Ecofeminism,* ed. Irene Diamond and Gloria Feman Orenstein (San Francisco: Sierra Club, 1990), 176.
28. Quoted by Nelson in ibid., 177.
29. Smiley, *A Thousand Acres,* 342–43.
30. See, for example, Roger Ebert, "A Thousand Acres," mini-review, *Ashland Daily Tidings,* Sept. 25, 1997, "Revels" sec. 5.
31. See Smiley, *A Thousand Acres,* 234.
32. Ibid., 95.
33. Ibid., 206.
34. Ibid., 85.
35. L. Teal Willoughby, "Ecofeminist Consciousness and the Transforming Power of Symbols," in *Ecofeminism and the Sacred,* ed. Carol J. Adams (New York: Continuum, 1993), 144–45.
36. Quoted in ibid., 142.
37. Smiley, *A Thousand Acres,* 85.
38. Ibid., 246.
39. Ibid., 247.
40. Ibid.
41. Ibid., 370.
42. *King Lear,* 3.4.95–96.
43. Plumwood, *Feminism and the Mastery of Nature,* 123.
44. *King Lear,* 3.4.84–85.
45. *King Lear,* 4.6.118–121.
46. Smiley, *A Thousand Acres,* 161.
47. Ibid., 198.

48. Gaard, "Ecofeminism and Wilderness," 11.

49. Vandana Shiva, "Development as a New Project of Western Patriarchy," in *Reweaving the World: The Emergence of Ecofeminism,* ed. Irene Diamond and Gloria Feman Orenstein (San Francisco: Sierra Club, 1990), 191.

50. Smiley, *A Thousand Acres,* 45.

51. Ibid., 43–47.

52. Ibid., 217.

53. Ibid.

54. Ibid., 368.

55. Ibid., 333.

56. Ibid., 335.

57. Plumwood, *Feminism and the Mastery of Nature,* 22.

58. Gaard, "Ecofeminism and Wilderness," 7.

59. Smiley, *A Thousand Acres,* 247.

60. Ibid., 16.

# 8

~❧~

# King Lear and A Thousand Acres: Gender, Genre, and the Revisionary Impulse

## Iska Alter

Jane Smiley has made it clear that her novel *A Thousand Acres* was conceived not only as a response to the masculine distortions of perspective that she finds in Shakespeare's most apocalyptic play, one that theatrically embodies and linguistically generates femaleness as the cause of the fallen world, but also as a response to that interpretation of *King Lear* "which privileged the father's needs over the daughters."[1] Not surprisingly, then, the narrative she constructs, voiced by Virginia Cook Smith/Ginny/Goneril rather than by the male participants in the revisionary events, is meant to counter the various forms of feminine silencing—motiveless villainy, public humiliation, sororal jealousy, redeemed duty, filial love, and death—that occur in the master('s) text.

That Smiley chooses narrative as the method and the novel as the instrument to articulate her transformed, female-centered version of the Shakespearean original makes available, indeed insists upon, modes of storytelling that manage the problems of causality, chronology, and character in ways markedly different from the ways in which dramatic representation functions. The assumptions and expectations embedded in this aesthetic shift of form allow the author to establish the necessary matrix within which "a habit of mind that perceives daughters and children as owned things . . . a habit of mind . . . in our culture of seeing nature and women in much the same way"[2] can be explored overtly rather than alluded to or buried in subtextual discourse.

However, fictional narrative as it operates in the more-or-less traditional, more-or-less linear, more-or-less realistic novel (a not entirely fashionable category these days for the artistic/moral/authorial claims made in its name, but the one in which I would nevertheless locate *A Thousand Acres,* fashion notwithstanding[3]) requires a density of detail and motive to fill the interstices of events, a linked network of facts that localizes, specifies, and explains what the flexible dimensionality of performance can leave open. To be sure, as Smiley suggests, there may be "a mainstream interpretation of the play" that dominates the study, whose apparent analytical continuity seems to fix the inherent instability of the performed drama, in which

> Lear changes—that he becomes more human and less proud, less self-centered and arrogant. He goes from being a man who has little self-knowledge to being a man who has gained self-knowledge over the course of his suffering.[4]

But in the movement from the study (or classroom, or journal) to the stage, such interpretive hegemony can be, and most often is, undermined, both at the center of a performance and on its margins, by the bodies, voices, and gestures of actors and by the supportive community who translates concept into production into theatrical experience.

Given the fact that the author has anchored *A Thousand Acres* in an ideologically resonant master-text governed by generic conventions distinct from, perhaps even in conflict with, those that determine the constituents of the novel, with complex and commingled hermeneutic, performance, and cultural histories, to what extent is the rendering of action and behavior in Smiley's work impelled by considerations of genre as well as by its overtly stated revisionary purposes? In addition, to what extent do the novel's effectiveness and its limitations emerge from its formal narrative pressures? Finally, to what extent does the structure of intertextuality serve to enrich Smiley's reconfigured analogue on the one hand while enforcing a new reading of *King Lear* on the other? This discussion provides some provisional answers to these questions.

## Daughters: Who Tells What Stories

Theatrical representation creates causality, motivation, and character not through explicit or implied narrative linearity, but primarily through dialogue; that is, an ongoing if complicated process of verbal interaction, gestural signification, and body language involving major and minor actors as well as members of the audience functioning as individual spectators and as a collective, observing unit. Although these dialogic exchanges establish who is central and who is peripheral in the stage action that shapes the story told, these categories often can seem unstable, less certain than the play titles or line counts might indicate, because they are contingent upon the actor who inhabits a given role, and/or the directorial blueprint, and/or authorial ambiguity.

While there is little question that Lear dominates the stage,[5] even if the story told is by no means exclusively his, and that Shakespeare might indeed be pleading for the character as Smiley asserts,[6] it is not always clear what case the playwright is arguing. The disintegrative, increasingly volatile interpretive activity that would seek to explicate the play weakens any notion of an abiding, secure, unitary critical attitude, as does its tangled textual history, and the ways in which both these factors further destabilize the already variable performance moment.

Nevertheless, Lear's daughters do assume an especially problematic authority in Shakespeare's ostensibly male text out of all proportion to their actual appearances in the tragedy: Regan and Goneril speak 187 lines and 181 lines respectively (each representing close to 6 percent of the total lines spoken) and Cordelia only 115 (approximately 4 percent of the total).[7] Although Regan's and Goneril's frightening power resides as much in Lear's demonizing rhetoric of characterization as in their own conduct, the audience is reminded that their cruelties may be the consequences of fatherly indifference, paternal favoritism for the youngest sibling, and the sovereign will to retain and control what in fact already has been surrendered. So, too, must the audience watch, in some discomfort, as the good daughter, Cordelia, betrayed first by the assumption that filial love within patriarchy will be rewarded by paternal/kingly affection, or at least understanding, is betrayed again when she reenters the play late in Act IV as the "good" daughter, no less a creature of her father's fantasies than her "wicked" sisters.

Given Lear's apparent theatrical imperium and his rhetorical license as the "onlie begettor" of his daughters' identities, it seems a legitimate analytical choice to name misogyny as the heart of the play since

> Shakespeare and the interpretive establishment have painted [Regan and Goneril] so bleakly that in every article it was *de rigeur* for the writer to set herself apart from Regan and Goneril, to characterize them as evil or label them somehow.[8]

But evaluative perspective and judgmental stance are more unpredictably fused in dramatic representation as the intersecting demands of the text as written artifact to be studied, and the more fluid requirements of the text as suggestive performance script create the permeable terrain of theatrical experience. What appears to be thoroughgoing misogyny in *King Lear* also can be read less conventionally or less conveniently. As Madelon Gohlke observes, in discussing Shakespearean tragedy more generally:

> The values that emerge from these plays are, if anything, "feminine" values dissociated from the traditional masculine categories of force and politics, focused instead on the significance of personal relationships or the fact of human relatedness. . . . In this structure of relation, it is women who are regarded as powerful and men who strive to avoid an awareness of their vulnerability in relation to women, a vulnerability in which they regard themselves as "feminine." It is in this sense that one may speak of a matriarchal substratum within the patriarchal text. The matriarchal substratum itself, however, is not feminist.[9]

Within the world authorized by the novel, the figure who controls point of view determines the patterns of narrative selectivity, devises the modes of access to causality, motivation, and character, and sanctions as well as conditions the reader's engagement with the text. And in *A Thousand Acres,* Ginny is that sovereign instrument of generic power. Virginia Cook Smith/Ginny/Goneril is the distinctive, sometimes fearful, sometimes frightening voice that tells the story of the shattered Cook family, of the poisoned community that is Zebulon County, and by extension, of the decaying country that is America. It is her vision, whose willed, even willful, blindness dissolves over the course of the novel, through which our response is focused and informed. Here are the eyes that see, the mind that judges, the self that learns, the words that expose.

But Smiley deliberately has constructed Ginny as an insecure, and therefore, a potentially untrustworthy or unreliable observer:

> From a narrative point of view, it is much more interesting to have a narrator who is uncertain of what she thinks or what should be done or what the future will hold. . . . Also the oldest child is often the one who, in any conflict, is torn between sympathizing with the parents and with the other siblings.[10]

Although such a narrator surely is necessary, given that the reconceived text seeks to accomplish what Shakespeare seems to elide, evade, or suppress, the structural price can be high, for it also means that uncertainty can become unsettling inconsistency or, worse, confusion, thereby transforming readerly belief into skepticism.

This narrative problem is most clearly evident in the ways in which Ginny establishes her relation to and position in the community after the fractures in the once-ideal/idealized Cook family become the public's property, especially in her claims that she and Rose are being condemned for their treatment of their respected, respectable father.

> Most issues on a farm return to the issue of keeping up appearances. Farmers extrapolate quickly from the farm to the farmer. . . . What his farm looks like boils down to a question of character. . . . The paramount value of looking right is not something you walk away from in a single night. . . . In fact, it is something you embrace, the broken plank you are left with after the ship has gone down.[11]

And it is an interesting ironic device to translate the discourse of gossip and Ginny's social perceptions into "the normal interpretation of *King Lear* as a counterpoint to what we know is happening."[12]

But the extent to which we actually hear that judgment voiced or can accept Ginny's evaluation of it is questionable. The supposed condemnation is all too frequently sensed, rather than uttered, save by speakers associated with forms of male institutional power whom we have grown to mistrust (Harold Clark, Ken LaSalle, Henry Dodge), and is generated by internal psychic pressures, not by fictively realized demonstrations of hostility. Neurotic overreaction to issues of guilt and shame, provoked by repressed, but no less present memories of incest and abuse, make Ginny's assumptions (and actions based on those assumptions) suspect, to say the least.

Further, although the self-sufficiency so valued by Larry Cook and imposed on the family by paternal desire and patriarchal tyranny has elevated his status in Zebulon County, it also has separated the Cooks from ordinary participation in the life of the community. Ginny's relative isolation from her neighbors and her lack of a network of sustaining friendships (excepting the sororal bond with Rose) deny her the familiarity with the circumstances of the communal present necessary to support more discerning assessments of individual and relational behaviors.

Another kind of difficulty emerges from the now-problematic quality of Ginny's position as author/observer/participant: that is, the occasional thinness of the explanatory tissue that the generic demands of the traditional linear novel seem to compel. This lack is particularly disturbing in the puzzling fictive depiction of the Caroline/Cordelia figure, although it is manifested in the ambivalent treatment accorded the familial and societal unwillingness to acknowledge, much less to accept, the fact of Larry Cook's physical and mental collapse, whatever its source.

There certainly are hints in the Shakespearean master-text that can be embodied and elaborated in the activity of production to explain why Cordelia becomes the "good" daughter when she returns to the play: she is the loved favorite—her straightforward and honest, if priggish, response to Lear's hectoring questions are those of a daughter certain of her place in her father/sovereign's heart, so that what appears to be rebellion can be read (and enacted) as filial allegiance and devotion; she is fully aware of and hostile to the reasons behind her sisters' excessive rhetoric of affection; she is able to marry a male figure who need not participate in what Gayle Rubin has termed "the traffic in women"[13] and is, therefore, not dependent upon Lear's authority for either his bride or his position. These factors, among others, free Cordelia to make emotional, familial, and political choices her sisters finally cannot.

However, the behavior of Smiley's Caroline—or, rather, Ginny's Caroline— remains as inconsistent as the explanations for it are unclear. With the collusion of her sisters, Caroline alone has been able to distance herself from the presumptive ideals of farm life and escape from its oppressive physical specificity. Ginny notes with approval that becomes increasingly ironic, "she made good grades, conceived large ambitions, and went off as we had planned, no farmwife, or even a farmer, but something brighter and sharper and more promising" (*ATA*, 64).

Ginny-as-narrator possesses no significant understanding of her sister's character though she and Rose served as Caroline's creators; nor is her insight enhanced because of the self-knowledge she has acquired by recovering, and then confronting, the memories of her own physical and sexual abuse. The reader cannot even be certain whether Caroline's actions are the result of the same abusive patterns that both Ginny and Rose have suffered. Given such equivocal fictive circumstances, Caroline's metamorphosis into the dutiful, caring "little girl" who believes that "'people are basically good, and sorry to make mistakes, and ready to make amends'"(*ATA*, 362), is not entirely convincing and continues to be unnecessarily mysterious.

These various fictive ruptures result from particular generic claims made by a certain category of novel. They cannot be filled, mended, or masked by the bodily presence of actors and the dispersed energies of performance as occurs in dramatic representation. Instead, such slippages of narrative voice call attention to discrepancy and make more tentative the daughters' stories as they unfold in this revisionary text.

## Father: The Madness of King Lear II

Shakespeare's Lear/*Lear* is enacted within and obtains power from a dramatic matrix whose fluid, unstable elements—ideological necessity, political intrigue, familial opportunism, linguistic play—not only are subject to the coercive weight of cultural need, or the fluctuations in critical fashion,[14] but also must constantly be renegotiated in the practical and creative tumult of production. Jane Smiley's (or is it Ginny's?) Larry Cook, resituated in *A Thousand Acres* because it is his daughters' story, is fixed into certainty, deliberately contained and diminished by the explanatory methodology of narrative—details of language that localize, stipulate, and justify.

Since the events of *King Lear* are located on the unspecified stage of prehistory, they seem to occupy a theatrical landscape and map an emotional geography that are infused with a sense of archetypal boundlessness not quite tamed by the conventions of the civil compact. Lear's double sovereignty as monarch and as father rules a kind of infant's kingdom where wish too easily can become fact and desire too readily becomes action. In this world of patriarchal gratification, his daughters, especially Regan and Goneril, necessarily have been obedient reminders of his authority, or have chosen to act such roles, children still, well into adulthood, and dangerously so, until Lear capriciously decides to "Shake all cares and business from our age, / Conferring them on younger strengths, while we / Unburthen'd crawl toward death."[15] Verbally and psychologically collapsing the limitless willfulness of infancy and the frightening constraints of old age, Lear releases the destructive momentum of tragedy. Because the play has been constructed in this way, we do not need to ask why these circumstances have arisen but must simply accept that it is so, although in performance reasons can be provided by amplifying suggestions in the text and/or externalizing the implications in the subtext.

Having first divested himself of titles, status, and the prerogatives they name, save the regressive one of fool—"*Lear.* Dost thou call me fool, boy? *Fool.* All thy other titles thou hast given away; that thou wast born with." (1.4.145–47)—Lear is then dispossessed of what remains of his fragmentary identity by the custodial arrangements with his ascendant daughters, free now to invert the naturalized order of his patriarchal power and gender and to satisfy their unmodified infantile appetites:

*Lear.* When were thou wont to be so full of songs, sirrah?
*Fool.* I have used it, Nuncle, e'er since thou mad'st thy daughters thy mothers;
for when thou gav'st them the rod and put'st down thine own breeches,

> *Then they for sudden joy did weep,*
> *And I for sorrow sung,*
> *That such a king should play bo-peep,*
> *And go the fools among.*

(1.4.167–74)

However, through what follows—terrible madness, brief reconciliation, possible redemption, even the more terrible murder of Cordelia, and, finally, Lear's own death—and although he is stripped of everything that once mattered, that still matters, that never mattered, Lear nevertheless retains majesty because his language is allowed to propel and control the play: the misogynistic diatribes directed against his "pelican daughters," the corrupted worlds they inhabit, the world he had made corrupt, the childlike/childish reconciliatory dialogue with Cordelia, the extraordinary, heart stopping "Never, never, never, never, never!" (5.3.308). Whatever the disintegration ultimately signifies, the linguistic energy unloosed by madness confers upon the character continued authority and forges the audience's response to the mad, despairing king.

Although Lear's centrality is reinforced by the generic dialogic structures of dramatic form, what this theatrical positioning establishes will vary with the requirements of performance and the strategies of interpretation; even so certain a characteristic as his advanced age becomes suppositional if it is perceived to be a fact of mind rather than the physical truth of chronology. However, Larry Cook's place in Smiley's reconstituted feminine text is more circumscribed, its qualifications derived not only from authorial decisions concerning chronology, setting, and occupation but also from the use of point of view, a generic agent of fictive narrativity, to establish modes of control over the aggressive masculinity exercised in the novel.

Because the plot of *Lear* has been inscribed so obviously within the action of *A Thousand Acres,* once the reader hears the retrospective female voice speaking the story, he/she knows from the first that Ginny survives her father's brutality and his death, although the education she has obtained and the wisdom she has inherited is bleak and only capable of articulation at the novel's end:

> . . . when I remember that world, I remember my dead young self, who left me something . . . which is her canning jar of poisoned sausage and the ability it confers, of remembering what you can't imagine. I can't say I forgive my father, but I now can imagine what he probably chose never to remember—the goad of an unthinkable urge. . . . This is the obsidian shard I safeguard above all the others. (*ATA,* 370–71)

However, the knowledge of female survival that the reader is given the moment Ginny's narrative voice is heard reveals that Larry/Lear's patriarchal authority will soon be limited.

Cook's diminished majesty is further contracted by the boundaries acknowledged in the novel's title—"a thousand acres." This and no more is the extent of his kingdom. Lear's power may seem immeasurable and his fall cataclysmic, but Larry Cook's imperium is confined to a narrow, restricted territory. That qualified sovereignty is made yet more tenuous as Smiley sets much of her story in 1979 at the beginning of a serious farm crisis in the United States, the consequences of which flash darkly through the work in the form of loss, failure, bankruptcy, and suicide, until the entire fabric of agrarian idealism that has sustained the vision of the family farm, especially in its American incarnation, is unravelled by the faltering agricultural economy. Nor is this particular crisis singular; rather, as the novel reflects back on the Ericsons and Mel Scott, it is part of a recurrent cycle of depressions that have marked the history of agriculture in the United States.

Indeed, Smiley's choice to have made Larry Cook a farmer-monarch relocates and subverts the justifying bases of Lear's kingship as well as his paternal authority in the refractory economic structures that govern agricultural production and in the radical instability of the natural world, forces that are surely outside the control of patriarchal will and that, ultimately, cannot be contained within the rationalizing ideology of American agrarian pastoralism.[16] In addition, while sovereignty can be embodied in and exercised by the single dominant figure of Lear, especially in the primal landscape the play imagines, farming is by definition a cooperative venture, particularly on a thousand acres. Whatever Larry Cook believes about the scope of his supremacy, Ty Smith and Pete Lewis are necessary to his "rule" in ways that Albany and Cornwall, who often seem like dramatic afterthoughts, both in text and performance,[17] are not. This factor not only dilutes Cook's tyrannical self-sufficiency, but also implicates the other male figures in the various forms of masculine exploitation and injury operating in the novel.

Finally, because Lear's preeminence in the hierarchies of institutional and cultural power, including, most critically, his dominion over language, invests his madness with a kind of cosmic destructive grandeur, its roots are never clearly articulated nor do they need to be. They remain unspoken, mysterious perhaps, to be teased from the level of subtextual discourse and subject to the generic mutability of performance. However, Larry Cook's fictively reconfigured decay, unfolding within the explicatory constraints of the novel form, requires the definition of illness; his progressive immobility; the arbitrary petulance transformed into nasty public tantrums; the decline into childishness. The retreat from language must be caused, whether it be Alzheimer's disease, arteriosclerosis, environmental poisoning, patriarchy, or playacting. For if reasons can be assigned, then Cook's place within the narrative, not to say his daughters' lives, can be contained and domesticated.

This process of individual and generic silencing that Cook undergoes (an ironic inversion of the daughterly silences of *King Lear*) could be said to reduce and flatten his character because of expectation instilled by the Shakespearean antecedent; but it could equally be said that such a revision, compelled by point of view, finally empowers the elder sisters generally, and Ginny in particular, because they have been allowed to seize custody of their own stories, and it is their voiced experiences that authorize and control the methods by which Larry/Lear is known and judged. This reinscription of feminine voices into a culturally valorized master('s) text is to certify survival: if *King Lear* is apocalypse, the end of days, then Ginny's narrative, because it is just that—her story—is "a step away from the abyss . . . a way for her life *not* to end, not to be destroyed by what her father has done to her . . . even in the face of the end of their life on the farm."[18]

## Mother Nature Versus Father Capitalism

By reinventing *King Lear* not simply as the daughters' novel but as the "wicked" daughters' novel while nevertheless relying so heavily on the primary Shakespearean original, Smiley has produced an unsettling experience, made even more so by increasing familiarity with the tragedy: the internal generic claims of the now-reconfigured story and the external correspondences to *King Lear* (especially the events and conventions of its plot devices) always will be disjunctive, opening gaps of trust and credibility that the explicatory pressures of narrative cannot always fill or sustain as might a play through the three-dimensional possibilities of theatrical practice. However, what the novel does effectively accomplish is to refashion, expose, and examine as cultural process what is enmeshed in the symbolic substructure of the drama.

Just as the discontinuities between the patriarchal text and the matriarchal subtext of *King Lear* license an interpretive space within which to explore the shifty and permeable relationships between the predatory feminine and the vulnerable masculine, between woman as gratifying/betraying mother and man as ever needy, appetitive son, between inchoate, absorbing nature identified as female and the ordering principle of will identified as male, so, too, does *A Thousand Acres* open the same ideological territory as it chronicles the inevitable dissolution of the American pastoral dream.

American pastoralism was initiated by the early explorer/exploiters and settlers who first viewed, then described, and finally colonized the paradisal landscape of the New World, behaving in ways that have been and continue to be read both as barbarous and as civilizing. The novel is linked to this ambiguous history by characters called Ericson, Cabot, Drake, Smith, and Hudson. Indeed, their tangled and ultimately ruinous desires for commercial gain, religious redemption, political liberty, and prelapsarian fulfillment suffuse a narrative inhabited by a population of major and minor figures called Lewis and Clark, LaSalle and Cartier, Stanley and Livingston, Amundson and Scott, Boone, Pike, Carson, and Crockett, all ironic and sometimes slightly comic embodiments of their greedy, contradictory spirits. American pastoralism ostensibly articulates a vision of

> harmony between man and nature based on an experience of the land as essentially feminine—that is, not simply as mother but the land as a woman, the total female principle of gratification. . . . America was experienced as the daily reality of what has become its single dominating metaphor: regression from the cares of daily life and a return to the primal warmth of womb or breast in a feminine landscape.[19]

However, at the heart of these seemingly benevolent aspirations there is a dangerous inconsistency:

> Colonization brought with it an inevitable paradox: the success of settlement depended on the ability to master the land, transforming the virgin territories into something else. . . . As a result, those who had initially responded to the promise of a feminized landscape were now faced with the consequences of that response: either they recoiled in horror from the meaning of their manipulations of a naturally generous world . . . or they succumbed to a life of easeful regression. . . . Neither response, however, obviates the fact that the despoliation of the land appeared more and more the inevitable consequences of human habitation.[20]

Successful farming—as it is practiced by Larry Cook and his neighbors in Zebulon County, Iowa,[21] and by the ironically named Heartland Corporation that replaces the failed system of family farms—thrives on exploiting this poisonous anomaly with toxic results for the womblike, watery, maternal body of the land, for the men who work/violate that body, and for the women who are her surrogates (" . . . goodness me, everything is toxic. . . . You can't avoid toxins" [*ATA*, 29] says the rationalizing New Age banker

Marv Carson). Smiley has observed that "Women, just like nature or the land, have been seen as something to be used"[22] and that agriculture, a capitalist enterprise in this novel, has become an agent of possessiveness and thereby licenses abuse. Even Jess Clark, the novel's spokesperson for a fashionable environmentalism, does not believe "that nature has its own worth, independent of its use for man,"[23] but instead sees land as an instrument upon which he can practice theory, just as he sees the bodies of women as sexual landscapes to test, to probe, to use.

Given the culturally authorized paradigm of gendered exploitation that the text provides and interrogates, it cannot surprise that Rose and Ginny are revealed as victims of incest, an act that is justified and naturalized as another form of ownership by the now-corrupted pastoralism of father and community. Ginny explains the strategies of normalization that the ideology employs, and the modes of resistance that they provoke:

> . . . I can remember when I saw it all your way! The proud progress from Grandpa Davis to Grandpa Cook to Daddy. When 'we' bought the first tractor in the county, when 'we' built the big house, when 'we' had the crops sprayed from the air, when 'we' got a car, when 'we' drained Mel's corner, when 'we' got a hundred and seventy-two bushels an acre. . . . It's good to remember and repeat. You feel good to be a be a part of that. But then I saw what my part really was. . . . I see taking what you want because you want it, then making something up that justifies what you did. I see getting others to pay the price, then covering up and forgetting what the price was. Do I think Daddy came up with beating and fucking us on his own? . . . No, I think he had lessons, and those lessons were a part of the package, along with the land and the lust to run things exactly the way he wanted to . . . poisoning the water and destroying the topsoil . . . and then feeling *that* all of it was 'right'. . . . (*ATA*, 342–43)

To be Daddy, to be a farmer, and, it would seem, to be a man, is to possess "a personality structure that supersedes every childhood influence" (*ATA*, 118). To be a woman is to see "without being afraid and without turning away" (*ATA*, 355) that Eden is, and perhaps always has been, irreparably spoiled. Ginny's task, then, is to escape, to survive, and to tell the story.

### Notes

1. Suzanne Berne, "*Belles Lettres* Interview" (with Jane Smiley), *Belles Lettres: A Review of Books by Women* (Summer 1992): 36.
2. Ibid., 26.

3. A brief but pertinent discussion of where to place Smiley's novel in a generic framework occurs in Diane Purkiss, "Uncovering Iowa," *Times Literary Supplement,* October 30, 1992, 36.

4. Smiley, in Berne, "Interview," 36.

5. Indeed, productions of the play either stand or fall (according to reviews) to the extent that any given actor is charismatic enough to beat the role into submission. Where *Lear* is concerned, and where Lear is concerned, competence is just not enough.

6. Smiley, in Berne, "Interview," 36.

7. This data comes from that most valuable book, T. J. King, *Casting Shakespeare's Plays: London Actors and Their Roles, 1590–1642* (Cambridge: Cambridge University Press, 1992), 223–26.

8. Smiley, in Berne, "Interview," 37.

9. Madelon Gohlke, "'I wooed thee with my sword': Shakespeare's Tragic Paradigms," in *Representing Shakespeare: New Psychoanalytic Essays,* ed. Murray M. Schwartz and Coppélia Kahn (Baltimore, MD: Johns Hopkins University Press, 1980), 179–180.

10. Smiley, in Berne, "Interview," 37.

11. Jane Smiley, *A Thousand Acres* (New York: Ballantine Books, 1991), 199–200. Hereafter, all citations will appear in the text.

12. Smiley, in Berne, "Interview," 37.

13. Gayle Rubin, "The Traffic in Women: Notes on the 'Political Economy' of Sex," in *Toward an Anthropology of Women,* ed. Rayna R. Reiter (New York: Monthly Review Press, 1975), 157–210. This groundbreaking essay continues to be a valuable, indeed indispensable, resource.

14. For a thorough discussion of the mutability of the critical enterprise and its effects on the interpretation of *King Lear,* see R. A. Foakes, *Hamlet Versus Lear: Cultural Politics and Shakespeare's Art* (Cambridge: Cambridge University Press, 1993).

15. William Shakespeare, *King Lear,* ed. Kenneth Muir, (Arden edition) (Cambridge, MA: Harvard University Press, 1959), 1.2.39–41. Hereafter, all citations will appear in the text.

16. Annette Kolodny's *Lay of the Land: Metaphor as Experience and History in American Life and Letters* (Chapel Hill, NC: University of North Carolina Press, 1975) has proved invaluable in helping to articulate the contradictory elements that constitute the American version of pastoral ideology.

17. In Q1608, Albany has 137 lines, Cornwall 86; in the Folio, Albany speaks 124 lines, Cornwall 110. Once again, this data comes from King, *Casting Shakespeare's Plays,* 223–26. Although there is some variation from Quarto to Folio, these roles remain minor ones, no matter how briefly memorable they might become when performed by a skilled actor.

18. Smiley, in Berne, "Interview," 37.

19. Kolodny, *Lay of the Land,* 4–7.

20. Ibid., 7. The sexualized vocabulary of Kolodny's definition of the elements constituting the pastoral ideal is obviously no accident.

21. Named after the explorer/adventurer Zebulon Pike, who did, indeed, travel through the Iowa Territory. There is, of course, no such county on the map of the state.

22. Martha Duffy, "The Case for Goneril and Regan," *Time,* (138: November 11, 1991), 94.

23. Ibid., 94.

## 9

~~~

# Shakespeare in Iceland

## *Jane Smiley*

I would like to dedicate this talk to the memory of Harriett Hawkins, a former teacher of mine, who died last autumn, and who was, as many of you know, an erudite and avid Shakespeare enthusiast, and without whose influence I might never have written *A Thousand Acres*.

Over the last few weeks, I've been privileged to enjoy one of the fruits of the literary life that Shakespeare himself seems not to have enjoyed, that is, reading academic papers that take seriously and thoughtfully my novel *A Thousand Acres*.[1] Some writers might conceivably consider this a torment, but as a sometime academic myself, who wrote many English papers, I appreciate not only the thoughts that I have read, but also the habit of mind that ponders a work, finds connections within it and between it and other works, and in other ways is stimulated and moved by that work. This is especially gratifying in the case of *A Thousand Acres* because that novel grew out of a very similar mental process. In one sense, *A Thousand Acres* is my academic paper on *King Lear*, while in another sense, it is my production of the play.

What I would like to do today is use this interesting opportunity that I have had to close the loop between artistic production and cultural response to investigate the nature of composition, using *A Thousand Acres* as a case study, drawing on my memories and thoughts. Let me call this an "as if" biography. I am going to try to consider the composition process as if from the outside, asking whether how *A Thousand Acres* seemed to come together for me actually accounts for what seems to be in it, according to the various papers upon it that I have read. It is my hope that this case study might shed some light on modes of composition in general, an area that, as far as I know, isn't much investigated. Conversations of critics and scholars with artists don't seem to me to get to the heart of this matter, and for lack of time or lack of interest or lack of perspective, most writers don't write much about how writing comes about.

First, let me suggest an image of the mind working at its novelistic task. I see an organic machine mostly immersed in darkness, but partly revealed. The machine is organic because it is not metal, has not been constructed, but it is machine-like, because it is orderly in its operations and predictable, when you know the principles by which it operates. It is these principles that are largely mysterious, because much of the machine, though present, is unseen and unknown even to the writer. The visible part is intellect, reason, and intention. But the larger part, lost in darkness, is made up of the body, the emotions, the remembered and the unremembered but still present, the DNA, the immediate environment, the passing currents of attention, dreams, half-thought thoughts, the impressions made by others. The organic machine of composition works 24 hours a day. It sucks in more than it puts out. The writer is aware of its working, involves herself more or less closely with it depending on the time of day and other pleasures or obligations, but also relies upon it to go on working without her. I would like you to keep this image in mind as I touch on other elements of composition.

Of course, the novelist has many intentions for her novel, and one of these is a straightforward one—an intention to enter into a relationship with a reader during which both contemplate a subject and some characters together. In my experience, this sense of the reader's presence sometimes gets lost when the writer's mind is taken over by the characters during the act of composing, but every novelist understands that writing is essentially a social exchange, and every writer to a greater or lesser degree brings a strategy for communicating to her side of the exchange. I stress this because I feel that certain critical schools portray the writer as more or less unconscious, as if reading were a form of eavesdropping on the author's inner life. This sort of criticism demeans the writer's quest for technical mastery and the writer's talent for making artistic choices. I think when we say that so and so is a genius, we imply that the writing was done through them rather than by them, while for the writer the very exercise of technique, the choice to employ one image rather than another, or to cast a scene from the point of view of one character rather than another, is the central delight of composition.

And so, I had an intention in *A Thousand Acres* that grew out of something less rational, a response to the play. I wanted to communicate the ways in which I found the conventional readings of *King Lear* frustrating and wrong. Beginning with my first readings of the play in high school and continuing through college and graduate school, I had been cool to both Cordelia and Lear. While I understood and accepted how I should feel about them, he struck me as the sort of person, from beginning to end, that you would want to stay away from—selfish, demanding, humorless, self-pitying. Even when cast low by events, he seemed to hog the stage—his self-effacement a pose, his strategies for calling attention to himself myriad and completely successful. In all the productions I saw, no actor, not even my favorite Olivier, could make him sympathetic to me. My acceptance of his tragedy was pro forma, the response of a good girl and a good student. I didn't like Cordelia, either. She seemed ungenerous and cold, a stickler for truth at the beginning, a stickler for form at the end. No amount of beauty in an actress warmed her up for me. On the other hand, the older sisters, figures of pure evil according to conventional wisdom, sounded familiar, especially in the scene where they talk between themselves about Lear's actions, and later, when they have to deal with his unruly knights. They were women, and the play seemed to be condemning them morally for the exact ways in which they expressed womanhood that I recognized. I was offended. Let me emphasize that these were visceral responses—semi-conscious "No's" that being a good student and a good girl didn't change. These responses made me find the play less enjoyable than my favorite Shakespeare plays—*Hamlet, Measure for Measure, Much Ado*. I felt an automatic resistance when people labeled *King Lear* Shakespeare's greatest tragedy, but I read my resistance as an idiosyncratic reaction, something not to mention in educated company—not exactly a failure in myself but more like a tiny tear in the social fabric that could be overlooked.

Responses, of course, are connected to some of the hidden parts of the machine, but let me speculate a bit about mine to *King Lear*.

Perhaps I was unsympathetic to fathers in general because I didn't live with a father and had never been trained to accept the fatherly qualities that Lear represents—command, power, self-centeredness. Although my grandfather was quite patriarchal, and I spent a lot of time with him as a child, he was much more charming than Lear, and in all events, he was a grandfather. His power had been diminished already before I knew him and he had accepted that with grace. Also, as a resident of the American Midwest, I found the extreme expression of emotion off-putting, which is not to say that in my family and among my friends extreme emotions were never expressed—they were, but afterwards we were ashamed of ourselves for saying rash things, hurting each other and threatening our relationships. When Lear, at the end, is ashamed of himself, I didn't see his shame as transcendent, but only as what it should be. I didn't think he should get any extra credit for it, especially since he becomes no more considerate of Cordelia than he had been—he still overrules her desire to go "see these daughters and these sisters," still wants her all for himself, and she no longer has the strength to resist.

And so these responses to the play formed a beginning, but their realization as a novel was hardly assured. I was a lot more interested in other things.

Perhaps every writer is molded by seminal texts. I certainly was. For me, the three books that formed my future writing were two novels, *Giants in the Earth*, by O. E. Rölvaag, which I read in eighth grade, and *David Copperfield*, which I read in ninth grade, and a science book, *The Web of Life*, which introduced me to the field of ecology, also in eighth grade. Each of these books, in its way, seemed entirely true to me at the time I read it. They were almost the first books I read that weren't series books for children. Though I remember very little of the style of the Rolvaag novel, I remember that the hardships endured by Per Hansa and his family, and the tragic outcome of their immigration to Minnesota, seemed absolutely right as a picture of the way the world worked—like the "westward ho" stories I was seeing on TV but more honest in counting the costs of western settlement and predicting that the probable outcome would be terrifying rather than happy. I do remember the style of *David Copperfield*. Who doesn't? I was enchanted by it, but the real lesson of Dickens was the complexity and liveliness of the novel as a form. In David's novel, David is the still center of a swirl of other characters, uncountable for me at fourteen. And *The Web of Life* reinforced that sense I had of the variousness and interconnectedness of land, animals, plants, people, town and countryside, prairie and civilization. From these readings I came to Shakespeare, who fit right in. Each year, we read a Shakespeare play, starting with *Twelfth Night* in seventh grade, going through *A Midsummer Night's Dream*, *Julius Caesar*, *As You Like It*, *Hamlet*, and *King Lear*. What I liked at first was the treasury of names in the list of dramatis personae, and what I kept liking was the action and liveliness on the stage—everything was interconnected; plenty was happening. It was almost Dickensian. But, though fond, I remained unpossessed by Shakespeare. Things in Shakespeare plays were not quite dark enough to be right for me and there was too much talk. Drama was not going to be my natural form, either. I grew up in a family of story-tellers, gossipers, natural narrators. We did not mimic voices or take parts or perform. We specialized in irony of tone. When I discovered the Icelandic sagas, I discovered us.

Here is another part of the authorial machine, the assimilation of the writer to a form. Perhaps the writer does choose, but it seems different from that to me, more like a taking in of the writer by the form, complete with a gentle sucking noise. Perhaps what I blamed Lear for was actually a feature of dramatic form that I was uncomfortable with—all the talk, especially talk about emotions, that seemed simultaneously to trivialize and make self-indulgent and shrill the passions being expressed. Narrative gives more direct access to the inner life, allows the writer to reveal the disjuncture between what is felt and what appears, and to suggest emotions so powerful that their complete expression must fail, resulting in silence. Each form makes a psychological assertion. Neither assertion is precisely true or complete, which is why each form is a compromise and why both forms exist. At any rate, narrative and I assimilated each other, and I made a career plan.

I have often thought how neatly Virginia Woolf foretold my generation of writers in *A Room of One's Own*, for we of the SAT generation, from, say, the early 1960s on, were the first generation of girls for whom education was so normal that we took our career choices for granted. I went to Vassar, my boyfriend went to Yale; we thought that the fight for women's education was a historical matter, already won. When we discussed our futures we automatically discussed our work. Mine was to be writing novels and his was to be building the revolution. Everyone took my education seriously—my parents, my professors, my boyfriend, myself. I was surrounded by other girls whose educations were also taken seriously, taught by women who were scholars and writers, given access to books and libraries. If the plan was for us to get married and raise children, it was not communicated directly to us. The boys I knew were no more or less ambitious than I was, than the girls I knew. I stress this demographic detail because, of course, no woman can think about Shakespeare after Virginia Woolf without being aware of Woolf's figure of Judith Shakespeare. Every novel is, in part, a demographic demonstration of what is possible during a writer's lifetime, and as I get older, I realize with more modesty than I felt as an eighteen-year-old, that my path, that is, my automatic assumptions about my choices and intentions, was cleared by others. What I was doing seemed normal, not radical. What my boyfriend was doing seemed radical.

My career plan was straightforward—to read as many books as possible and to get as much praise for my own writing as possible. My only system was taste, and my tastes, as I mentioned above, were largely formed. In college, I took courses almost entirely in English literature, from Old English to the beginning of the twentieth century. Courses at Vassar were almost all year-long courses, and so investigation of a subject was intensive. At Vassar I met Harriett Hawkins, to whom this talk is dedicated. She taught me freshman English for a year and then taught me Renaissance and Restoration Drama. She was a wonderful teacher—compelling, enthusiastic, friendly, and supportive. I liked her and I felt that she liked me, so I showed her a few of my poems, which she reacted to with enthusiasm. It was in Harriett's class that I read *King Lear* with real seriousness for the first time, and where I became aware of how my reaction to the play did not conform to the standard interpretation of it. Harriett's was, simultaneously, a voice of authority, dispensing the conventional wisdom about the play, but also a woman's voice, slightly recasting the whole argument. I clearly remember what she had to say about Goneril and Regan, and I remember noticing what she said because she was a woman talking about women in a way that I do not remember what she had to say about *Everyman*, for example. I also continued to like big complex novels—

*Pamela, Emma, Tom Jones,* the Russians. I got some praise for my writing. My education, in other words, moved smoothly forward.

The only things my boyfriend and I talked about were class warfare, racism, endangered species, whether Marxist analysis was appropriate to the history of the Merovingian period, in what ways literature and music were inherently political, and whether the workers actually wanted an alliance with the students. Another demographic detail—he was a member of the notorious Yale class of 1970, the first class that was predominantly middle class and public school educated, whose admission was primarily based on merit examinations. I now think that the visceral reaction of my boyfriend and his friends in finding themselves in the bastion of privilege that was Yale University in 1966 was from the beginning to the end rage at finding what was behind those closed doors, that their forebears had been shut out of. My reaction, once I gained access to the facilities through him, was more goofy, more Virginia Woolfian—I saw what they had that I, even at Vassar, did not have—for example, William Blake's real works at the Beinecke Library, compared to what we had, postcards. I was more amazed that they had them than I was angry that we did not. But I noted the difference. Politics had not been in my educational or career plan, but one thing I have noticed is the profound effect a young man with ideas can have upon a young woman with desire. He would say that I argued with him about every mote and dust particle. I would say that he changed and shaped my sense of the world from top to bottom. Of course, all of our discussions were juvenile, partial, half-baked. But they came at a significant moment for me, at a moment where sexual awakening and intellectual awakening coincided, and however right or wrong the conclusions we drew, what was learned did not later get unlearned. I now had a political consciousness. Soon feminism would flow into it, both as a response to feminist writing and as a recognition of the realities of my first experience of intimacy with a man.

I do not want to give into the temptation of chronology here, only to reflect for a moment on how certain things I did in my teens and twenties began to form the mold that *A Thousand Acres* was finally struck from in my forties.

Let's return to the organic machine, and shine a different light on it, seeing it now not as a solid object, but as a large, three-dimensional web, with filaments running everywhere, so numerous and variously connected that we can follow only a few of them out.

My boyfriend and I, now married, went to the University of Iowa, he in medieval history, me in nothing. I hadn't been accepted to the Writer's Workshop, and so found myself as a graduate student wife making teddy bears in a factory. At the first party of medievalists in October of that year, I met a man named John C. McGalliard, who was teaching Old Norse. I had loved Old English in college, so I asked if I could join his class. He agreed, and I began rearranging my teddy bear schedule to accommodate *Hrafnkels saga*. Here is where, in my life, Shakespeare set sail for Iceland.

While I was not possessed by Shakespeare as I was by the great English novelists, every writer of English has a relationship to him, both direct and indirect. English cannot be written without Shakespeare, or, for that matter, read without Shakespeare. My officemate in grad school seriously considered Shakespeare to be an incarnation of the deity, and so every discussion of Shakespeare that we had, and there were many, proposed his universality. I took this as a question I had to answer but could not, as well as a characterization of what it meant to be a writer that I had to grapple with. If Shakespeare was not God, then he certainly was a writer, and therefore a model of what a writer should be—adept at comedy and tragedy and irony and characterization and poetry and prose, a person of wide-ranging interests and skillful at the illusion of expertise, lively and sober by turns, familiar with the full range of emotions, able to believably extrapolate from the quotidian life of a citizen to the epic life of a king or a queen. Why not, I felt, try for that? Why try for less? Shakespeare did not seem confessional, more investigative, a writer who used his instrument to explore the world and not himself. That's how I thought of him, anyway. So while I did not feel particularly close to the plays, as my officemate did, I did feel inspired by Shakespeare the writer as a model. Why in the world I felt I could dare to take this particular model I will never know; it is one of those filaments of the web that runs away into the darkness.

I read all of *Njáls saga*, word by painstaking word, line by translated line. Some of you lucky ones in the audience may be familiar with the Icelandic sagas. Of them, *Njáls saga* is the longest and grandest, detailing the ramifications of a marriage and an ever-widening feud while at the same time depicting the panorama of life in Iceland. The words of *Njáls saga* were so engraved on my brain by my translating process, that ten years later when I reread the saga in translation, I remembered it almost line for line. I was not a good student of Old Norse, in that I never memorized grammar rules or vocabulary, and often relied on a more general sense of the burden of the prose than I should have. But the result of my lack of facility was that the sagas that I worked on dripped very slowly into my brain, and the images that they made there were ones that I pondered over and over.

In graduate school, I also took a course in Shakespeare's problem plays from Miriam Gilbert, at the University of Iowa. I wrote a production paper in which I attempted to solve the problems of *Measure for Measure*, my favorite, most dark, cynical, and ironic play. I set my production in the medieval period, and a certain way of looking at Shakespeare, as a generation or two removed from the middle ages, opened up for me. I realized that I had always assumed that Shakespeare knew he was the great precursor, as if when he held out his arms, he could see all of English history and literature to come flowing from his fingertips. But now I imagined him looking backward, as I looked backward to him. When I returned to *King Lear* later on, this sense of Shakespeare attending to the mysterious past was important in my inspiration.

So far, I have talked a great deal about school, coursework, books. As I reveal these mundanities, I feel a little uneasy, even here, or perhaps especially here, in front of you. It sounds like I read some books and kind of understood them, then wrote some books, straining mightily over any number of gnats. I was no scholar of Shakespeare, even of Dickens, even of the Icelandic sagas. I was just a reader, and a slow one at that. When I was studying Middle English for my Ph.D. exams, I napped over my work morning, noon, and night. It took me a week to read *Sir Gawain and the Green Knight*. Some of what I learned about the Middle Ages wasn't from sources at all, but from *The Seventh Seal* and *Virgin Spring*. I was and am hardly the reader that Virginia Woolf was—perhaps, unlike Shakespeare, she was the model who intimidated me. Even so, I read enough to form my notion of what a writer does, a literary theory, and here it is. A writer is first a reader, who enters the realm of literature and soon forms a reciprocal relationship with it, work by work, and not only with works she has read, but also with works she has not read, but heard about or even just seen on the shelf. She carries with her emo-tional, intellectual, spiritual, physical baggage, but she isn't even, at first, seeking a form. At first she is seeking the most basic ideas. In fact, until she finds a form, her mind is a blank; she has no ideas at all. Later, there are some aborted, unimag-ined, failed ideas. The specific forms each work takes, not just the novel, but the novel *Pride and Prejudice*, for example, give her the very ideas that she thinks are her own, but as soon as she has those ideas, she has other slightly different ideas that are the fruit of her non-Pride-and-Prejudice life. The relationship builds on itself, so that more experience of forms creates more ideas, which whets the ap-petite for more precisely suitable forms, that is, a specific novel that is not any novel that the novelist has ever read before. What is available even to not very good scholars such as myself is the passion of this reciprocal relationship. I can-not count the times I have put down a book because I was too inspired by it to keep reading. I could feel some sort of joy or power flowing from the book to me, filling me with the yearning to write, which felt like a desire to form something like clay or music. Most of these times, I had nothing to write about, and so I took a few deep breaths and picked up the book again. The writer in the realm of lit-erature is first and foremost a reader, or perhaps maybe a listener also, for whom the giving back of the energy received from the text is an almost physical need. Writing is a social act, a social response, a effort to make a connection, an act of love that is sometimes frankly libidinous, but other times friendly, sisterly, affec-tionate, or merely interested. The realm of literature excites these social feelings as much as the writer's associates do. But in addition to the possibility of con-nection, the writer is excited by technical mastery.

I have often noticed that I am less moved by my works than my readers are—that is, I pass through a phase where I am moved by the plight of the characters and into a longer and more interesting period where, whatever is happening to them and however bad it is, I am excited and pleased at the writing process. Once Mark Strand, the author of *Darker*, among other volumes of poetry, and I had a whale of a time laughing at how funny we found our work, though we were both known in general for gloom and doom. I later thought that it wasn't the work it-self that we found funny, but the way the technical process delighted us. Writing a novel or a poem is playing a game, and it puts the writer in a similar mood to chess or baseball—serious and playful at the same time, a separate mental region. And so, in the realm of literature, the reciprocal relationship between the writer and the works is both emotional and technical, and at times one side is more ex-citing and at times the other side is more exciting. I always felt that I sensed this joy in technical mastery in Shakespeare's writing, a kind of click click of words and images and scenes and themes falling neatly, clearly, meaningfully into place. After I sensed it in his writing, I sought the same feeling in my own.

Although I didn't become famous until *A Thousand Acres*, the most important period of my life as a writer so far was the fourteen months, from May 1984 to July 1985, when I was writing my novel *The Greenlanders* and then my novella *The Age of Grief*. By then, I had been obsessively focused on writing and publishing novels for about seven years or so, since taking my degree from the Iowa Writer's Workshop and going on a Fulbright to Iceland. In Iceland, I exchanged the socia-ble, coupled, communal life I had lived in Iowa City for a solitary one, my many companions and amusements for reading, reading, and only reading. I read, among others, *Anna Karenina*, *War and Peace*, *Madame Bovary*, *The Brothers Kara-mazov*, *The Grapes of Wrath*, Christina Stead's *The Man Who Loved Children*, every Icelandic saga translated into English, and two or three books by Halldór Laxness, including *Independent People*. I wrote some short stories and conceived my first two novels as well as *The Greenlanders*. By the spring of 1984 I had two children, had been married for six years, owned a house, had tenure in an academic job, and was otherwise firmly fixed in my writing and childcare routine. In June of 1984, I went to England, Denmark, and Greenland on a research trip. Before I left, I had 68 awkward pages of my manuscript written. I got back on the first of July. By Labor Day, I was up to 130, by Christmas, I was up to 385. I was 35 years old and dissatisfied with my marriage. Somehow connected to that but not was the fact that writing *The Greenlanders* was taking hold of me, seemingly from the outside. My characters were in part historically attested by the Icelandic chronicles, and they seemed to be coming through me onto the page from outside myself.

Though I kept to my writing schedule of only a few hours each day, I was frantic with inspiration—filled with energy and interest in things, so gripped by narrative flow that I could go in and out of the novel at will. I thought of Shakespeare constantly. I was very aware of how old I was in comparison to him in 1600, when he was writing the great tragedies. I was convinced that what I was going through would be the only way a writer could do so much work in a short period. It was a *kind* of literary madness in the sense that the normal haphazard and contingent conditions of life had suddenly organized themselves, probably through the obscure agency of the id, into an entirely meaningful and fully realized symbolic universe. I was the concentrating point for the creation of *The Greenlanders*, and that was all that mattered, really. By 1 June I had about 720 pages, and when I finished, on Midsummer's Eve, I had over 1100. At the end, I was writing all day, 20 pages a day. In retrospect, a day's work seems to have lasted the usual two hours. After I finished *The Greenlanders*, I woke up the next morning, full of momentum, and for the next month wrote *The Age of Grief*, employing all of the figurative, introspective language I had been storing up while writing in the plain style of *The Greenlanders*. Both works are for all practical purposes rough drafts, as I imagined Shakespeare's works from the first years of the seventeenth century were. I'll admit here that while I was writing *The Greenlanders*, I was convinced that it was my masterwork, and that the process I was going through was a necessary process for such a work. I also have to say that I didn't like it, that what it had done to my life, my routine, and my sense of myself appalled me, and I thought, though I loved *The Greenlanders* itself and still do, that I never wanted to go through that again, even for another masterwork. I learned my lesson, and the lesson was that literature wasn't everything, didn't deserve to be everything.

In studying Old Icelandic and in writing and researching *The Greenlanders*, I engaged for ten years or so with a distinctly pre-modern mind, as expressed in the stories and the style of the Icelandic sagas and the poetic Edda, and yet, because the sagas were written prose narratives about the social consequences of unrestrainable conflict in the polity, they were also strangely modern, strangely American. I always thought of *Njáls saga* as the great proto-American novel, halfway here in place and time. After I turned in *The Greenlanders*, I was still reeling from the experience of writing it—I thought about the characters and incidents daily for about three-and-a-half years, until they were driven out by the composition of *A Thousand Acres* during the fall of 1988. For the purposes of this paper, that means that almost every literary thought I had for something like 15 years, from 1973 to 1988, was linked to or influenced by medieval Icelandic literature. Lear's heath, in my mind, was not in populous, voluble, green England, but in treeless, distant Iceland. The conflict between Lear and his daughters, primal and so quickly going out of control, so isolated and depopulated in feeling, seemed Germanic and even Nordic to me, by contrast to, let's say, the distinctly Italian feel of *Romeo and Juliet*. I had found medieval literature to be very close to its folkloric sources, so it was automatic for me to imagine Shakespeare cocking his ear backward when he was writing *King Lear*, probing the Germanic side of his English heritage rather than the Latin side.

Nevertheless, it took a few accidents to precipitate *A Thousand Acres*. One of these was a visit to McDonald's in Delhi, New York, in the summer of 1987. For some reason, that McDonald's was decorated with pictures of the Midwest, and the one in the booth we sat down in had a man standing in a barn in what seemed to be wheat country. While I was looking at the picture, I described, idly and briefly to my husband, the idea of rewriting *King Lear*. He said, "You could set it on a farm in Kansas," and I said, "I don't know anything about Kansas." Pooh. Dismissing him! Right around that time, I had a visit from the actress Glenn Close, who had enjoyed *The Age of Grief* and written me a note. Sometime late in the evening, after the children were in bed and we had already eaten and I was casting about for something to say, I began to describe a production of *King Lear*, or a movie, done as if from the older daughters' point of view, in which, of course, Miss Close would star. A good role for a woman. Though I was describing this in order to connect with her somehow, I didn't feel that I was successful in that, and I fell silent. Still, having my own *King Lear* was now more than a thought, though less than a project. That did not happen until the following March, when, for the first time since moving to Ames, I happened to drive with my husband to Minneapolis. As we were coming home in what we called "the iron season"—that is, everything frozen and dead and unattractive—I looked out the window somewhere around mile 170, and said, "You know, I could set that *King Lear* book around here. I know about this area." And there we were; as had happened to me with each book, a sight of the place where the novel was set caused the ideas and the characters to jell, as if all at once. *A Thousand Acres* was now a presence. The actual writing of it seemed more like a manageable detail than an effort of creation.

Three other threads that tied up for me in *A Thousand Acres* were feminism, environmentalism, and a vaguely Marxist materialism. No longer a student, I was now a teacher, and one course I was assigned to teach was a course of world literature in translation for nonmajors. My reading list started with some parts of *Don Quixote*, galloped apace through four centuries, and ended with short stories by modern Latin American women writers. In addition to literary works such as *Candide*, *Taras Bulba*, *Claudine at School*, and *The Metamorphosis*, my class read and reported on Fernand Braudel's three-volume history, *Civilization and Capitalism*. By the end of the semester, the students knew what capitalism was and how the works we read expressed and critiqued it. By the end of three semesters teaching this course, I had a much clearer idea of how our times have evolved out of Shake-

speare's times, and how ideas and questions posed in his works have been answered and modified by history. I developed a thought or two about the intrusion
of notions of ownership and commodification upon familial and romantic relationships, and a thought or two about the specificity, as opposed to universality,
of Western European ideas of family order, of ownership and exploitation of land,
resources, and the services of other human beings, of conflict, literary form, ego,
power, gender, and the finality of death. Most of my ideas were suggested by
Braudel but realized through the literary readings and our class discussions.
While I was teaching this class, I was writing *A Thousand Acres*.

In addition, I was living in Iowa. When my first husband was accepted to graduate school, he was accepted to Iowa and Virginia. We discussed where he should
go extremely briefly. Iowa seemed nicer and more rural, somehow, and it was
closer to Wyoming, his home state. That was just about all we said about it. And
yet, of course, as it turned out, all sorts of agricultural issues and environmental
issues became a part of my daily life once I moved to Iowa, lived in small towns,
started reading the *Des Moines Register*, began to know people who lived on farms
or had been raised on farms. My absolutely first ecological concern when I got to
Iowa was to wonder, as a result of reading Barry Commoner's *The Closing Circle*,
whether the well water on the farm we were renting was contaminated with ni-
trates, and whether, if I got pregnant, I would be able to carry the baby to term.
My second one was to wonder how often over the years the bees who were living
in our house had been poisoned with DDT. A lot of times, as it turned out. When
we first moved there, I went for nature walks, but of course, the only place to walk
was down the gravel road. Nature, as I had known it elsewhere, was missing, and
large fields of crops had been put in its place.

And then there was feminism. Women's education made feminism inevitable. The rise of the left insured its almost immediate emergence. The outward flow of college women into work and family life disseminated it. When
women of my generation became writers, editors, publishers, and literary critics
they could not help but express feminism because they could not help but express the right they felt to be doing what they were doing. And, I think, they
couldn't help but express anger of the same sort that the Yale class of 1970 expressed, not gratitude that they had been allowed in the gates, which I think is
what those already inside thought we should express, but resentment at how
long the gates had been barred, and how deluxe the accommodations inside the
gates turned out to be.

When I looked out my car window at mile 170 and thought I might set my
production of *King Lear* right there, these were the main ideas that fell together so
suddenly and so completely. I had a global apprehension of the entire book that
did not change significantly afterward, and I thought the book would be easy to

write, but it wasn't. Of all my books it was the most difficult, and for that I blame Mr. Shakespeare.

After writing *The Greenlanders*, I rather prided myself on my cruelty to my characters. I was pleased at how readily I could sacrifice them to principle. Sudden, accidental death, for example, is a prominent feature of the Icelandic saga, often followed by the saga-writer's remark, "And now he is out of this story." Boom, you're dead; doesn't matter how good or useful or interesting you are, that's life in the Middle Ages. And, I thought, in the modern period, too. Russell Banks once told me that it was his ambition to write the saddest novel ever written, in *Continental Drift*. I thought, that, except for *The Greenlanders*, he had succeeded. NO REDEMPTION, the characteristic failure of artistic integrity of all Western European authors. Every time you thought someone really great, like Tolstoy, was going to look straight down into the abyss, at the last minute, he stepped back—there was that little streak of light, even in Kafka, even, for God's sake, in Gogol. Only the Yiddish writers we read had the courage to fall at last into total darkness. The Yiddish writers and me. That was my claim to artistic respectability. I had read *King Lear* four or five times by the time I reread it to begin *A Thousand Acres*, and I had seen three productions of the play as well as Kurosawa's *Ran*. But I had never entered into a relationship with the play or the author like the one I entered into when I began writing through my version.

My intention was to stick as closely to the plot as I could, given one or two caveats. The first was that family battles in the twentieth- century rural Midwest are more likely to be fought in the courts than with weapons—actual fighting with guns, say, would be too melodramatic. The second was that I wanted Goneril and Regan to live through to the end, so that they could reflect upon their experiences. That, too, I felt would be characteristic of life as we know it. The world population explosion shows us that survival has become the norm, survival even of terrible cataclysms like the genocide in Rwanda. Otherwise, though, I planned to play the game of following the storyline. When I began, I had a particular vision of Shakespeare—mentally healthy, passionate but also funny, smart, balanced, essentially good. A guy I could relate to. I thought that following his dramatic logic would be easy. And remember, I brought a suspicion of all that talk into the project, so I half wasn't listening to the particulars of what the characters were saying.

But I didn't find writing *A Thousand Acres* at all easy. Instead, I found myself, an author who had killed off hundreds of characters in *The Greenlanders* and ended a whole little world, recoiling from the cruelties of Shakespeare's twists and turns of plot. At first this wasn't conscious. I would be writing along, and discover that some plot point didn't quite fit, that is, that I had become confused, or that I didn't know how to progress the action. Then I would read over what I had written, and compare it to the play, and discover that I had diverged slightly from what was happening in the play. I attributed this to lack of attentiveness on my part. But as the play progressed and the stakes got higher with each scene, I realized that what I was doing was avoiding the crueler judgments of the play upon its characters. Where Shakespeare had a character do something intentionally and coldly self-serving, I would resist it. But the plot was always the test, a puzzle that had to work out. The challenge was sticking to the plot but substituting what I considered a truer but what many would say was simply a more congenial view of human nature. As I followed him into the story, the Shakespeare that I thought I knew rapidly metamorphosed into a harsher, more alien, and more distant male figure. I felt very strongly our differences as a modern woman and a Renaissance man. At the root lay the question of the nature of evil. His view I read more and more as Machiavellian—cold, irreducible self-interest, unashamed, unsoftened by any sense of connection with others or of any common humanity. That these feelings should be present in a man of the Renaissance did not surprise me, but that they should be so forcibly expressed by the man who had also written *Much Ado, As You Like It,* even *Macbeth,* a treatise on the power of remorse, disturbed me because the cruelty of *King Lear* that I felt like I was experiencing by rewriting it called into question all the softer and more humane insights of the other plays. Having to wrestle with his vision forced me to assert my own—not to knuckle under but to redouble my efforts to counter his characters' cold evil with my characters' hot passion, his characters' clear agenda of self-interest with my characters' ill-thought-out confusion. I could not allow his universality, but instead, as a rhetorical mode, had to counter it with assertions of the universality of my vision. My tool, the ace in my deck, was narrative form itself.

Drama privileges action over point of view. This privilege can sometimes be mitigated by asides, soliloquies, prologues, epilogues, and other devices, but for sheer relentless inescapable immersion in subjectivity and point of view, you can't beat narrative. Narrative, in my opinion, always calls into question the validity of appearance, always proposes a difference between the public perception of events and their actual meaning. We see this all the time in our adversarial court system, where an event of apparent criminality has taken place, and the jury or the judge must decide which narrative of the event is more likely to be true. As the lawyer for Goneril and Regan, I proposed a different narrative of their motives and actions that cast doubts on the case Mr. Shakespeare was making for his client, King Lear. I made Goneril my star witness, and she told her story with care. I made sure that, insofar as I was able to swing it, she was an appealing witness as well—cautious, judicious, ambivalent, straightforward. I didn't, for example, dare to make Regan my star witness. She was too outspoken and full of spleen. The jury would have reacted negatively no matter whether what she had to say was true or not. The goal of the trial was not to try or condemn the father, but to gain an acquittal for the daughters. The desired verdict was not "innocent," but rather "not guilty," or at least, "not proven." One thing I learned from *Hamlet* is that none of us are innocent, but one thing I learned from narrative is that all of us have something to say in our own defense.

I would not say that I won the wrestling match with Mr. Shakespeare by any means. He exhausted my inventiveness, my theoretical underpinnings, my spirit. Where I had found writing *The Greenlanders* exhilarating though frightening, I found writing *A Thousand Acres* laborious. The work did not speed up as it went along, but rather slowed. When I was finished, I was both dissatisfied and at the end of my artistic rope. I felt that I was stopping rather than finishing. While I thought I had worked through the plot well enough, I knew that I had failed with Cornwall, who was so much a creature of his time and social class that he was not translatable at all; with Oswald, whose servility I could do nothing with; and to some degree with Cordelia, who just wouldn't talk to me. I thought I could solve these problems with another draft, but I didn't have another draft in me.

Even so, I felt that I had not given in to Mr. Shakespeare's alleged universality, but had, in fact, cut him down to size a little bit. I was happy to have made my case about what it means to be a father, what it means to be a daughter, about the asymmetry of power in patriarchal capitalist Western European society, about the attempt to possess other persons as objects and to call that love. I knew that the mind of the reader-jury would be influenced by the order in which it encountered the two works. I hoped that the minds of adolescent girls would encounter *A Thousand Acres* first, and that it would serve them as a prophylactic against the guilt about proper daughterhood that I knew *King Lear* could induce.

At the same time, I pondered my new image of Shakespeare, and I thought of him doing just what I had done—wrestling with old material, given material, that is in some ways malleable and in other ways resistant. I thought about how all material, whether inherited or observed, has integrity. The author doesn't just do something with it, he or she also learns from it. The author's presuppositions and predispositions work on the material and are simultaneously transformed by it. I imagined Shakespeare wrestling with the "Leir" story and coming away a little dissatisfied, a little defeated, but hugely stimulated, just as I was. As I imagined that, I felt that I received a gift, an image of literary history, two mirrors facing each other in the present moment, reflecting infinitely backward into the past and infinitely forward into the future. I knew that the wrestling I had done had not been only with Shakespeare, but also with his nameless predecessors, who carried forward this question of the nature of evil from the earliest human times. Since to me the greatest joy of writing and reading is connecting, this sense of connection through Shakespeare with the distant past has been the loveliest reward of writing *A Thousand Acres*.

Once the novel was out of my hands, it entered into the publishing process and then into the hands of readers. My feeling about it was different from my feeling about *The Greenlanders*—I didn't live with the characters day after day, but instead lived with its success. The fact that *The Greenlanders* had had a devoted but narrow readership and had not made me famous meant that my private experience of it remained the most important one for me. In some sense I was its ideal reader as well as its author, and this bolstered the sense I had of it coming to me from the outside. *A Thousand Acres* was much different. As soon as I turned it in to the publisher it began becoming public. They began planning its promotion and I began talking officially about it. This, again, went right along with my sense of the novel while I was writing it—it was my production of *King Lear*, but hardly mine any more than any production belongs more than temporarily to any theater company. Since it had also exhausted me and I had found it difficult to write, I didn't exactly revel in its success—it wasn't dear to me. This sense of an impersonal relationship to the novel (though accompanied by a fondness for Ginny and Rose) was new and unlike what you might call the afterbirth of any of my previous novels. I therefore read with interest, but some detachment, the letters and papers that I began to get, analyzing various aspects of the novel, and it is to that response that I would now like to turn, as another way of regarding the composition of the novel.

I would say that the dozen or so analyses that I have read (this includes only papers written in the academic mode, not book reviews, which are a separate category) fall into three groups. The first of these discusses the novel in a way that I never thought of. An example would be the analysis I received not too long ago of my use of names in the novel. The writer considered "Zebulon," the county where the novel is set, and "Ginny," and "Rose," the names of my main characters. I had chosen Zebulon for a concrete reason. Iowa has 99 counties, and I did not want to pinpoint any of them, so I made an impossible geography and named it with the only Z word I could think of quickly, so that it would come after all the other counties (Wright is the last one in Iowa). I was surprised and gratified to learn that the land of Zebulon, in the Bible, is a land of Godless gloom, where the people of Israel have gone wrong. It fit in nicely, but I hadn't thought of it. The same reader felt sure that I was likening Ginny to a Jenny, or a female mule, because it was her burden to carry the weight of the family history, and that in Rose's name, I was referring to Blake's line, "Oh, Rose, thou art sick!" I wish I had been! In my novel *Moo*, I found out only after publication that "Gift," the name of my villain, means "poison" in German. Gosh, I think, whenever I read one of these logical analyses that adds something to my understanding of the novel, I certainly am smart!

What I really think is only partially a fudge of the theoretical problem that these interpretations raise, and that is that since the novel exists in a cultural soup, it has references even to parts of the cultural soup that I am not conscious of but am possibly aware of on some level. The image of the sick rose was common in medieval literature, for example, and I did know what a Jenny was. An author cannot use either the language or a wide array of images apart from their other appearances in the culture, and in many cases, as in this one, the work demonstrates a productive relationship to the culture that is partly independent of the conscious intentions of its author. The reader's analysis is neither right or wrong—it notes a true connection, but doesn't understand its source. There are in fact at least three logical systems at work in any piece of literature—there is the one that the author knowingly constructs, the one that the book makes in relationship to the rest of the culture, and the one that the reader constructs. These probably more or less overlap, but they are not identical. Recognition of these three separate incarnations of my work has helped me accept its independence, made me a bit more cautious as a reader, and also made me more accepting as a writer. I do think, though, that scholars need to be aware of all three incarnations in order to really understand a given work.

The second category is that of papers that seem to understand everything I tried to do, but don't go beyond that. These papers appeal to my pedagogical instincts—they please me because they make me feel that I was clear and cogent in my presentation. I also feel that the reader passed the test and understood what I put in there. If he or she liked it, so much the better. They gratify my ego, but they leave me feeling a little bad, as if the novel was only a simple communication, like a chart with names down one side and characteristics down the other, and all a good reader has to do is draw lines correctly from elements in one line to elements in the other. I suppose what I am saying is that these papers don't recognize and then reveal the darkened parts of the authorial machine outside consciousness and intention, and so there is nothing surprising in them, and therefore, nothing surprising in me.

The third group of papers takes more risks, and is, in my opinion, the sort of criticism I really like to read, both of me and of others. This group of papers is drawn to, and tries to come to terms with, the paradoxical other in the text. All my greatest reading experiences have had one thing in common, and that is that at some point I am made aware of how irreducibly different from me an author speaking through a given work truly is, and how completely alluring and marvelous it is to accept that difference. I am reading along, sensing the common humanity of author, narrator, characters, and me, and suddenly there is something entirely meet and fitting in the text that I would never have thought of, were I the author, and yet I understand and appreciate it. Dickens does this for me on almost every page, especially in my favorite of his, *Our Mutual Friend*. His style displays a way of organizing the world that is utterly alien from mine, yet perennially fascinating. I want to read and write criticism that explores how he came up with that style—that is the crux of Dickens for me.

I will say that in this group of papers, I have found a few where the writer of the paper seems resentful and antagonistic toward the otherness of the author—complaints of what the author should have been doing, how the novel might have been more to the taste of the critic, descriptions of mistakes and prescriptions of how to avoid them in the future, or even theories of how authors in general are severely wanting. But apart from these, I think that papers that openly acknowledge the literary paradox of otherness-simultaneous-with-kinship-or-affinity are getting at the heart of what I consider to be my experience as a reader who writes who reads who writes, the heart of why I started writing and keep writing, the literary mystery.

In closing, I would like to emphasize the tentative nature of the observations I've made here. The typical structure of scholarly and critical discourse is based on the presumption that the author's experience of the process and the text must be divined from often fragmentary evidence. The freedom the death of the author gives his or her readers, I think, amply compensates for its inconvenience. At the same time, though, I am reminded of Freud's question, "What do women want?" Why, I have always thought, didn't he ask? One reason, perhaps, was that the women he might have asked could not have answered him in a language that he understood. In some ways, the language he used about women precluded an answer that he would have credited. Authors, too, have not developed a language for talking about what is going on inside them. For example, I have often felt that I could sense the physical effort of composing a novel, and that what it felt like was movement from one side of the brain to the other, back and forth, a form of physical exertion not unlike any other pleasurable but tiring exercise, though more subtle. Perhaps this is an actual perception of a physiological process, perhaps it is only an image; perhaps, with the brain, one gives rise to the other, or is the other. I haven't really discussed this with other authors because when we talk, it doesn't come up, or it sounds stupid to say it. I certainly have not discussed it with scholars, because no one has ever seemed interested. Additionally, the confessional mode is, of course, rhetorically, the trickiest of all modes, self-reflection the trickiest of all forms of observation. Nevertheless, I thank you for listening to these attempts I have been making to narrate the creation of *A Thousand Acres*, and I thank you for inviting me to think about it.

## Appendix

The second scariest thing I learned in graduate school was that William Butler Yeats continually rewrote his poems all the way until his death.[2] I always thought this sounded like a doubling and tripling of labor—how would you produce anything new if you had to keep updating the old, and how would you ever know when to stop? It was a Borgesian nightmare. But the scariest thing I learned in graduate school was that Geoffrey Chaucer disavowed almost all of his works on his deathbed, even, and maybe principally, *The Canterbury Tales*, because they were too secular. However awful it would be to have your life's work turn into a cascade of revision tasks, it would be far worse to regret it entirely, an act of retrospective despair and a rejection of the reader. I didn't want Chaucer to have disavowed his works. It shook my faith in them.

I expect writers whom I love to agree with me about the lovable qualities of their writings. They may evince a becoming modesty, but deep in their hearts, I want them to find the same truths and beauties I find there. I may love this character a little less whom they love a little more. I may see greater depths of style in this book while they see it in another, but what can literature be but a form of communication so extended and elaborate that after the author and I have contemplated the subject at sufficient length through his work, we must surely be in agreement about it? Isn't my special love of that particular book evidence of the congruence of my mind and the author's?

And yet, in spite of my old fear and my perennial wishes on this subject, I find myself having to disavow my most famous and admired novel, *A Thousand Acres*. All this spring, at lectures and on my book tour, I have had questions about *A Thousand Acres* that I have had a hard time answering, and, worse, I have had reader after reader thrust the novel at me with the remark that this is their favorite novel of mine, one of their favorite novels of all, and I have had to say that my interpretation of *King Lear*, the very source of the novel, has changed in significant ways, and that *A Thousand Acres* is not a novel I could write today in the same way I wrote it ten years ago. I suppose it should not come as a surprise to me that I have changed over the years—better that I have, for me as a woman and a citizen—but it does come as a shock. I was so sure of my interpretation, and I wrote with such conviction!

Two years ago, I was invited to give a talk on my novel at the International Shakespeare Congress, and then sit in on a seminar on twentieth-century women's rewritings of Shakespeare plays. At the very end of the seminar session, an older English scholar whose name I do not know said, "I don't think you can understand *King Lear* until you have seen your parents go into decline. Shakespeare's father was in decline for a long time, possibly with Alzheimer's or something like it." At that very moment, I felt my interpretation, which had just been accorded all kinds of attention and respect, shift. Whereas I had interpreted *King Lear* as a brief for the patriarchy, with the author identifying with Lear himself, and allowing him all sorts of leeway as a father in comparison to the daughters, who were narrowly defined as either brutes when they didn't give him his way, or angels if they sacrificed themselves for him, with no intermediate choices, I now felt that perhaps in looking at his father's troubles and his responsibilities as a son, Shakespeare was identifying with the daughters, and doing what we often do when we are required to ameliorate pain that can't be ameliorated—that is, to propose a solution that isn't humanly possible. Goneril and Regan, who seem in the beginning of the play to be rather normal women, are found to be inhumanly vicious, and Cordelia's self-sacrifice is the only daughterly response that is moral, that is, the only one that expresses sufficient love for the father. My interpretation shifted from a political one to a psychological one that I felt was truer and more subtle, in the process answering the question of why Cordelia is an impossible character to play sympathetically—she is a projection of ideal virtue that even the author didn't understand. Well, I kept this new interpretation to myself, though I quite liked it.

And then, this spring, my interpretation shifted again, from psychological to philosophical. This time, I wasn't thinking of the characters at all, but of the definition of love that Lear proposes in the first act—a quid pro quo exchange of goods for love, based on a sense of obligation on both sides that quickly transforms into resentment when the love proves insufficient to satisfy Lear's unsatisfiable neediness and the goods prove insufficient to satisfy everyone else. In the airless, animal, physical world of the play, this definition of love cannot be escaped, and must result in death. The tragedy results from a failure of imagination or spiritual vision—no one in the play, even Cordelia, ever knows what love is or where it comes from, and so the final remarks of the surviving characters are peculiarly meaningless.

How would I write *A Thousand Acres* now? The fact is, I probably wouldn't. The inevitability of the characters' downfall, the almost mechanical working out of their fates, doesn't appeal to me anymore. I just don't believe it. I am more drawn to *The Winter's Tale*, and, in fact, I would love to see a rep company do *The Winter's Tale* and *King Lear* together, same actors, same sets, same costumes, because I think Shakespeare wrote *The Winter's Tale* to answer *King Lear* with hope. The crucial difference between Leontes and Lear is that Leontes lives to regret and rethink his early selfish definition of love (of course he has the help in this of the delicious nag Paulina, who says, "It is required/ You do awake your faith. . . .") and to accept the miracle of Hermione's revival. The play redefines love as a miracle and a gift, which, once accepted, allows all things, not only reappearances and resurrections, but even total forgiveness.

But whatever I think of *A Thousand Acres*, and however I go on with my own work, the book has legs, as they say, and it is ever more with me.

Perhaps political, psychological, and philosophical interpretations of the play are not mutually exclusive, but mutually enlightening. That would let me off the hook, wouldn't it? But I don't really believe it, and don't have the Yeatsian energy to bring the novel in line with my current thinking. Like Shakespeare, I only have the energy to go on to new things and to hope that some future reader might see the evolution in what seems to me a revolution, the *même chose* in the *change*. I am not sorry I am no longer attracted to the dire mechanism of tragedy, but I see that one's life and one's literature perhaps inevitably must part. To those readers who adore *A Thousand Acres*, I have to say, it is more your book now than mine; I have run out of things to say on the subject, and, more importantly, I have run out of the desire to say them. I have made way in my mind for something else that may not have the same legs or the same impact. The paradox of literature is that everything must be written with total commitment, or the work reads falsely and insincerely, and yet all total commitment is to partial knowledge. As writers age and learn, they can't help rethinking and perhaps regretting earlier commitments. Perhaps readers forgive them more readily than they forgive themselves for taking on the mantle of "authority." At any rate, I know a little better why Chaucer disavowed his writings. The wholesale nature of his choice still scares me, but now it seems courageous rather than frightening, the last literary act of a mind that never stopped working over the largest questions life has to offer.

### Notes

1. This essay was originally delivered as a talk at the International Shakespeare Association World Congress held in Los Angeles in April 1996.
2. The appendix first appeared in the *Washington Post Book World*, June 21, 1998, 1.

# 10

---

# "Out of Shakespeare"?:
# Cordelia in *Cat's Eye*

## Suzanne Raitt

It is not until some way in to Margaret Atwood's 1988 novel, *Cat's Eye,* that we are explicitly told the derivation of Cordelia's name:

> Cordelia's two older sisters are Perdita and Miranda, but nobody calls them that. They're called Perdie and Mirrie. . . . Cordelia ought to be Cordie, but she's not. She insists, always, on being called by her full name: Cordelia. All three of these names are peculiar; none of the girls at school have names like that. Cordelia says they're out of Shakespeare. She seems proud of this, as though it's something we should all recognize. "It was Mummie's idea," she says.[1]

Shakespeare's play, for the little girl Elaine who is describing this scene, is some strange archaism, his characters' names trivialized by abbreviation into the comical "Perdie," "Mirrie," and "Cordie." *King Lear* is presented as an anachronism, a frame of reference that has outlived both its significance and its relevance.

*Cat's Eye* is constructed as a series of flashbacks on the part of the narrator, Elaine, who is visiting her childhood city of Toronto to attend the opening of a retrospective of her paintings, themselves the subject of considerable attention in the text and mostly figuring scenes from the childhood she is remembering throughout the book. Elaine is obsessed with the possibility that she may see Cordelia, her childhood enemy, whom she last saw in a psychiatric hospital after Cordelia's suicide attempt. Cordelia haunts Elaine throughout the text—nothing more can be said about her than that she *might* be there: "she could be within a mile of me, she could be right on the next block" (*CE,* 8). Repeatedly Elaine thinks she sees Cordelia, only to realize that she is mistaken.

> On the other side of the glass, Cordelia drifts past; then melts and reassembles, changing into someone else. Another mistaken identity.
>     Why did they name her that? . . . The third sister, the only honest one. The stubborn one, the rejected one, the one who was not heard. If she'd been called Jane, would things have been different? (*CE,* 263)

Among the "mistaken identities" of the book—the passersby Elaine hopes and fears are Cordelia (*CE,* 419), the woman with Cordelia's eyes on the sidewalk in Toronto (*CE,* 152–53)—is the naming of Cordelia after Shakespeare's heroine. Yet even mistakes are misrecognized here, retaining their own form of rightness: "Is it wrong to be right?" (*CE,* 124) wonders Elaine after being teased for getting too many correct answers in Sunday school. We—and Elaine—are never sure that Cordelia has not been there: she could be dead, or she could be "right on the next block."

Insofar as it revolves around Elaine's obsession with Cordelia, then, *Cat's Eye* is centrally defined by the absent presence of *King Lear.* But its invocation is far from straightforward: *Cat's Eye* is in no sense a "revision" of Shakespeare's play. When she wrote *Cat's Eye,* Margaret Atwood had already produced one book, the poetic sequence *The Journals of Susanna Moodie* (1970), that was explicitly a revisiting of an earlier work, pioneer Moodie's autobiography *Roughing It In the Bush* (1852). The context for *Cat's Eye* was rather different, however. In the intervening 18 years, Canadian literature, and especially the novel, had increased both in volume and in confidence: Atwood herself identified the late 1960s as pivotal years, and this view is echoed by Linda Hutcheon and W. H. New.[2] Atwood's project in *Cat's Eye* was not primarily to develop the specificity of a Canadian literary tradition, as she had sought to do in *The Journals of Susanna Moodie:* that labor was almost over. *Cat's Eye,* unlike other recent revisions of *King Lear* such as Elaine Feinstein and the Women's Theatre Group's 1987 play *Lear's Daughters,* or Jane Smiley's 1991 novel *A Thousand Acres,* neither follows the narrative framework of the original play nor gives voice to silenced characters, as a feminist intervention into patriarchal cultures and scripts. Rather, *Cat's Eye* develops a typically postmodern form of intertextuality in which an engagement with Shakespearean commonplaces—Cordelia's famous "nothing"—

becomes the basis for an alternative epistemology, one built on uncertainty, relativity, and disjunction. The relationship between *King Lear* and *Cat's Eye* cannot be reliably mapped as far as the correspondences between characters go. Sometimes Atwood's Cordelia seems to come directly "out of Shakespeare"; sometimes she seems to stand for Canada; sometimes she seems to be a figure for England; and Elaine at various times recalls Lear and again Cordelia herself.[3] Intertextual relations are contingent and shifting, like postcolonial cartographies. "Postmodern intertextuality" here becomes a way of figuring the provisionalities of a postcolonial, "postfeminist" world.

The relation between the two texts is anchored in *Cat's Eye*'s repeated recall of the opening exchange between Lear and Cordelia in the first scene of Shakespeare's play. Lear's demand for a form of ritual speech echoes throughout many of the encounters in *Cat's Eye* between fathers and daughters, and between Elaine and Cordelia. Cordelia at the dinner table cannot respond adequately to her father's banter:

> Cordelia can never come up with it, because she's too frightened of him. She's frightened of not pleasing him. And yet he is not pleased. . . . nothing she can do or say will ever be enough, because she is somehow the wrong person. (*CE,* 249)

Cordelia's "nothing" is the response of a stammering child who knows she's making a mistake: "how can she be so abject?" (*CE,* 249) wonders Elaine, enraged. But she too cannot speak to order. Cordelia challenges her:

> *What do you have to say for yourself?* Cordelia used to ask. *Nothing,* I would say. It was a word I came to connect with myself, as if I was *nothing,* as if there was nothing there at all. (*CE,* 41)

Through its meditations on Elaine's brother's work on quantum physics, the novel worries away at the idea of "nothingness," the incommensurability of the matter that goes to make up human flesh and the human world. As contours and objects dissolve, so does the literary past. Allusion here is uncomfortable: *Lear* cedes its authority just as Lear does. But there is also a family resemblance between Shakespeare's play and *Cat's Eye:* both invoke troubled national histories shaped by invasion and resistance. In Atwood's hands "Cordelia"—her name, her textual origin, scraps and fragments of her speeches from *Lear*—becomes a way of figuring the complex and ambiguous dynamics of both patriarchal and colonial relations. Shakespeare's Cordelia is asked to speak the script her fathers (and her sisters) have written for her—she must learn their language: "what can you say to draw/A third more opulent than your sisters. Speak."[4] By resituating this demand in the context of late twentieth-century Canada, Atwood implicitly asks us to reread *King Lear* in a colonial frame. Shakespeare has long been seen as the guarantor of a certain kind of Englishness, and even as the nature of that Englishness and of Shakespeare's stake in it is contested by critics such as Alan Sinfield and Jonathan Dollimore, "Shakespeare" and "England" continue to be seen as tangled terms.[5] *King Lear* itself retells an episode in English history. Recontextualizing Shakespeare in Canada is also a way of thinking about Canada's relation to Englishness and its own colonial past. Lear in *Cat's Eye* thus becomes an image of colonial, as well as patriarchal, power. Like Cordelia, native Canada has had to learn another language, even two other languages. As Coral Ann Howells puts it, women's stories "seem the natural expression of the insecurity and ambitions of their society and in many ways they provide models for stories of Canadian national identity."[6] Cordelia's "nothing," as Atwood deploys it in *Cat's Eye,* embraces at once women's muteness, colonial subordination and negation (as Atwood says, "Canada for us was not-America"), the indeterminacy of matter, and the haunting silences of absence and death.[7]

Shakespeare is explicitly associated with the character of Cordelia throughout the novel. Cordelia performs in a number of Shakespeare plays. She prepares the props for a visiting company's production of *Macbeth;* later, after she leaves high school, she has nonspeaking parts in *Measure for Measure, Richard III,* and *The Tempest.* But the plays themselves are not a focus of critical attention in the novel. Cordelia's involvement with stagings of Shakespeare is significant for the way it throws her ineptitude into relief. She allows the towel-wrapped cabbage that is to represent Macbeth's severed head to rot, so that it bounces off the stage into the audience; when Elaine goes to watch her perform in *The Tempest,* she cannot even distinguish Cordelia among all the other attendants of Prospero. There is no place for Cordelia in Shakespeare: the dramas are indifferent to her, erasing her individuality and rendering her, at times, ridiculous.

It is in this sense of superfluity that the drama of Canada's—and Cordelia's—relations to their own cultural histories is played out. As Colin Nicholson has pointed out, Canada's "ability to tell its distinctive varieties of story has always had to contend with powerful and in some mediums overwhelming discursive economies originating elsewhere."[8] Cordelia too is literally overwhelmed by Shakespeare: she can find no home in these texts from across the ocean that in some crucial sense take precedence over more familiar scripts. As Atwood remarked of her own education (roughly contemporary with Cordelia's), Canadian schoolchildren got the impression that "all literature was written by dead Englishmen."[9] In refusing to engage in detail with Shakespeare's plays, Atwood is partly repudiating the ties of Canada's colonial past. Not only Cordelia but the plays themselves are mocked as muted texts that no longer have anything of importance to say.

But the presence of Shakespeare in the text at all, and especially in the name of the character with whom Elaine is obsessed, signifies vividly the ambivalent but crucial residues of colonial cultural presence—its "disjunctive" authority, to use Homi Bhabha's term.[10] Shakespeare may be opaque, recalcitrant, unyielding, like a particularly sullen Cordelia, but he also, like Elaine's Cordelia, refuses to be forgotten. Bizarre as it may seem, the England of *King Lear* has certain parallels with late-twentieth-century Canada. Modern Canada is the product of a centuries-long struggle between England and France.[11] *King Lear* too describes a conflict between the English and the French: when Cordelia returns to save Lear and rescue her country from the depredations of her two sisters, she comes back as Queen of France, supported by the French army. In Holinshed's chronicles, one of the sources for the play, Cordelia is explicitly the figurehead for a French invasion:

> Aganippus caused a mightie armie to be put in a readinesse, and likewise a great nauie of ships to be rigged, to passe ouer into Britaine with Leir his father in law, to see him againe restored to his kingdome. It was accorded, that Cordeilla should also go with him to take possession of the land, the which he promised to leaue vnto hir, as the rightfull inheritour after his decesse, notwithstanding any former grant made to hir sisters or to their husbands in anie maner of wise.[12]

Kenneth Muir notes that Shakespeare takes pains to establish Cordelia's disinterestedness in his own version of the play, but, nonetheless, the specter of French invasion flickers throughout the text and establishes Shakespearean England as an island with a history of French settlement—if not in Leir's time (around 300 AD), then certainly later, after the Norman invasion of 1066.[13] Haunting *Cat's Eye* is the ghost of a colonial power that itself has a bicultural history, albeit in the long distant past. This is perhaps the source of the uneasiness around England and Shakespeare as sources of cultural authority: England, like Lear, is troubled, its identity heterogeneous and contingent. *Cat's Eye* imagines a Canada that still contends with its own secondariness, its failed mimicry of Britain: Elaine is taught that "because we're Britons, we will never be slaves. But we aren't real Britons, because we are also Canadians. This isn't quite as good" (*CE,* 80). But Britain is unreliable too, invoked, as Derrida would have it, as a contingent and unknowable space: "if [the supplement] represents and makes an image, it is by the anterior default of a presence."[14] In emphasizing Canada's "supplementarity," *Cat's Eye* also exposes the failure of colonial power. Shakespeare's *Lear,* with its drama of kingly authority undone by narcissism and paranoia, shows an England unraveling in a way that Bhabha suggests is intrinsic to the practice of colonialism: "the *other* side of narcissistic authority may be the paranoia of power."[15] In invoking Lear's England, *Cat's Eye* calls on the specter of England's own self-undoing and thereby invokes the narcissistic absence of colonial power itself.

*Lear* is an ideal play through which to question the priority and vigor of a colonizing culture. As the play opens, Lear is apparently in the process of giving up his claim to England, ceding his kingdom to his daughters in anticipation of his approaching death. But of course in the very act of handing over his authority he continues to exercise it, demanding from his daughters a kind of rhetorical performance. They must repeat the words he already knows he wants to hear, mouthing the conventional formulae of Elizabethan love-poetry: "a love that makes breath poor and speech unable," in Goneril's familiar words (1.1.60). Regan openly admits that she simply echoes her sister: "I find she names my very deed of love" (1.1.71). Their repetitions are strategic, of course: they play their father's game in order to overthrow him in the end. Insofar as they are not what they seem, they practice a form of the kind of subversive mimicry that Bhabha has described in *The Location of Culture:* the sisters' speeches "[articulate] those disturbances of cultural, racial and historical difference that menace the narcissistic demand of colonial authority."[16] Many of Bhabha's models for the exercise of authority are in fact far from specific to colonial discourses and their successors; within a patriarchal context, women too can play the game of "the *ambivalence* of mimicry," as Bhabha calls it.[17] In playing up to their father's fantasies, Goneril and Regan are mimicking the behavior of obedient daughters, as well as of obedient subjects.

Cordelia, on the other hand, is best known for being a woman of few words. Lear's demand is not so much for love as for its rhetoric: "what can you say to draw/A third more opulent than your sisters? Speak" (1.1.85–86). It is Cordelia's linguistic performance that is at stake, her ability to imitate. Her answer resonates ambiguously throughout both the play, and Atwood's novel: "nothing, my lord" (1.1.87; *CE,* 9). Just as Lear asserts his authority even as he stages its transfer, so Cordelia, as she refuses to give her father what he wants—by saying "nothing"—paradoxically acknowledges her respectful and loving subordination to him—"my lord." In naming him thus, she draws attention to the double fealty she owes him, both as her father and as her king. Her challenge is framed by her marking Lear's rightful place as "lord" of his kingdom and his family. But at the same time Cordelia is mutinous; by the end of the play she will be leading an army against the country to which she was originally subject, in the name of another "England" than the one she sees before her. Kent's intervention shortly after the exchange between Cordelia and Lear demonstrates even more clearly the overdetermined and contradictory nature of Cordelia's words:

> Royal Lear,
> Whom I have ever honour'd as my King,
> Lov'd as my father, as my master follow'd,
> As my great patron thought on in my prayers (1.1.139–42)

King, father, master, patron: the political, the familial, the social, and the economic are all part of the same order of subjection within which both Kent and Cordelia struggle to speak. Kent's words carry the menace of contingency: Lear is not Kent's father, but Kent has loved him as if he were. Is kingship similarly a kind of mimicry, an illusion in the eye—or the heart—of the beholder? In refusing the cheap rhetoric, the "sly civility" of her elder sisters, Cordelia perhaps unwittingly opens up a fissure in the discourse of political subjection itself.[18] She will not indulge in the kind of "ambivalent" mimicry that they practice, but neither will she reflect back Lear's discourse simply as it is. In Lacanian terms, her speech is the field of the Other in which Lear's lack opens up. Lear allows what Julia Kristeva would call the "void" of primary narcissism to overwhelm him (the Anglo-Saxon "Leir" is derived from the German "leer," or "empty"), but when he makes a quasi-incestuous demand on his daughters, he is also asking something excessive from them as political subjects.[19] Goneril and Regan realize that they can use his narcissism and his paranoia to political ends; Cordelia too recognizes that more is being asked of both a family and a nation than either should have to supply, but her response is to try and show Lear that his confusion will cause the whole social fabric to unravel.

The key word in Cordelia's response is "bond": "I love your Majesty/ According to my bond; no more nor less" (1.1.92–93). A quick reading of this sentence might reasonably conclude that "bond" here refers to the ties of affection and loyalty that usually bind daughters to their fathers. But "bond" has a range of other meanings too, especially in the early seventeenth century. Its basic meaning, a binding agreement or contract, gives rise to a number of more specific usages that are still current today, including a promissory note (as in "stocks and bonds") or a financial surety (as in "bail bonds"). In the fourteenth, fifteenth, and sixteenth centuries the word also referred to a vassal, or serf: one in bondage to a superior. When Cordelia uses the word "bond," then, she calls up a range of connections and obligations. In asserting the primacy of the "bond," she implies that in misrecognizing his relationship with his daughters and subjects—in abusing their "bonds" with him—Lear is undermining the foundations of the society of which he is the keystone. If one bond can be broken, why not all? In pitting the language of "bondage" against the language of false sentiment, Cordelia asserts her role as a political subject simultaneously with her role as a daughter. It is in this discursive context that *Cat's Eye*'s play on the word "nothing" needs to be read: not simply as a feminist revisiting of Shakespeare's play—although it is that too—but as part of a political discourse that explores the limit of the subject's bond and the relation between "bond" and "bondage": the ambivalent interface of power itself.

But if it is possible to see how the rhetoric of the "bond" can be political, it is much more complex to imagine the political ramifications of negation, of Cordelia's "nothing." Centuries later, in *Three Guineas,* with its dream of an "Outsiders' Society," Virginia Woolf would suggest a form of feminist political agency that depended on a similar form of indifference and refusal to respond to the demands and the ideas of men.[20] Is Cordelia's refusal to play her father's game just such an assertion of her rights as a woman? As Janet Adelman points out, Cordelia does not want even to pretend that she is in emotional or even sexual thrall—"bondage"—to her father: "why have my sisters husbands, if they say/They love you all?" (1.1.99–100).[21] Regan specifically suggests that her love for her father displaces other pleasures:

> I profess
> Myself an enemy to all other joys
> Which the most precious square of sense possesses,
> And find I am alone felicitate
> In your dear highness' love. (1.1.72–76)

Of course, Lear swiftly moves in to legislate for Cordelia's desire, offering her to the Duke of Burgundy and the King of France in turn. But for a brief moment, Cordelia is able to assert her sexual independence from her father, her right to name her love for herself.

Her response also serves, however, to highlight the impossibility of a faithful language of love, either filial or sexual. Love has as troubled an ontology as the matter—the human body—on which it so often depends. At first Cordelia simply says "nothing"—a way, of course, of staying silent. When she does finally speak, it is only by analogy—"according to my bond." The audience is thus encouraged to read her "nothingness" in the context of previous asides: "What shall Cordelia speak? Love, and be silent" (1.1.62). Cordelia distinguishes between speech and action, between language and event: "what I well intend /I'll do't before I speak" (1.1.225–26). Her words imply that for her, to recite love's script is not the same as to feel or to live it. But perhaps those distinctions—between emotion and event, between substance and act—are not so easily made. Even in this early aside, affect and action are elided in the word "love." When Cordelia says "love, and be silent," does she use "love" as a verb or a noun? Does she mean that her only response can be to love in silence, or that the only word she can utter in response would be "love"?

If love can say nothing, what speaks in its place? The answer, of course, is "nothing." In the original ending of Jean Rhys's 1934 novel, *Voyage in the Dark,* the protagonist Anna's death is preceded by a vision of negation as she dreams of visiting the ruined plantation owned by her mother's family:

> now I see I see the moon looking down on stones where nobody is the trees and the moon looking down on a place where nobody is there was a cold moon looking down on a place where nobody is full of stones where nobody is[22]

Both Cordelia's "nothing" and Anna's "nobody is" intensify their own negative force by making it palpable. The repetition of "nobody is," which occurs only in the early version of *Voyage in the Dark* (rejected by Rhys's publishers as too depressing), pushes the reader to feel absence as an intolerable form of presence. Cordelia's "nothing" is similarly chilling because, as David Willbern notes, it graphically speaks the presence of absence, announcing her withdrawal from language and anticipating her later murder.[23] "Nothing" acts like a harbinger of death, anticipating Lear's as well as Cordelia's own. As Lear enters carrying Cordelia's corpse in the final act, he cries out "howl, howl, howl!" (5.3.258), and his "howl" echoes Cordelia's initial "love, and be silent"(1.1.62) in being at once a noun and a verb. This is the grammar of mortality, articulating the possibility that the animation—the "life"—of the verb may be reduced to the inert substantiality—the "thingliness"—of the noun.

Substance—"thingliness"—is centrally on *Cat's Eye*'s postmodern agenda. The nature of matter itself—"something"—is called into question in the novel through the figure of Stephen, Elaine's physicist brother. He explains to Elaine that time is a dimension, that "if you knew enough and could move faster than light you could travel backwards in time and exist in two places at once"(*CE*, 3). Matter is not co-terminous with itself. When Elaine asks what an atom looks like, Stephen responds:

> "A lot of empty space," Stephen says. "It's hardly there at all. It's just a few specks held in place by forces. At the subatomic level, you can't even say that matter exists. You can only say that it has a tendency to exist." (*CE*, 242)

Something may in fact be nothing; existence itself could be merely a tendency. Cordelia herself may, in fact, be nothing: "Stephen considers Cordelia. 'Cordelia has a tendency to exist,' is what he says"(*CE*, 242). Cordelia figures the possibility of a cosmic confusion of substance and nothingness, of an absence that is experienced as a ghostly form of presence. *Cat's Eye* thus reworks Shakespeare's "nothing" in ways that both recall and extend its meaning.

Atwood commented in an interview that "*Cat's Eye* is partly about being haunted."[24] Elaine is haunted by Cordelia, and Cordelia herself is haunted by a literary past to which she has at best a random and anecdotal relation: "'it was Mummie's idea'" (*CE*, 73), she tells Elaine. Cordelia's name alienates her from herself in ways of which she is not even aware, but which she cannot help but express. When she calls Elaine from the mental hospital, "her voice on the phone did not sound like her" (*CE*, 356). Like the night sky in Stephen's lecture, Cordelia is composed of "fragments of the past" (*CE*, 332): she is shadowed by her own name, by fragments of a script that she cannot utter because it is already too late. Elaine knows this: "everything is post these days, as if we're all just a footnote to something earlier that was real enough to have a name of its own" (*CE*, 86). Cordelia is a cultural postscript, lonelier than ever because she has strayed into a text that has no real place for her. Indeed she is doubly lost: in the labyrinth of colonial Canada and in the world of Shakespearean drama that gave her her name. Here postmodern intertexuality is only an experience of "post-ness": a disappointing rather than an enabling condition.

Cordelia's double exile figures both the secondariness of women's position and of colonial identity. Elaine's feeling of being a "footnote" (*CE*, 86) is partly derived from her education, which, as it is described in *Cat's Eye*, is concerned almost exclusively with Britain and its empire.

> Over the door to the cloakroom, so that you feel you're being watched from behind, there's a large photograph of the King and Queen . . . Things are

more British than they were last year. We learn to draw the Union Jack, using a ruler and memorizing the various crosses, for St. George of England, St. Patrick of Ireland, St. Andrew of Scotland, St. David of Wales. Our own flag is red and has a Union Jack in one corner, although there's no saint for Canada. We learn to name all the pink parts of the map. (*CE,* 79)

The Canada to which Elaine and Cordelia are introduced, then, is one that is dependent for its identity on Britain. It does not even have a saint of its own, and its flag is marked with the sign of ownership: a Union Jack in the corner. Traces of conflict are reflected in the anecdotes the girls are told about indigenous peoples:

> The Indians in Canada did not have the wheel or telephones, and ate the hearts of their enemies in the heathenish belief that it would give them courage. The British Empire changed all that. It brought in electric lights. (*CE,* 79)

The tone is ironic, of course, but the sense of a kind of indeterminacy in the conceptualization of Canada itself persists into the description of Elaine's own identity that I quoted earlier: "Because we're Britons, we will never be slaves. But we aren't real Britons, because we are also Canadians" (*CE,* 80).

This characterization of Canada as a place of negation appears in the work of numerous critics and writers of Canadian literature. Diana Brydon, writing in 1981, comments that Canadians were still "[wondering] if they had a national identity," and Gayle Greene, more recently, notes that constructions of a "Canadian tradition" are "to some extent a response to the *absence* of past or community."[25] Atwood, however, would appear to reject these sentiments. In the same volume in which she describes Canada as "not-America," she also ridicules as "nonsense" talk in the late 1960s about "the absence of a Canadian identity."[26] The question is, of course, how an identity based partially on negation might be built—an issue central to any exploration of the colonial and post-colonial predicament. In both *King Lear* and *Cat's Eye* such identities are built on conflict and division: Cordelia withdraws into saying "nothing" in the course of a confrontation with her father; the image Cordelia gives Elaine of herself ("Cordelia, I think. You made me believe I was nothing." *CE,* 199) grows out of their radically conflicted childhood relationship. To some extent Canada's history too repeats this pattern: if there is any truth in Coral Ann Howells's statement that "it has always been easier to define 'Canadian' negatively," this is because modern Canada is the product of numerous conflicts and wars over the control of different territories.[27] The new constitution, ratified by the government of Prime Minister Pierre Trudeau in the 1982 Canada Act, which established Canada as a fully sovereign state, was partly defined by Trudeau's vision of "one Canada with two official languages." Consensus around Canada's "oneness," however, was and is fragile. Quebec opposed the Canada Act, although the Quebec Court of Appeal ruled twice in 1982 that it possessed no right of veto over constitutional change.[28] Currently, battles over the question of "Canadianness" are largely fought out over language—whether to use English or French.[29] These divisions mean that Canada's national unity is partly symbolic—in spite (or even as a result) of its parliamentary endorsement. Elaine in *Cat's Eye* finds the notion of "one Canada" puzzling: "Wolfe's name sounds like something you'd call a dog, but he conquered the French. This is puzzling, because I've seen French people, there are lots of them up north, so he couldn't have conquered all of them"(*CE,* 80). As young Elaine, at school in the 1940s, muddles her way through Canadian history and the cultural texts of British dominance, the idea of "Canada" becomes more confusing than ever. The Union Jack and the British national anthem get oddly associated in Elaine's mind with the idea of her teacher's bloomers, which frighten her because "whatever is wrong with them [the bloomers] may be wrong with me also, because although Miss Lumley is not what anyone thinks of as a girl, she is also not a boy" (*CE,* 81). Canada, like Miss Lumley, is neither one thing nor the other. National and gender identities even converge in the playground chant the children sing: "*I see England, I see France,/ I can see your underpants*" (*CE,* 77). Elaine fears living in this kind of furtive transitional space, between English and French, masculine and feminine. Her fear of, and preoccupation with, Cordelia's absence is also a fear of her own indeterminacy, a sense that she, like Canada, must continually resist division and dissolution.

Both *King Lear* and *Cat's Eye* (and indeed many of Atwood's other texts) are haunted by the idea of division. As Janet Adelman has remarked, *King Lear* is "everywhere a play of division": it opens with "the division of the kingdom" (1.1.4); the "twoness" of Goneril and Regan is continually opposed to the singularity of Cordelia; and Cordelia, describing Lear's madness, refers to it as a "breach" in his nature (4.7.15).[30] The structures of the play mirror its plot, and Lear's psychic disintegration is imagined—at least by Cordelia—as another manifestation of this "fall into division," as Adelman puts it.[31] Separation is a key concern of Atwood's work as well: in an early interview Atwood spoke of her interest in ghost stories in which "the ghost that one sees is in fact a fragment of one's own self which has split off."[32] The protagonist of her classic novel *Surfacing* (1972) is obsessed with the fetus she has aborted: "a section of my own life, sliced off from me like a Siamese twin, my own flesh canceled."[33] Throughout the novel the protagonist imagines herself as a twin whose sibling has been lost, as if she can conceive of herself only as the product of some kind of primal division.[34]

In *Cat's Eye* the image of twinship continues to figure some kind of primary separation, an internal splitting. But it serves a number of other purposes as well. It is invoked both in the context of the theory of relativity and of the colonial relationship between Canada and England. In Shakespeare's comedies, separated twins—Sebastian and Viola in *Twelfth Night,* for example—are reunited as part of a vision of a reintegrated world. But in *King Lear* the doubleness of Goneril and Regan is annihilating: their interdependence insists both on a horrifying and fatal division and on the grotesquerie of the inability to separate. In *Cat's Eye* the image of twins is used to work through the violent intimacies of colonialism. Elaine imagines the relationship between Canada and Britain as a kind of twinning, or Bhabhaesque mimicry: when she has to send old clothes over to war-torn England, it gives her "a strange feeling to think of someone else, someone in England, walking around in my clothes. My clothes seem a part of me, even the ones I've outgrown" (*CE,* 81). Here England is the weaker twin, superseded by its more robust—and, during the war, safer—colony. Twinship is a metaphor for the uncomfortable entanglements of post-coloniality: like identical twins, like Elaine and the English girl who wears her clothes, Canada and Britain are, in Bhabha's formulation, "almost the same, *but not quite.*"[35]

Twins are part of the nightmare of an Einsteinian universe, too. As Stephen says, explaining relativity: "if you put one identical twin in a high-speed rocket for a week, he'd come back to find his brother ten years older than he is himself" (*CE,* 219). In part this is an image of the disjunctions of colonial time: Canada and England, the non-identical twins, age differently. The separated twins are also a way of thinking about Elaine's inner world. She, too, is "post," outliving her brother Stephen, her parents, and her childhood world. After Stephen dies, she thinks of how she will age, and he will not (*CE,* 392); and towards the end of the novel she begins to realize why she has been so haunted by the idea of Cordelia.

> Really it's Cordelia I expect, Cordelia I want to see. There are things I need to ask her. Not what happened, back then in the time I lost, because now I know that. I need to ask her why. . . .
> She will have her own version. I am not the centre of her story, because she herself is that. But I could give her something you can never have, except from

another person: what you look like from outside. A reflection. This is the part of herself I could give back to her.

We are like the twins in old fables, each of whom has been given half a key. (*CE*, 411)

Elaine's childhood conflicts with Cordelia are both expressed and transcended in this image of someone who attacked and yet "reflected" her. The division between them is the central theme of the book: Cordelia taunting Elaine, controlling her, leaving her to die in a frozen ditch. And yet at times they seem the same person: "I'm not afraid of seeing Cordelia. I'm afraid of being Cordelia" (*CE*, 227). The concluding pages of the book dramatize the ways in which Elaine's identity is dislocated by her identification with Cordelia. Imagining she sees Cordelia coming toward her down the ravine in which, so long ago, Cordelia left Elaine almost frozen to death, Elaine thinks:

> There is the same shame, the sick feeling in my body, the same knowledge of my own wrongness, awkwardness, weakness; the same wish to be loved; the same loneliness; the same fear. But these are not my own emotions any more. They are Cordelia's; as they always were.
>
> I am the older one now, I'm the stronger. If she stays here any longer she will freeze to death; she will be left behind, in the wrong time. It's almost too late.
>
> I reach out my arms to her, bend down, hands open to show I have no weapon. *It's all right*, I say to her. *You can go home now.* (*CE*, 419)

But it is Elaine, not Cordelia who, in the following chapter, is on a plane back to the house she shares with her husband in Vancouver. Even as she invokes and speaks to Cordelia, she is also invoking and speaking to part of herself, laying her memories to rest. In the final chapter, she recognizes the temporal paradox in which she must live: "this is what I miss, Cordelia: not something that's gone, but something that will never happen" (*CE*, 421). Here the time of "postness" is seen also to be a form of tragic anticipation, the endless waiting of mourning.

Postmodern intertextuality is realized here as a kind of disorientation. In a late-twentieth-century, postcolonial world, Atwood suggests, allusion no longer calls up any kind of meaningful cultural priority. Instead, it is a recognition of separation, the separation that Canada's independence from Britain entailed. With the exhilaration of autonomy comes also the flatness and disappointment of survival. In rereading *King Lear* as a text about the instabilities of England and the paranoid narcissism of both patriarchal and colonial relations, Atwood also recognizes the unsustainability of colonialism itself. *Cat's Eye* is not a revision of *King Lear* because in *Cat's Eye*'s version of the play there is little that it would make sense to revise. And yet Atwood's Canada is as haunted by its loss of Shakespeare as Elaine is by her loss of Cordelia. The alternative epistemology that Shakespeare's phrase generates in *Cat's Eye* is one that empties out meaning, that disorders all our maps. Cordelia's "nothing" means just that in a postmodern universe: that there might simply be nothing here.

### Notes

1. Margaret Atwood, *Cat's Eye* (1988; London: Virago, 1990), 72–3. All further references to this edition will appear in the text.
2. Margaret Atwood, *Second Words: Selected Critical Prose* (Toronto: Anansi, 1982), 384–85; Linda Hutcheon, *The Canadian Postmodern: A Study of Contemporary English-Canadian Fiction* (Toronto: Oxford University Press, 1988), 1; W. H. New, *A History of Canadian Literature* (London: Macmillan, 1989), 213.
3. As Gayle Greene comments, in this version of *King Lear* Elaine is the Lear-figure, waiting endlessly for a Cordelia who, this time, does not return. See Gayle Greene, *Changing the Story: Feminist Fiction and the Tradition* (Bloomington: University of Indiana Press, 1991), 209.
4. William Shakespeare, *King Lear,* ed. Alfred Harbage, in *William Shakespeare: The Complete Works* (New York: Viking, 1974), 1.1.85–86. Further references to this edition will appear in the text.
5. See, for example, the essays in Alan Sinfield and Jonathan Dollimore, eds., *Political Shakespeare: New Essays in Cultural Materialism* (Manchester: Manchester University Press, 1985).
6. Coral Ann Howells, *Private and Fictional Worlds: Canadian Women Novelists of the 1970s and 1980s* (London: Methuen, 1987), 26.
7. Atwood, *Second Words,* 84. W. H. New also notes that the name "Canada" has sometimes been taken to echo the Spanish phrase *acá nada,* or 'nothing here'. See New, *History of Canadian Literature,* 2.
8. Colin Nicholson, ed., Introduction to *Margaret Atwood: Writing and Subjectivity: New Critical Essays* (New York: St. Martin's Press, 1994), 1.
9. Atwood, *Second Words,* 378.
10. See Homi Bhabha, *The Location of Culture* (New York: Routledge, 1994), 177: "the authority of customary, traditional practices—culture's relation to the historic past— . . . [is] revalued as a form of anteriority—a before that has no a priori(ty)—whose causality is effective because it returns to displace the present, to make it disjunctive."
11. The French claim to Canada was made in 1534, and the French settled Nova Scotia in 1605. The English formed the Hudson Bay Company in 1670, gained Nova Scotia and Newfoundland from the French in 1713, and es-

tablished the Dominion of Canada in 1867. The Canada Act of 1982 gave Canada control over its own constitution and severed all legal ties between Britain and Canada. Quebec continues to fight for its independence.

12. Quoted in the Arden edition of *King Lear,* ed. Kenneth Muir (London: Methuen, 1972), 236.

13. In *King Lear,* Cordelia defends her mission: "No blown ambition doth our arms incite,/But love, dear love, and our ag'd father's right" (4.4.27–28).

14. Jacques Derrida, *Of Grammatology,* trans. Gayatri Chakravorty Spivak (1967; Baltimore, MD: Johns Hopkins University, 1976), 145.

15. Bhabha, *The Location of Culture,* 100.

16. Ibid., 88.

17. Ibid., 86.

18. See ibid., 93–101.

19. See Julia Kristeva, "Freud and Love: Treatment and Its Discontents" (1983) in *The Kristeva Reader,* ed. Toril Moi (Oxford: Basil Blackwell, 1986). Both the 1987 play *Lear's Daughters,* by Elaine Feinstein and the Women's Theatre Group, and Jane Smiley's 1991 novel *A Thousand Acres* represent Lear's relationship with his daughters as actively incestuous. Janet Adelman, in *Suffocating Mothers: Fantasies of Maternal Origin in Shakespeare's Plays, "Hamlet" to "The Tempest"* (New York: Routledge, 1992), argues that Lear's demands come out of an displaced infantile desire for complete possession of the mother (103–29).

20. Virginia Woolf, *Three Guineas* (1938; Oxford: Oxford University Press, 1992), 309–14.

21. See Adelman, *Suffocating Mothers,* 118: "As Goneril and Regan develop into monsters, they become exfoliations of what Lear's imagination has made of Cordelia: it is Cordelia's sexuality, her insistence on her own separateness, that first strike Lear as monstrous."

22. Jean Rhys, *Voyage in the Dark* (1934); reprinted in Bonnie Kime Scott, ed., *The Gender of Modernism* (Bloomington: University of Indiana Press, 1990), 388.

23. See David Willbern, "Shakespeare's Nothing," in Murray M. Schwartz and Coppélia Kahn, eds., *Representing Shakespeare: New Psychoanalytic Essays* (Baltimore, MD: Johns Hopkins University Press, 1980), 244–63. Freud, analyzing the fairy-tale structure in which a man must choose between three women, the third of whom (the correct choice) is often dumb (Grimms' stories "The Twelve Brothers" and "The Six Swans") or silent (Shakespeare's Cordelia), comments: "the third one of the sisters between whom the choice is made is a dead woman." Later, Freud is even more explicit: "Lear is not only an old man: he is a dying man. . . . But the doomed man is not willing to renounce the love of women; he insists on hearing how much he is loved. Let us now recall the moving final scene, one of the culminating points of tragedy in modern drama. Lear carries Cordelia's dead body on to the stage.

Cordelia is Death. If we reverse the situation it becomes intelligible and familiar to us. She is the Death-goddess who, like the Valkyrie in German mythology, carries away the dead hero from the battlefield. Eternal wisdom, clothed in the primaeval myth, bids the old man renounce love, choose death and make friends with the necessity of dying." See Sigmund Freud, "The Theme of the Three Caskets" (1913) in *The Standard Edition of the Complete Psychological Works,* trans. James Strachey, vol. 12 (London: Hogarth, 1958), 296, 301.

24. "Waltzing Again" (interview with Earl J. Ingersoll), in Earl J. Ingersoll, ed., *Margaret Atwood: Conversations* (Princeton, NJ: Ontario Review Press, 1990), 237.

25. Diana Brydon, "Landscape and Authenticity: The Development of National Literatures in Canada and Australia," *Dalhousie Review* 61 (Summer 1981): 286; Greene, *Changing the Story,* 24.

26. Atwood, *Second Words,* 84; 385.

27. Howells, *Private and Fictional Worlds,* 26.

28. Quebec's first challenge to the authority of Ottawa was its opposition to the Canada Act itself. Later in 1982, Quebec's controversial language law, Bill 101, which required English-speaking Canadians who moved to Quebec to send their children to French-speaking schools, was ruled unconstitutional because it violated the newly instituted Charter of Rights, which provided for minority language education in all Canadian provinces.

29. Quebec's language laws stipulate that English lettering on outdoor commercial signs must be half the size of the French. Many bilingual signs have been replaced with signs written in French only.

30. Adelman, *Suffocating Mothers,* 123.

31. *Ibid.*

32. Interview with Margaret Atwood in *Eleven Canadian Novelists,* ed. Graeme Gibson (Toronto: Anansi, 1975), 29.

33. Margaret Atwood, *Surfacing* (1972; New York: Warner, 1983), 56.

34. See, for example, ibid., 10, 129.

35. Bhabha, *The Location of Culture,* 86.

~~~~

# 11

# Tempest Plainsong:
# Retuning Caliban's Curse

## *Diana Brydon*

In her survey of work addressing the vexed issue of "Shakespeare and cultural difference," Ania Loomba, recognizing that *The Tempest* "has now become an allegory of colonial relations," concludes that for postcolonial readers "Caliban's curse became an evocative symbol of native articulation, but it was a symbol that suggested a specific model of that articulation . . . a 'derivative discourse.'"[1] Such a view may explain why so few First Nations (indigenous Canadian) writers have been interested in appropriating *The Tempest* for their agendas: they have no need for a derivative discourse to state their case. In Canada, rewriting *The Tempest* has been primarily a white Anglophone enterprise.[2] Yet Loomba's explanation seems inadequate for many postcolonial works that "recycle" Shakespeare's *Tempest* into different forms.[3] This essay examines one instance of how Caliban's curse has been reconfigured by white settler culture in Canada as a way of trying to hear indigenous voices without either appropriating or distorting their complexity.[4] In *Plainsong* (1993), Nancy Huston employs what Jonathan Dollimore might call "creative vandalism" to turn the potentially "derivative discourse" of Caliban's curse into haunting "plainsong." She counterpoints indigenous, Haitian creole and settler stories against the recurring theme of the ways in which the past continues to haunt the present.[5]

Like the revisionary texts that Susan Bennett examines in *Performing Nostalgia: Shifting Shakespeare and the Contemporary Past,* Huston's *Plainsong* could be seen as essentially nostalgic in that it stages what Susan Stewart describes as "a desire for desire"[6] through a text that explores the process of remembering the history of invasion that the settler colony has repressed, and the longing for the other that the settler has demonized. But *Plainsong* is also haunted by interior and exterior doublings and spiralings that complicate this pattern. *Plainsong*, the English book, is half of a whole made complete by its French twin, *Cantique des Plaines*.[7] These parallel texts, each written in its own language by this bilingual author, were published simultaneously, but as twinned texts, they "perform" their nostalgia differently for the differently situated cultural audiences they address.[8] In this essay, I examine the English text's participation in English-Canadian recyclings of *The Tempest*. (*Cantique des Plaines* performs a different dynamic for readers in Quebec that is not examined here.)

Both versions, however, appropriate Canadian First Nations' stories through the imaginary figure of Miranda, who is a mixed-race, native woman (part Blackfoot, Sarcee, and white), while appropriating and shifting Shakespeare to tell their own national stories.[9] Furthermore, both texts are highly self-conscious about their performances, as interventions into the recording of imperial history and as aesthetic constructions.

## What's in a Name?

Huston's novel *Plainsong* signals *The Tempest* as intertext most obviously through its focus on a character named Miranda and her involvement with two others, Paddon Sterling and his granddaughter Paula, both of whom are engaged in constructing "*P's Book*" (5), the final text of which becomes the novel *Plainsong*. But *Plainsong* also recalls *The Tempest* in more complex ways through its metaphoric arrangement around musical motifs, its thematic arrangement around "the dark backward and abyss of time,"[10] its invocation of the magic of Haitian *marasa* consciousness, and its organization around the lives of three central characters whose family dynamics reflect the larger political issues of colonialism. Paddon, Paula, and Miranda are each trying to reconcile their individual needs for creative expression with the impact of colonialism's legacy in the Americas on their lives.

In Gillian Beer's terms, the novel develops an "argument" with multiple intersecting pasts: with Canadian history and white settler guilt; with colonialism and missionary activity in the Americas (particularly in Haiti and Alberta); and with European literary, philosophical, and theoretical traditions, which it sees as implicated in European imperialism, racism and the violence that led to the Holocaust and the Cold War.[11] Paula, the novel's narrator, adopts an alternately accusatory and loving tone, literally addressing her dead grandfather in the second person throughout the narrative, insisting that he explain his actions (and more often inaction) and account for her heritage, which she finds a source of embarrassment if not outright shame. Her book, a work in progress, examines a hundred years of Alberta history through the lives of her ancestors, at the time of the Oka crisis in the summer of 1990, when Mohawk warriors confronted the Quebec provincial police and the federal army over ownership of the land in Quebec (191–92). This context inevitably invokes Caliban's claim, in *The Tempest,* that "This island's mine by Sycorax my mother" (1.2.331). But it is Paula who recalls this claim in her restating of the Mohawk stand: "this whole fucking area is our property including the city of Montreal itself and this time there's no two-timing treaty you can whisk out of your back pockets to prove differently. . . ."(192). Miranda, dead before Oka, prefers "laughter-spiked sarcasm" (162) to cursing, and Paula, after imagining the Mohawk position, immediately interrupts herself to exclaim: "Ah but somehow the dead are more alive to me than the living" (192).

In making this assertion, Paula reveals her desire to understand present conflicts by reexamining the past, recognizing that one can hope to live fully in the present only when the past has been laid to rest. At Oka, the Mohawk were fighting to prevent the conversion of their ancient burial grounds into a golf course, also recognizing the claims the past makes on the present. Paula's narrative restages the past to exorcize its demons just as Prospero does in *The Tempest.* And just as Prospero arranges a second, abortive coup that he can frustrate as a way of redeeming and canceling the first coup that had led to his exile, thus clearing the way for his return, so Paula reruns her grandfather's life backwards to redefine an apparently conformist life as resistant.

In analyzing *Plainsong*'s argument with the past, this essay attempts two related tasks: first, to understand the implications of Huston's rewriting of Miranda as, on one level, a manifestation of invader-settler society wish-fulfillment and guilt; and, second, to suggest how that reconstituting of Miranda might also be read more generously, as an attempt to imagine a fuller entitlement for native peoples by recognizing the legitimacy of their claims to ownership and the "wonder" of their survival. *Plainsong* can perhaps most usefully be read in terms of Mark Fortier's argument about reading *The Tempest.* In asserting that "romance and post-colonial readings of the play need not be based on mutual denial," he implies a way of reading *Plainsong* beyond seeing its romance elements as undermining its politics. Instead, Fortier suggests that "romance in Shakespeare works by a full and open engagement with conflict": conflict that is staged in part through the range of songs in the play.[12] In an earlier version of this essay I struggled to reconcile Howard Felperin's claiming of the play's allegory for a universalized idealist reading[13] and Ania Loomba's claiming of its allegory for a particularized postcolonial reading because both seemed necessary to understand *Plainsong.* Fortier's essay, however, makes it possible to read *Plainsong* within the "broad range of possible post-colonial readings of *The Tempest* as romance."[14] I argue that Huston is trying to appropriate this double-barreled allegorical power—of the utopian drive behind romance and the postcolonial critique—for herself as a woman writer living in exile, working within and across two languages, and struggling to reconcile biological and intellectual creativity, maternity and authorship. In her engagement with what Laura Donaldson has called the "Miranda Complex," Huston negotiates multiple territories divided by uneven power relations created by linguistic, political, and cultural differences over the past century.[15]

Caliban, often envisioned as native, is usually the center of postcolonial reinterpretations of *The Tempest.* Canadian rewritings, however, tend to diverge from this pattern, privileging Miranda as the dutiful or rebellious daughter of Empire, although few write out the role of Caliban entirely. In earlier articles, I have suggested that Canadian settler nationalism could not afford, either politically or psychologically, to acknowledge openly that Canadian territory was stolen from the First Nations.[16] Instead, earlier uses of *The Tempest* masked that open secret, one that could be not acknowledged, through indirections that displaced Caliban's presence from the figure of the colonized native onto animals or the land itself. Huston's conflation of the usual roles of Miranda and Caliban is an interesting but troubling innovation. Through her deployment of Miranda, she conflates the usually disarticulated categories of gender and race, colonizer and colonized, recurrently opposed in postcolonial *Tempest* discourse, into the single figure of Miranda. An indigenous Miranda disturbs the oppositions traditionally drawn between Caliban and Miranda, as if Caliban had been successful in impregnating Miranda but had created a subject beyond his full control, a new being who embodied something of both her parents (although in fact this Miranda derives her ancestry from the historically more common impregnation of a native woman by a white man). This conflation is troubling because the allegory as traditionally mobilized equates Miranda with white women's privilege and Caliban with native or black male victimization. Here the name Miranda clashes with the reality of a native woman's oppression.

Notably, Huston's character was not born Miranda; she has become Miranda through the process of colonial renaming. The nuns assigned to teach her at the residential school for native children could not pronounce her proper name, which was initially Shining Star, and then with the onset of a clumsy adolescence, Falling Star. (The humor offsets any New Age-inspired desire to sentimentalize her.) They christened her Miranda, which became the name by which she goes throughout the novel. Like Shakespeare's Miranda, she retains her capacity for wonder in the face of trials that grind the other characters down. And like Caliban, she rejects the education offered by those who have usurped her land and denied her original naming. Forced to copy the Ten Commandments as punishment for sharing her father's version of the creation story in the nuns' classroom, she learns to hate reading and writing, and eventually leaves school after the fourth grade. Effectively, then, Miranda remains outside the space of literacy, barely able to read or write. But like Caliban, she tells stories and is attuned to the music she hears around her; she also paints. This innovation makes her the novel's artist figure, redefining creative power and taking it from Prospero, who in his incarnation as Paddon is redefined as the failed educator who has lost the power to change lives and make things happen. Despite her creative spirit, Miranda suffers from a degenerative disease that eventually kills her. It is hard not to see this allegorically as the disease/dis-ease that is colonialism, but, unlike Caliban, Miranda refuses to curse or blame individuals for her misfortune, reserving her anger for the interrelated institutions of church and school.

What happens to Caliban's political force when he is transformed into a forgiving, feisty, and conveniently doomed part-native woman? What happens to Prospero's daughter when her name is taken by another? Because Paula's mother, Ruthie, gives birth to Paula out of wedlock without telling the father, Paddon, (Ruthie's father) effectively becomes Paula's father. But Paula is not the novel's Miranda. Instead, Paula's name places her firmly within a patrilineal line of descent: her first name recalls that of her father, the Québecois Paul, whom she has never met; her last name is the same as Paddon's—Sterling, implying the assumed moral worth and economic power of her English heritage and erasing the Irish and Québecois elements to which she is also heir (instant signals of postcolonial intertexts to any reader educated in the now substantial body of criticism associated with postcolonial *Tempest* studies). Both Paula and Miranda, then, are shown as heir to hybrid heritages, although their society seeks to label them in terms of airtight categories: self and other, settler and native, colonizer and colonized.

Huston shifts the gender dynamic of *The Tempest* from two men (Prospero and Caliban) competing over control of the sexuality of a white woman—Miranda—into a story about two women (one part native; one white but heir to francophone and anglophone histories) who love the same man. Paddon Sterling is the Prospero figure who enjoys the physical love of his mistress Miranda, the wifely love of Ruthie, and the intellectual love of his granddaughter Paula, who aspires to succeed as a writer where he has failed. Clearly, such a rewriting complicates any attempt to read the novel as postcolonial allegory. To the extent that this novel's Miranda is a Caliban figure, what does it mean to imagine her loving and forgiving Prospero while continuing to contest the legitimacy of his rule? And what does it mean for the Prospero figure's granddaughter to seek mastery over his role?

Huston also shifts *The Tempest*'s political dynamic of two men competing over ownership of an island into that of three people competing over the ownership of history and how it is to be recorded. But only two of these characters—Paula and Paddon—speak for themselves. Miranda is almost always spoken for, and Paddon's fragments of text are inherited, reinterpreted, and rearranged by his granddaughter into an invented narrative of her own. His text mentions Miranda, but it is Paula's text that represents her to the reader, putting words in her mouth. Paula's novel becomes the version we read: she positions herself as the inheritor of both Paddon's and Miranda's legacies.

If in rewriting Shakespeare we are also rewriting ourselves, as Peter Erickson suggests, then whose selves are being rewritten in Huston's text?[17] The politics of the debate concerning the appropriation of voice in English Canada made English critics uneasy about a white author creating a native character, although this unease is seldom expressed directly in reviews of Huston's novel.[18] The politics of sovereignty, national identity, and separatism in Quebec made Quebec critics downplay the politics of nonnative writing of a native character in favor of contesting the legitimacy of an anglophone writer (however bilingual) creating a character who is part-Québecoise, ostensibly locating the text in Quebec but publishing it from Paris.[19] Huston writes as someone raised in Alberta who has preferred to live in Paris for the last 20 years, but by locating the site of Paula's narration in Montreal and publishing the book in French, she threatened Quebec cultural sovereignty as much as she did English Canadian sensibilities, although in different ways. Anglophone Canadians did not like the ways in which they felt themselves interpellated in this text. The English-Canadian reviews were lukewarm at best and the novel was not nominated for the Governor General's Award in English, Canada's most prestigious literary prize. The francophone Canadians who selected the French version of this novel, *Cantique des Plaines,* published simultaneously, for the Governor General's

Award in French, thought the book a masterpiece. The book was a bestseller in France, where Huston indeed found herself mistaken for Québecoise. Now, several years after the literary scandal around the prize has subsided, Huston is well known and widely read in Quebec and more slowly gaining attention in English Canada. *Plainsong*'s engagement with *The Tempest* intertext thus raises important questions about literary power, exile, and cultural representation. Huston's Parisian credentials still carry weight in Quebec and, to a lesser extent, in anglophone Canada and the United States, testifying to the lingering power of a colonial mentality in both locations.

Paula, like Huston, has fled anglophone culture to write in a francophone environment, but despite her centrality as the novel's narrator she reveals very little of herself as a fictional character. The self she projects is almost entirely public, refracted through the major events of the time and the dramas she imagines the other characters enacting. Intellectually, she is fully aware of the various traps of imperialist nostalgia and exoticism that inscribe the colonial territory her text revisits; yet emotionally, her text seems to repeat the very patterns it critiques. She describes the Calgary Stampede[20] as an astute capitalist response to "the city's potential for instant nostalgia" (137), and shows Miranda laughing at white audiences' need for "ethnic and colourful" natives (163); yet her own story as it unfolds seems unable to avoid repeating these stereotypes, and not always in parodic form. When Paddon first meets Miranda, she is literally "colourful," with flecks of paint in her hair because of the problems with coordination brought on by the advance of her disease. Here, the stereotypic expectations are exceeded and thus mocked. But the narrative in its entirety seems to endorse the validity of these stereotypes, delighting in Miranda's censored creation myths and shrinking in distaste from the dominant Christian stories upheld by the nuns. As so often in English-Canadian fiction, Paula's revolt from her middle-class origins leads her to idealize cultural "others": the natives, French Canadians, and Haitians she was brought up to look down upon. And there is little space in the text to distance the reader from either Paula's judgments or her enthusiasms, except perhaps in the very elegance of her phrasings and self-conscious construction.

## Plainsong

The punning metaphor of plainsong establishes a structure for the text that implies intertextual weavings around a single theme. When Paula hears plainsong, she describes it as "a single plaintive melody hovering around one note" (147). The pun thus destabilizes and conflates traditional reference points: is it the song of a place or the song of a people? Is it a "plains song," the song of the plains, or "plainsong," song of the European Christian tradition that silenced the songs of the people of the plains? Just as the novel's Miranda conflates gendered and racial readings of an allegorical opposition between Shakespeare's Caliban and his Miranda, so this title implies a merging of North American plain song into European plainsong. Does such a merging blur important distinctions between different songs or does it imply the beginning of something genuinely new, a doubling that could lead to a spiraling of cross-cultural interaction? If Caliban's identity is merged in Miranda's and if his curse is retuned into plain song, does this mean that allegorically his resistance is blunted or that it assumes a more subtle and liberating form of expression?

Huston makes much of a third use of the word "plain": to designate what is flat, ordinary, and unbeautiful. She saw a challenge in trying to make a work of art, a beautiful song, out of such unpromising material: the life of a man who never accomplished anything in a land with no history. The dominant ideologies of beauty, so constraining especially for women, and of Eurocentric belief in the equation of Europe with civilization and art, shape the ambivalences expressed by Huston and her characters, Paula and Paddon, about Canada, exile, and theoretical understanding.[21] Paddon cuts himself off from the life of the land and his family to study philosophy; even when forced to abandon university study to earn a living as a schoolteacher, he locks himself away with his books in a futile attempt to write. His exile is internal; Paula's is external. She leaves Alberta for Quebec, where she sees that Paddon's obsession with the theory of Time deprives him of the ability to live in and through time. Like Prospero, he suffers violent rages that can make him appear a tyrant, but Paula forgives him, seeing his violence as an expression of his frustration with the flatness of his world, a frustration she shares. Miranda, in contrast, is at home on the plains as Caliban was on the island. She sees both beauty and history in the landscape and finds frustration only in her dealings with the dominant white society.

Desiring to desire, Paula imagines Miranda pouring "colour back" into her grandfather's life, giving him the gift of living entirely in the present through "the unique way in which [she] inhabited the here and now" (93). As Paula describes her, Miranda becomes the exotic "imaginary Indian" of white desire described by Daniel Francis and Marcia Crosby.[22] Miranda rails at length against this role, but structurally, through the romance pressures of the text and Paula's desire, she seems doomed to fulfill it nonetheless. *Plainsong* makes it possible, however, to read Miranda against Paula's desire as a character who combines Ariel's freedom with Caliban's earthiness, and to see

Paula's attempt to reinscribe her within a more limited role as itself implicitly a critique of the white nation's need to "swallow and to mourn an aboriginal other who has died."[23]

### P's Book

Shakespeare's Caliban knew that Prospero's power lay in his books and advised his co-conspirators to steal them first. In Huston's retelling, Paddon's granddaughter not only legitimately inherits "P's Book" (5) but has promised to pull its fragments together and get it published. The task that has structured her life since the age of nine eventually becomes a nightmare from which she begs to be released. Ultimately, however, the writing frees her, helping her to see that she has used her promise to him as an excuse for avoiding her own choices in life. She begins by disavowing responsibility for her work, describing it as reading rather than writing: "I'm trying to read the manuscript." When she finds most of it "indecipherable" (9), she moves more confidently from reading to magic. Her raising of Paddon from the dead becomes, as she tells him proudly, "this gradual pulling of your existence from the void like coloured scarves from the hat of a magician" (39). (The metaphor inevitably recalls not only Prospero's magic but also Sycorax's sorcery as a source of alternative power.) The pretense of listening to Paddon's voice and telling his story finally breaks down completely when Paula confesses: "All right. I know. I'm the one doing the singing" (192). The novel thus becomes Paula's claiming of the plains, her plainsong. Paddon's life as she reconstructs it ends in the devastating realization that "*This is the crowning irony; my children destroyed my book and my book destroyed my children*" (194). This is the closest Paula has Paddon come to claiming responsibility for his life. He could not choose between the book and the body and so he lost both. Her own parallel moment of insight comes when she acknowledges that his wisdom will never be hers: "You have left me your words and I am stitching them into a patchwork quilt that will serve you as a shroud" (203). Paula thus succeeds where Paddon had failed: he had dreamed of writing an ambitious philosophical treatise on the history of time; she has written a novel that particularizes time, showing its embodiment in human lives and history. She has stolen and rewritten his book.

Paula has also stolen Miranda's story. In trying to redress the wrongs of the past, as she sees them, she acknowledges fearing that she may have perpetuated new violences of her own. A few pages after admitting that she has reshaped Paddon's book into Paula's book, she dreams that Miranda returns to earth as a giant corpse, a Golem. As Paula looks at various parts of Miranda's body, they are destroyed by the very power of her gaze. She turns her eyes away in fear and confesses: "The dream appalled me because it suggested that what I'm doing here is just the opposite of what I had hoped to do—not stitching a shroud but defiling cadavers" (214). The ambivalence of the woman artist finds its classic expression in this Frankensteinian motif, which is here combined with the need of a settler society to deal with its guilt. Death and birth are intertwined. In seeking to lay to rest the violence of the past, she finds herself perpetuating it beyond the grave: stealing the soul after the land has been taken. *Plainsong* asks whether it is possible to expiate a heritage of genocide by trying to see it from the point of view of the conquered, when the descendents of the usurpers insist that the telling remain in their control. One cannot help recalling Hélène Cixous's "Laugh of the Medusa" in the account of Paula's nightmare.[24] As in Cixous, Paula's text conflates racialized stereotypes of a dark continent with feminist revisions of the myth of Medusa.[25] Paula is defensive about her creation of Miranda, arguing, "Admittedly a character like Miranda is exceptional not to say far-fetched but she exists, there's no doubt in my mind about that and I hope there's none in yours either" (192). Her dream, however, reveals her intuitive understanding of the violence that projecting her desire on another continues to perpetrate.

### "This thing of darkness I Acknowledge mine"
#### (*The Tempest* 5.1.275–76)

Just as Prospero's claiming of Caliban has given rise to contradictory interpretations, so Paula's claiming of Paddon and Miranda as her own spheres of darkness may be read as both imperialist and revelatory of her own dawning self-knowledge. The novel begins by addressing the dead Paddon: "And here is how I visualize the moment of your death . . . lying flat yes flattened at last into the plain from which you'd struggled to arise . . ." (1). It ends with the moment of his conception, as God "lethargically dragged you from nothingness, Paddon, against His better judgement and your better interests, then heaved a sigh and, staring off into space, continued drumming His fingers on Eternity" (226). God is the Joycean modern artist, removing himself from his text as Huston removes herself from hers, through assigning the narrative to Paula.

But Paula takes Prospero, not this distant God, as her model. The single note of Paula's plainsong is the Prosperian confession: "This thing of darkness I Acknowledge mine." Paula's claiming of Paddon as her own depends on God's abandonment of him. Through Paddon, she both claims and exorcises the guilt for what their ancestors did to native peoples and their land. This guilt is reaffirmed and solidified in the climactic scene of the novel. Paddon, in 1942, decides he must make reparations for the past by teaching his students the truth about colonization in Canada, by retelling Miranda's story about Father Lacombe's betrayal of her people. When parents complain and he is reprimanded by the principal, fears about losing his job combine with doubts about which version of history can finally be trusted. When Paddon shares his doubt with Miranda, she is angry and hurt. The fantasy of their union is broken, and shortly afterwards, she suffers the final attack that leads to her death. Paddon, though well-intentioned, is unable to expiate his people's guilt through teaching history from the point of view of the indigenous nations, erased from the official histories. His failure reflects Europe's failure to acknowledge the Nazi holocaust as its own civilization's heart of darkness, in some ways an unanticipated culmination (however much we might wish to disavow it) of the attitudes to otherness that led to conquest in the Americas.

Through Paddon's affair with Miranda and its sorry conclusion, Paula allegorizes the history of betrayal that marks Canada's past and its tainted European legacy even as she claims through the affair a connection with native culture, with the vitality and authenticity she finds in the exotic other. As "woman, native, other,"[26] Paula's Miranda confirms these stereotypes even as she also raises doubts about the limits of cross-cultural imaginings and the reach of authorial hubris. At the same time, she seems to represent an attempt to think beyond binaries. Her own race is mixed, and she is willing to share her history and her love with a descendent of the people (whose ancestry she may also claim) who dispossessed her native ancestors.

This pattern is repeated through the introduction of the part-Haitian twins, Pearl and Amber, the *marasa,* whose intervention prevents the exposure of Paddon's affair with Miranda from disrupting his family birthday party. Although *marasa* is the Haitian word for any twin, it also signifies the divine twins of Voodoo (or Vodoun) practice. Huston employs the term to imply Paula's need to access an imaginative realm beyond the reach of her puritan Canadian heritage. Vévé A. Clark explains "*marasa* consciousness" as "a mythical theory of textual relationships based on the Haitian Vodoun sign for the Divine Twins, the *marasa.*" She elaborates: "*Marasa* consciousness invites us to imagine beyond the binary. The ability to do so depends largely on our capacities to read the sign as a cyclical, spiral relationship . . . the *marasa* principle points to the transformation of cultural oppositions in plantation societies." Clark claims *marasa* consciousness as a "third stage in diasporic development" that follows earlier historical moments of racially

conscious movements and anticolonial struggles. Unlike these earlier movements in their assertion of difference, the *marasa* consciousness inaugurates
a tradition of "imagining beyond difference."[27] In Clark's mobilizing of
*marasa*, I see an equivalent to Fortier's interest in reconciling postcolonial interpretations with romance traditions through their shared search for alternative imaginings of a better world beyond oppression.

Huston invokes the *marasa* principle to support Paddon and Paula's attempts to move beyond the destructive binaries of their inheritance.
Through *marasa*, Sycorax's magic joins Prospero's in the quest to move beyond the destructive colonial legacy of the Americas. Paula writes: "That
party was also the only time in my life I saw what I would call magic with
my own eyes" (208). Paula not only witnesses this magic but immediately
claims it as partly her own. The twins' intervention makes her "jubilant" because she sees it as evidence that "the twins were on our side, the side of deep
secret against shallow fact, the side of glimmering contradiction against
glassy certainty; the side of tremulous Crowfoot against triumphant Lacombe" (210). Here the magic links the descendents of slaves and slavers,
colonized and colonizer, in a new alliance against philistines and fools, big-
ots and bourgeois moralists.

What troubles me here are the recurring binaries in Paula's invocation of
the *marasa* even as she acknowledges that their consciousness celebrates the
"deep secret" and the "glimmering contradiction," formulations of experience hostile to binary modes of thinking. I am also troubled by the immediate effects of *marasa* intervention at the party. By preventing Paddon's son
from exposing his secret life, and therefore circumventing an opportunity for
Paddon to publicly acknowledge his love for Miranda alongside his love for
his wife, the twins enable the binaries to continue unreconciled and en-
courage the silencing of truth. Just as Paddon was prevented from continuing to speak an alternative history in the classroom, so he is here prevented
from speaking an alternative private life to the public facade of the monog-
amously married man. But perhaps this is the point: Paddon was incapable
of such a speaking, and so the truth had to wait until Paula could tell it. The
*marasa* thus save Paddon from having to speak the unspeakable: that the
racially pure white bourgeois family depends for its prosperity and integrity
on the father's unacknowledged dependence on and exploitation of the native woman. Only Paula can eventually speak this truth in her *Plainsong*,
after she has been privileged to witness the spiraling of *marasa* magic.

With *marasa* intuitiveness, Paula imagines her grandfather Paddon in bed
with his dying mistress, Miranda, tracing the loss of feeling in her limbs:
"Tracing the outline of the numb island. Paddon the cartographer, the sur-

veyor" (53). The native woman is body, territory, unconscious; man is mind, shaper, and knower. She is; he does. This is the *Tempest* model—woman and native as island. But in *Plainsong,* this pattern arouses unease. Paula must take on the task of moving beyond such models.

### "Graves at their command/Have waked their sleepers, oped, and let 'em forth/By my so potent art" (*The Tempest* 5.1.48–50)

In recreating the lives and voices of Paddon and Miranda, Paula metaphorically raises the dead and rewrites her own origins. *Plainsong* is particularly self-conscious about its "working through" of its intractable materials: how to write what Huston calls the boring history of a utilitarian, brutalized, and ugly culture into the literary tradition; how to write women's lives beyond the limits imagined for them in traditional mythologies of what she calls "Mothers and Heroes."[28] In "Novels and Navels," Huston addresses a related problem that she sees for women who wish to be writers: the apparent incompatibility of maternal ethics and fiction.[29] Paula can take on the father's task because she is not a mother. "Mothers must not kill their children. . . . Novelists, on the other hand, must be prepared to kill their characters" and, she implies, their ancestors as well.[30] In Huston's words, "All novels say, 'Look Ma, no navel'"[31]—that is, no umbilical cord to the past; no literary parents; no imbrication in the bodily process of giving birth and dying. No wonder *The Tempest* is both there and not there as an intertext—Shakespeare is too powerful a progenitor to be named.

Chantal Zabus speculates that "If the Unknown, the unsaid is feminine, then perhaps this is why Prospero in Shakespeare's play speaks the lines of Medea, Ovid's witch."[32] In Huston's novel, Paula becomes the sorcerer who can raise the dead and choose not to have children, combining the powers of Sycorax and Prospero into a *marasa*-like consciousness. Miranda becomes the woman resolute enough, like her own grandmother, to contemplate killing her children because she will not bring them into the world on the conqueror's terms. Although Miranda has one daughter she loves from her husband, another white man, she aborts the child she has conceived with Paddon without consulting him. It is that abortion that indirectly leads to Paula's birth, since it is in reaction to it that Paddon decides to persuade his daughter Ruthie not to abort her own illegitimately conceived child. Huston has argued that "Only mothers who are capable of comprehending the gesture of Medea—facing death, including the death of their own children—can invent great stories."[33] And what of the children who must kill their parents? "In 'family romances,'" Huston writes, "children reinvent their origins."[34]

*Plainsong* also reinvents origins, installing the dominating, anguished, and angry figure of Paddon, a man who lives his entire life on the edge of despair, as Paula's nurturer, teacher, and model. Paula invokes the story of Heidi and her grandfather " . . . how fervently I loved you, just as Heidi loved her own misanthropic misunderstood grandfather in the Alps, and you rocked and wept and held me in your confidence. . . ." (202). None of the women in her family play such a maternal role; none of them need her as he apparently does. Indeed, the women confirm the worst stereotypes of English Canadians: Paddon's mother, wife, and sister are puritanical, cheap, moralistic, unimaginative, and frumpy. The text drips disdain as it speaks of them: "these people have spent their lives scouring spontaneity from their souls" (4). Despite Paula's late admission that she spurned marriage "only because my love of women was too strong" (203), her text shows no evidence of it. Like Athena springing from the head of Zeus, she models her creativity on that of her progenitor. Her desire, too, is modeled on his longing for completion through the exotic native other.

In *Plainsong,* Huston creates Paula as a narrator who is producing a new family romance for Canadians who are not of the First Nations, a romance that symbolically redeems a history of colonization through imagining a magical act of transcendence achieved through art. But Paula's text deconstructs itself. Miranda explicitly links the history of colonial oppression to contemporary New Age idealizations of a noble savage. Paula shows her telling Paddon: "I'm talking about I'm sick and tired of whites feeling so guilty they destroyed us they have to say we were perfect. . . . We were good and bad just like you guys" (126). Yet in her very sensible wisdom, as well as her beauty, her knowledge, and her talent, Paula's Miranda inevitably does seem to be characterized through Paula's need for the native woman in her text to be "perfect." And one cannot help the nagging feeling that part of her "perfection" for Paula lies in the fact that she is dead. Paula is now the custodian of Miranda's legacy as well as Paddon's.

In these ways, *Plainsong* inscribes a colonialist ambivalence about belonging; a fear of the "plain," of what is flat and unattractive; a desire for acceptance; a need to shape and impose a self-generated song on "the keyboard of the century" (6), and especially a need to control how that song is interpreted. These ambivalences are reproduced in the dramatic differences between the covers of the text in English and French. The English cover is a realist prairie landscape (sky, plain, and railroad), but with fragments of a text blowing in the breeze: a postmodern collage somewhat reminiscent of early scenes in Peter Greenaway's film *Prospero's Books*. Here book and land-scape are juxtaposed in a self-conscious relation. The French cover, a portrait of a highly exoticized native woman in traditional dress, recalls the ambiance of nineteenth-century pioneer sagas and claims "Miranda" as its center, con-flating woman, territory, and nation.

Both covers represent components of *Plainsong*'s vision. For Huston, exile is "the fantasy that allows us to function, and especially to write."[35] Perhaps such a text could only be written in exile, since it is so uncomfortable for con-temporary English-Canadians to read its reworking of a settler society's re-pressions and desires. In many ways, *Plainsong* seems closer to colonialist than to postcolonialist rewritings and to operate within a modernist rather than a postmodernist frame of reference. Its feminism, too, fits more closely with contemporary French feminisms than it does with postcolonial or Anglo-American traditions. Although it is politically much more self-conscious than most English-Canadian novels, *Plainsong* invokes *The Tempest* primarily to claim the power of art as magic to transcend differences and effect reconcili-ations. It rests its faith in language and metaphor, celebrating the "rough magic" of the artist with the power of effecting "a sea-change/Into something rich and strange" (*The Tempest* 1.2.401–2). This, too, was the dream of suc-cessions of immigrants to North America. *Plainsong*, like *The Tempest* itself, reveals the troubling dimensions within all such utopian longings.[36]

## Notes

1. Ania Loomba, "Shakespeare and Cultural Difference," in *Alternative Shake-speares 2,* ed. Terence Hawkes (New York: Routledge, 1996), 171, 173.
2. Although Max Dorsinville makes a case for Quebec as Caliban in *Caliban Without Prospero: Essay on Quebec and Black Literature* (Erin, Ont.: Press Porcepic, 1974), contemporary Quebec revisions of Shakespeare have more often taken Hamlet as a figure for their thwarted nationhood.
3. See Charles Marowitz, *Recycling Shakespeare* (New York: Applause, 1991).
4. For a study of how the Caribbean-Canadian writer Marlene Nourbese Philip has created a black Miranda who retunes Caliban's cursing and takes on his resistant role, see Leslie Sanders, "Marlene Nourbese Philip's 'Bad Words,'" *Tessera* 12 (Summer 1992): 81–89, and Sanders's "'The Mere Determination to Remember': M. Nourbese Philip's 'Stop Frame,'" *West Coast Line* (special issue titled *North: New African Canadian Writing*), no. 22 (Spring/Summer 1997): 134–42; see also Diana Brydon, "No (Wo)man Is an Island," *Ku-napipi* 15.1 (1993): 48–56.
5. Nancy Huston, *Plainsong* (Toronto: HarperCollins, 1993). Quotations from this work will hereafter be cited in the text. Jonathan Dollimore's phrase is

cited in Susan Bennett, *Performing Nostalgia: Shifting Shakespeare and the Contemporary Past* (New York: Routledge, 1996), 1.

6. Susan Stewart, *On Longing: Narratives of the Miniature, the Gigantic, the Souvenir, the Collection* (Durham: Duke University Press, 1993), 23. Stewart's description here fits perfectly the perceived inauthenticity of colonial life in an invader-settler colony as reproduced in Huston's narrative: " . . . longing for an impossibly pure context of lived experience at a place of origin, nostalgia wears a distinctly utopian face, a face that turns toward a future-past, a past which has only ideological reality" (Stewart, 23).

7. Nancy Huston, *Cantique des Plaines* (Paris: Leméac Editeur/Actes Sud, 1993).

8. Huston analyzes her own perception of this dynamic in "Festins Fragiles," *Liberté* (1984): 7–15 and "Les Prairies à Paris," *Liberté* 35.4–5 (Aug.–Oct. 1993): 24–35.

9. The occluded native presence is the absence that creates the sadness of Paula's nostalgia. As Margery Fee explains, "A complicated process, simultaneously a confession and a denial of guilt—an identification and a usurpation—ensues when white writers choose Native people as literary material." See Fee, "Romantic Nationalism and the Image of Native People in Contemporary English-Canadian Literature," in *The Native in Literature: Canadian and Comparative Perspectives,* ed. Thomas King et al. (Toronto: ECW, 1987), 15. This is the dynamic I seek to explore here.

10. William Shakespeare, *The Tempest,* ed. Stephen Orgel (Oxford: Oxford University Press, 1987), 1.2.50.

11. Gillian Beer, *Arguing with The Past* (New York: Routledge, 1989).

12. Mark Fortier, "Two-Voiced, Delicate Monster: *The Tempest,* Romance, and Post-Colonialism," *Essays in Theatre* (special issue titled: Shakespeare and Postcolonial Conditions, ed. Denis Salter) 15.1 (November 1996): 94, 98.

13. Howard Felperin, "Political Criticism at the Crossroads: The Utopian Historicism of 'The Tempest'" in *The Tempest,* ed. Nigel Wood (Buckingham: Open University Press, 1995), 29–66.

14. Fortier, "Two-Voiced, Delicate Monster," 90.

15. See Laura E. Donaldson, "The Miranda Complex: Colonialism and the Question of Feminist Reading" in *Decolonizing Feminisms: Race, Gender and Empire-building* (Chapel Hill: University of North Carolina Press, 1992), 13–31.

16. See Diana Brydon, "Rewriting *The Tempest,*" *World Literature Written in English* 23 (1984): 75–88.

17. See Peter Erickson, *Rewriting Shakespeare, Rewriting Ourselves* (Berkeley: University of California Press, 1991).

18. For the debate, see Rosemary J. Coombes, "The Properties of Culture and the Possession of Identity: Postcolonial Struggle and the Legal Imagination" and Leonore Keeshig-Tobias, "Stop Stealing Native Stories" in *Borrowed*

*Power: Essays on Cultural Appropriation,* ed. Bruce Ziff and Pratima Rao (New Brunswick, NJ: Rutgers University Press, 1997), 74–96, 71–73. See also Daiva Stasiulis, "'Authentic Voice': Anti-racist Politics in Canadian Feminist Publishing and Literary Production" in *Feminism and the Politics of Difference,* ed. Sneja Gunew and Anna Yeatman, (Sydney: Allen & Unwin, 1993), 35–60. For anglophone reviews of Huston's novel, see Don Gillmor, "Even Cowgirls Get the Boos," *Saturday Night* 110.5 (June 1995): 85–88 and Jeannie Marshall, *"Plainsong," Paragraph* 16.2 (Fall 1994): 36–37.

19. For the francophone debate see Caroline Barrett, "Écrire Le Temps," Corinne Durin, "Traduction et Médiation," and Régine Robin, "Speak Watt: Sur La Polémique Autour du Livre de Nancy Huston," all in *Spirale* 132 (April 1994): 5, 6 & 3–4. See also Mathew Manera, "Plainsong and Counterpoint," *Canadian Forum* 73.831 (July–August 1984): 36–38, and Gilles Marcotte "L'Alberta devenue personnage mythique," *L'Actualité* 19.2 (February 1994): 74–75.

20. This annual agricultural fair and rodeo began in 1912 and remains a popular event for both locals and tourists today.

21. Huston's ambivalence about her own beauty is most famously expressed in "Dealing with What's Dealt," *Salmagundi* 106/107 (Spring/Summer 1995): 257–269.

22. Marcia Crosby, "Constructions of the Imaginary Indian," in *By, For & About: Feminist Cultural Politics,* ed. Wendy Waring (Toronto: Women's Press, 1994), 85–114, and Daniel Francis, *The Imaginary Indian: The Image of the Indian in Canadian Culture* (Vancouver: Arsenal Pulp, 1992).

23. For an analysis of this pathology, see Christopher Bracken, *The Potlatch Papers: A Colonial Case History* (Chicago: University of Chicago Press, 1997), 231.

24. See Hélène Cixous, "The Laugh of the Medusa," in *New French Feminisms: An Anthology,* ed with introductions by Elaine Marks and Isabelle de Courtivron (New York: Schocken, 1991), 245–64.

25. For a perceptive analysis of this troping in Cixous, which is also of relevance to Huston's method in this novel, see Uzoma Esonwanne, "Feminist Theory and the Discourse of Colonialism," in *ReImagining Women: Representations of Women in Culture,* ed. Shirley Neuman and Glennis Stephenson (Toronto: University of Toronto Press, 1993), 233–55.

26. See Trinh Minh-ha, *Woman Native Other: Writing Postcoloniality and Feminism* (Bloomington: University of Indiana Press, 1989).

27. Vévé A. Clark, "Developing Diaspora Literacy and *Marasa* Consciousness," in *Comparative American Identities: Race, Sex, and Nationality in the Modern Text,* ed Hortense Spillers (New York: Routledge, 1991), 43–46. For Huston's interest in twinship as an analogy for differences in how men and women relate to their bodies, their art, and each other, see "Les pièges de la gémellité: Sartre/Beauvoir et Plath/Hughes," *Liberté* 29.4 (August 1987):

18–38 and "Castor and Poulou: The Trials of Twinship," *L'Esprit Créateur* 29.4 (Winter 1989): 8–20. A graphic instance of moving beyond the twinship of English and French in the naming of Canadian places occurs when Paddon teaches the eight-year-old Paula "to hear the different melodies playing in the names of your world, a structure which had been shakily erected on three unequal columns" (6). The following page inscribes Alberta place names in uneven columns moving from the left to the right, from the native, through the English (the longest list) to the French (7).

28. Nancy Huston, "The Matrix of War: Mothers and Heroes," *Poetics Today* 6 (1985): 153–70. On Canadian history, see Huston, "Les Prairies à Paris."

29. Nancy Huston, "Novels and Navels," *Critical Inquiry* 21 (Summer 1995): 708–21.

30. Ibid., 712.

31. Ibid., 713.

32. Chantal Zabus, "What Next Miranda?: Marina Warner's *Indigo*," *Kunapipi* 16.3 (1994): 89.

33. Huston, "Novels and Navels," 714.

34. Nancy Huston, "A Tongue Called Mother," *Raritan* 9 (Winter 1990): 100.

35. Manera, "Plainsong and Counterpoint," 37.

36. Thanks to Christine Bold, Susan Brown, Donna Palmateer Pennee, and Ann Wilson for advice on how to revise earlier versions of this paper. Thanks also to my research assistants, Christine Viinberg and Jessica Braden, for locating sources. I am grateful to Marianne Novy and Gillian Beer for inviting me to contribute to the seminar they organized on Women's Rewritings of Shakespeare for the International Shakespeare Association conference in Los Angeles in April 1996, for which this paper was first prepared, and to all the participants in that seminar, whose feedback and discussion were invaluable. I am also grateful to Denis Salter, who gave me a second chance to present the paper and further develop it by accepting it for presentation at the special session on Postcolonial Shakespeare jointly organized by the Association for Canadian Theatre History and the Association of Canadian College and University Teachers of English at the Learned Societies Meetings in Newfoundland in June 1997, and to the audience there.

*12*

———～⁓ぐ～———

# Sycorax Speaks: Marina Warner's *Indigo* and *The Tempest*

## Caroline Cakebread

In her 1992 novel, *Indigo,* Marina Warner uses Shakespeare's *The Tempest* in order to examine the legacy of British imperialism at the end of the twentieth century. For her, Prospero's seizure of Caliban's island becomes a catalyst for a fictional discussion of the legacy of colonialism in modern British life. The novel jumps from the twentieth century to the sixteenth century and back again as Warner works to chart the experiences of the Everard family and their role in the expansion of the British empire. Here, the providential Caribbean voyage of Kit Everard, a sixteenth-century explorer, leads him to the shores of Liamuiga, a fictional island that shares its Carib name and geography with the actual island of St. Kitts Warner. Warner peoples this island with characters who take their names from Shakespeare's play: Sycorax, a wise-woman and healer, and her two adopted children, Ariel and Dulé (later renamed Caliban by English settlers). In claiming the island in the name of England and in subjugating its people in the service of his plantation, Kit becomes a Prospero figure, exploiting the landscape in order to accrue greater power and prestige back home and perpetuating a family legacy that is founded upon a whole series of inhuman acts. While the novel opens in twentieth-century London, Warner depicts the parallels between the sixteenth-century lives of the islanders and the settlers and the problems faced by Kit Everard's descendants, as Miranda Everard struggles to find love and happiness in the modern world.

The "indigo" of Warner's title refers to Sycorax's trade: the making of indigo dye through a churning method that colors the wise-woman's skin, creating an underlying reason for the blue-eyed status of the witch in Prospero's history of the island. But the process of dyeing also serves to underline Warner's own approach to the concept of history in the novel, a sense of time that is nonlinear, somewhat churn-like, merging stories and histories "in the continuous present tense of existence."[1] In accordance with the melting pot of Sycorax's churn, *Indigo* is a novel that is self-consciously constructed as an intertext, and Warner signposts her connections to other writers through the many epigraphs from poets and academics alike that she places at the beginning of the novel's chapters and sections: Derek Walcott, Paul Celan, William Empson, Emily Dickinson. That the novel is a palimpsest in and of itself is made clear throughout.

But it is the novel's alternative title, *Mapping the Waters,* that, in many ways, best illustrates Warner's role as an author at the center of so many divergent stories of the past. For although the rhythms of Sycorax's life on the island are characterized by the indigo churn with which she works, the twentieth-century figure of Miranda Everard (named for Prospero's daughter) must struggle to decipher a whole series of markers and codes that govern her view of her family's history, from the overwhelming white body of Kit Everard in the painting that dominates her grandfather's sitting room to Warner's fictionalized, cricket-inspired creation of "flinders," a male-dominated game that retells the violent takeover of Liamuiga by the English. Warner's recreation of Prospero's island, scarred by violence and the imposition of a plantation economy that destroys its natural landscape, produces the soil in which the Everard family is rooted. Like her fictional island (for which a map is provided at the beginning of the novel), *The Tempest* becomes another sort of map for Warner, as she uses Shakespeare's characters as a means of creating her own. Their names and traits provide her with a map through which she can portray the effects of the elder Everard's actions upon his modern progeny.

The idea of mapping is important in terms of Warner's relationship with Shakespeare for, in many ways, cartography is also an act of negotiation, an attempt to find a system of names, signs, and signals through which to mediate one's experience of any given landscape. The idea of mapping water, a substance that is constantly changing shape from one moment to the next, calls upon the idea of sea-changes in Shakespeare's play. But in mapping a body of water, one must necessarily turn toward the surrounding land—to the solid, jagged, and often irregular fringes along which bodies of water take their shape. Through Warner's negotiation between her own work and Shakespeare's, the reader can see a new territory taking form, one that is both bound to the past and yet distinctly her own.

Full fathom five thy father lies.
   Of his bones are coral made;
Those are pearls that were his eyes;
   Nothing of him that doth fade
But doth suffer a sea-change
Into something rich and strange.
(*The Tempest*, 1.2.399–404)[2]

The fragmented, tattered collection of dead slaves that are washed up on the shores of Liamuiga embody just the sort of sea-changes with which Warner is concerned. Transformed from human beings into nearly unrecognizable body parts, they act as fleshy memorials to the inhumanities of the slave trade. Thrown overboard from a slaveship, their journey between the old and new worlds cut off, these bodies signify a future that Sycorax and the other islanders are unable to see: "It was the beginning of a new world for her and her people, the start of a new time, and as yet Sycorax did not know it" (82). Significantly, characters throughout *Indigo* seem unable to read the signposts that surround them. Miranda, upon first visiting her family's island hundreds of years later, finds herself unable to adequately place herself in relation to her family's past. Touring the island, oblivious to the military coup taking place on the other side, she hears only "scraps of sounds falling around" her but is unable "to piece together their meanings" (319)—she is completely unaware of the impending political turmoil. For both Sycorax and Miranda—one unaware of the future, the other unaware of the past— these signs can only be read as presaging doom.

As Adrienne Rich asserts in coining the term "re-vision," the act of rewriting the past for women entails an effort to "understand the assumptions in which we are drenched." Until that point, "we cannot know ourselves."[3] In returning to this nascent point of first contact between new and old worlds, and in re-imagining that connection by using a Shakespearean text, Warner makes her novel a site of recovery for the marginalized voices of the past at the same time that she seeks to map out new directions for the future. The dead bodies speak out to Sycorax in a dream, echoing the language of Shakespeare's play, warning her about the tide of subjugation and slavery that is about to land on the shores of the island: "From our flesh, mermaid's purses, dolphin garlands. . . . Blood roses for the coral, black dust for the sand. . . ." (83). As their bodies become grist for the empire, the slaves' stories, though inscribed upon their flesh, are articulated only in the wise-woman's dreams. Prompted by these voices to return to the grave where the bodies are buried, Sycorax cuts open the belly of a dead slave to rescue the infant, Dulé. Pulling out new life from the carnage of the slave trade, Warner, like Sycorax, is returning to the wreckage of the British empire in order to salvage for herself a positive sense of connectedness to a past filled with pain and suffering.

*The Tempest* is certainly not the only blueprint Warner uses in her novel. As a writer, her stake in the legacy of British imperialism is substantial. The fictional island she creates, beginning at the moment of its colonization and ending with its new, twentieth-century role as a tourist resort, has its roots in her own family's past. The author's ancestor, Sir Thomas Warner, the original colonizer of the Caribbean island of St. Kitts, becomes the inspiration for Kit Everard, whose name acts as a constant reminder of the connection between Warner's narrative and the island at the center of her family's history. Sir Thomas's tomb, which still stands on St. Kitts, bears an inscription in which his exploits are memorialized in glorious terms:

First Read then Weep when thou art hereby taught
That Warner lyes interr'd here, one that bought
With loss of Noble bloud Illustrious Name
Of a Commander Greate in Acts of Fame
Trayned from his youth in Armes, his courage bold,
Attempted brave Exploites and uncontrold
By fortunes fiercest Frownes, he still gave forth
Large Narratives of Military worth
Written with his sword's poynt, but what is man
In the midst of his glory, and who can
Secure this Life A moment since hee
Both by Sea and Land, so long kept free
[At Mortal Strokes] at length did yield
[Grace] to conquering Death in the field
                              fini Coronat.[4]

The inscription is echoed in *Indigo,* in which Sir Thomas's "Large Narratives of Military Worth" are rewritten in the form of an epitaph for Kit Everard that is distorted by age and the large crack running through it: "Weep in Arms . . . uncontrolled . . . Narratives of . . . shame" (317). Like her protagonist in the novel, Warner herself is a Miranda figure, implicated by birthright in the imperial fortunes of her family's past. Weaving a narrative of shame from the narrative of military worth that has been passed down to her by her ancestors, Warner makes her novel a site of recovery for a family history marred by its involvement in the slave trade and the subjugation of the island's indigenous people, the Caribs. By integrating her own family's history into the literary palimpsest of her novel, Warner undermines the solid structures of Britain's imperial history, approaching the past as a series of fragments and reconstructing it in terms that question the received "narratives of military worth" that characterize her family's role in the history of the British empire.

The many books produced by members of the Warner family exist as testaments to their role in the European colonization of the Caribbean and their predominance in British history since the seventeenth century. From the author's famous cricket-playing grandfather, Sir Pelham Warner, to her great-uncle Aucher Warner, she has another strain of textual evidence to draw on for her novel—the edges along which her own vision of the past has taken shape. That Warner rewrites the quasi-religious sport of cricket (the ultimate game of the Empire) as a game called "flinders" comments upon her grandfather's how-to books about the sport. Aucher Warner's book, *Sir Thomas Warner: Pioneer of the West Indies,* contains a vindication of Sir Thomas who, in suppressing a native plot to reclaim the island, gathered together his compatriots and, heavily armed, "determined that their only safe course was to rid the island altogether of Caribs, and divide it between them."[5] As he writes,

> This regrettable incident has been made the ground of an accusation, originating with foreign writers, and ignorantly and carelessly followed by others, to the effect that the plot had no existence in fact, and it was invented by the English as a justification or excuse for their action.[6]

Aucher Warner's book, chronicling as it does Marina Warner's violent and bloody family history, is central to the novelist's attempts to portray the many voices of Britain's colonial past and her own place in that history. But in *Indigo,* the indigenous population isn't exterminated in the same, systematic way. Instead, Ariel lives to be an old woman, Sycorax dies a slow and painful death, Dulé has his hamstrings slit for his part in the rebellion, and the language of the Carib population is gradually subsumed into the "Large Narratives" of generations of colonizing powers that continue to impose themselves on the island for centuries to come. As Warner herself has written of her family history:

> Inviolate Englishness, in a family like my father's and his father's before him, was kept up by methods both subtle and brutal, conscious and unconscious acts of convenient memory and sins of omission.[7]

These sins of omission are expiated in *Indigo,* in which the rebel islanders are mowed down by cannon fire while still in their boats.

> The dead lay in rows under fans of palm and banana, so many dead, the survivors wept that they had been spared. The massacre was shameful, the losses piteous. The blood of the wounded trickled from the bank, spilling like one of the showers that freshened the earth each day, and flowed downstream towards the sea, which was not so far that its rich scarlet could diffuse before it met the waves. (203)

Warner's rewriting of Sir Thomas's massacring of the Caribs in her own family history takes place on the shore, the point of contact between the new and old worlds. The "regrettable incident" chronicled by Aucher Warner is humanized by one of his descendants, for whom the water that washed away the indigenous islanders' blood does not wash away her family's sins. Here, Warner reinscribes the islanders onto her family's narratives of shame.

Warner makes her fictional island speak, as the voice of Sycorax wells up through the cracks in the land: "The isle is full of noises, so they say, and Sycorax is the source of many" (77). The Warner dead, memorialized by the official tombstone of Kit Everard, and in the texts of her forefathers, are resurrected through the author's retelling of her family's history in the Caribbean. Sycorax's grave, marked only by an ancient saman tree, provides a natural site of resistance to the solid structures of imperial Britain, from the Everard tomb to the five-star hotel maintained by Ant Everard's daughter, Xanthe, and her husband, Sy. Although in *The Tempest,* the witch of Prospero's story imprisons Ariel in a tree, in *Indigo* the voice of the dead Sycorax emanates through the branches of the tree underneath which she is buried, an organic challenge to the structures left upon the island's landscape by generations of British and French colonial powers and to capitalist markers like The Hotel des Bains and The Spice of Life.

In this sense, Shakespeare's *Tempest* provides Warner with a mouthpiece through which she can vocalize the bloody and inhuman acts committed by her forefathers on the island of St. Kitts. In place of Aucher Warner's book, Ant Everard's memoir, *How We Played,* provides Miranda with one of her only windows onto her family's past on Liamuiga.[8] *How We Played* contains an extract from one of Kit's letters to his fiancée, Rebecca, in England.

> God himself has blessed this land with fruitfulness and beauty. You cannot count the features of loveliness here, but I attach some pages from my note-

book to discover to you the ingenious flora of this fair isle and their many productive and rich uses. (151)

Weighted with religious imagery, the letter describes the flora and fauna of
the island and the cooperativeness of "the natives" while omitting the most
troubling aspects of his actions during his occupation: the fact that he has
taken Ariel and Sycorax hostage, the destruction of the natural landscape of
the island in the development of his plantation, and his sexual relationship
with Ariel. He writes, "Fly here to stand by my side, sweet lady, for we can
further the walls of Christendom on this isle in goodly state" (153). Like
Gonzalo's providential vision of the island in *The Tempest*, Kit's vision of
Liamuiga is idealistic on one level and yet hopelessly skewed by his own desires, the "productive and rich uses" to which the land will soon be put.
"Treason, felony,/Sword, pike, knife, gun, or need of any engine/Would I
not have" (2.1.166–67): Gonzalo's Edenic vision of a landscape that is un-
marred by violence gives way to Warner's island, in which power is seized
and maintained at "Sword's poynt" and by "Mortal Strokes," to echo the
tomb of her forefathers. Although he works to sanctify his vision of economic prosperity on the island in Christian terms, the many features of love-
liness that characterize Kit's plantation—his "Everhope," as he calls it—are
undercut by the blood harvest of the rebellion. Inherent in the contrast between Warner's novel and Shakespeare's play is a new sense of history made
up of contrasting versions of the past. From Gonzalo's vision to Kit's
island—a space in which the natural flora and fauna are being destroyed by
the cutting down of trees—Warner is creating a dialectic between multiple
voices as she seeks to destabilize the version of history contained in Shakespeare's text as well as in the texts of her family.

Along with her grandfather's books, the young Miranda is given another
window onto her family's history on Enfant Béate through the painting that
hangs in his sitting room. Seen through the eyes of a Renaissance artist, Kit's
exploits on the island are revised in whitewashed terms, and it is the aspect
of his luminous white torso, "plunged into the sea naked to the waist," grip-
ping a "volcano-tipped island" (48) with one hand that dominates the foreground of the painting. The tiny figures on the island "in feathered skirts
and headdresses digging and planting the land" (48) are barely recognizable.[9] The painting serves as a backdrop for Ant's stories of life on Enfant
Béate—his "reverie of colonial sunniness" (42)—with which he entertains
his guests. But the presence of Serafine, the family's black servant from the
island, undermines the authority of these tales. Although Prospero's books
are the main source of Miranda's knowledge in *The Tempest*, Serafine's oral

stories—told to the young Miranda in the kitchen or in the nursery—become an alternative family history in *Indigo*. Like the novel itself, Serafine's tales weave together a host of other stories, from the King Midas-inspired story with which the novel begins to other stories through which she touches upon the history of the Everard family and their relationship to the other islanders. At the same time as the voice of Sycorax wells up through the cracked landscape of the island, Serafine's stories notably emanate from the fissures within the Warner family texts themselves: "Feeny's hands were dry and hard like the paper in a storybook, and when they handled Miranda she felt safe" (4). A living site of resistance to the printed narratives of the Everard family, Serafine's stories—nuanced with her island accent—offer Miranda an alternative to the version of her family's past authenticated in the printed accounts of her forefathers: the plight of slaves, the customs of the islanders, and the unarticulated stories of women. Serafine acts as a counterpart for Warner, who makes her way through the categories of race and gender by assuming a range of voices in the colonial experience.

Warner's place at the nexus of several divergent versions of the colonial experience calls into question her novel's role within the context of other twentieth-century, postcolonial re-visions of *The Tempest*, re-visions that almost always use Caliban as the focal point of Prospero's oppression. As Kate Chedgzoy points out, discussing *Indigo* in her book *Shakespeare's Queer Children*:

> Where they notice Miranda's existence at all, they usually take her to be complicit in Prospero's oppressive project, if only by virtue of her passivity and willingness to function as a token of exchange between the empire-building patriarchal dynasties.[10]

Chedgzoy's discussion of *Indigo*'s role within a greater dialogue of postcolonial writing is helpful in discussing the means by which Warner locates the female voices in *The Tempest* as sites of resistance to Prospero's power. In *The Pleasures of Exile* (1960), George Lamming was one of the earliest writers to link the postcolonial experience to Shakespeare's play. Positing a link between himself and the figure of Caliban, he writes that, in the modern Caribbean, "The old blackmail of language simply won't work any longer. For the language of modern politics is no longer Prospero's exclusive vocabulary. It is Caliban's as well."[11] But for Warner, the newly shared political language of Prospero and Caliban with which Lamming is concerned is still marked by exclusivity: it is male-dominated. In *Indigo*, she engages with a multiracial combination of voices—male and female—but her central characters are primarily female. At the same time, her island, from which the voice of Sycorax emanates, is more akin to the type of feminized landscape theorized by feminist critics like Hélène Cixous who, in *The Newly Born Woman,* writes of emerging female voices that will "crack the foundation" of the patriarchal order.[12] Examining some of the deeper female-centered fissures in Shakespeare's play, Warner focuses her attention upon the silent or dead women of *The Tempest:* Miranda's dead mother, the absent, silent Claribel, and the Sycorax of Prospero's history. In *Indigo* these women are replaced by female characters who give the novel its focus and power. Their stories literally well up through the cracks in the mapped-out landscape of Warner's island, to use Cixous's concept:

> Sycorax speaks in the noises that fall from the mouth of the wind. It's a way of holding on to what was once hers, to pour herself out through fissures in the rock, to exhale from the caked mud bed of the island's rivers in the dry season, and mutter in the leaves of the saman where they buried her . . . (77)

In challenging Prospero's skewed version of Sycorax's history with her own character, and in re-gendering the figure of Ariel, Prospero's shape-shifting servant, Warner moves beyond the vocabulary of master and slave implicit in Lamming's work and takes up the curse of silence that characterizes the female experience of colonization. Indeed, Warner cites her indebtedness to Peter Hulme's book *Colonial Encounters: Europe and the Native Caribbean 1492–1797* in the acknowledgments to her novel, indicating the way in which she has utilized Hulme's account of the colonial Caribbean in formulating a feminized re-vision of *The Tempest.* Warner's approach to the play rests on Hulme's assertion that the very presence of Ariel, Caliban, and, through Prospero's story, Sycorax, serves to undermine the power structure that has been imposed upon the island. Moreover, as Hulme asserts, the alternative history of the island represented by Caliban and, to a great extent, by Ariel, serves as a constant reminder to the audience that "Prospero's narrative is not simply history, not simply the way things were, but a particular *version.*"[13] As he writes:

> Prospero tells Miranda (and the audience) a story in which the island is merely an interlude, a neutral ground between extirpation and resumption of power. Ariel and Caliban immediately act as reminders that Prospero's is not the only perspective, that the island is not neutral ground for them.[14]

The variant versions of the island's history—with the figure of the sleeping Miranda at the center—opens up the Prospero-Caliban struggle to include two new and important presences: Miranda and Ariel. As the main focus of her own novel, Sycorax, Ariel, and Miranda are used by Warner to portray the effects of Prospero's power upon female characters, as each struggles in various ways to overcome the silence imposed upon them by two hierarchical systems, patriarchy and colonialism.

And while Lamming believes that the language of modern politics is now shared by Caliban, Warner depicts the way in which that language not only eludes her disenfranchised women—both black and white—but is also essentially flawed. The legacy of the unburied men who died in the rebels' fight for the island is a language of victimization and revenge that rises up to dominate the minds of the living:

> . . . the victims would become phantoms and speak to the living without ever finding rest. Though the ghost army would also persecute their murderers by their chatter, their relatives would have preferred that they find quiet. (203)

As Caliban-like characters in the novel, both Dulé and his descendants in the form of The Shining Purity are circumscribed by their unwillingness to relinquish the language of entitlement that fuels the expanding empire. Caliban's cursing takes the form of a struggle centered upon the futile assertion "This island's mine" (1.2.331) as the language of modern politics becomes a nationalistic language that still necessitates the same demeaning roles.

Against this background of male territorialism, Ariel and Sycorax become hostages at the center of a violent fight to take over the island. Mere pawns in the eyes of both the settlers and the islanders, these two women effectively characterize the female position in the new hierarchies being imposed upon the island. Warner links her female characters to the subject of territorial imperialism by creating parallels between their bodies and the changing space of the island. The treeless space that the island becomes is mirrored in descriptions of Ariel and Sycorax in their prisoner state, from that of the old woman's dry and burnt skin to Ariel's mouth when Kit tries to kiss her, "dry and hollow, a socket, no longer a well, as if she had no tongue to kiss with" (174). The passive position of women in the colonial dynamic is portrayed in a way that links them directly to the space of the land that is being exploited for economic gain. Ariel's reaction as she is shot and captured by the settlers represents the newly contained state of non-white women in that exploitation: "She came together at the shot's touch of ice, her borders all defined in tension, her limbs and frame her own, but breached" (132).

Just as the landscape is mapped out with new place names and new features, the women on that island are similarly re-mapped and redefined through their gradual metamorphosis into the figures in Shakespeare's play. The new borders being imposed upon Sycorax and Ariel can be seen in the series of unsettling parallels that Warner creates between the two women and their Shakespearean counterparts. Sycorax's fate at the hands of the British settlers is particularly violent as her body is burnt, broken, and physically contorted into a new shape. The injuries she sustains when she falls from her burning tree house gradually transform her into the shape of Shakespeare's witch, the withered crone of Prospero's story:

> Hast thou forgot
> The foul witch Sycorax, who with age and envy
> Was grown into a hoop? Hast thou forgot her? (1.2.258–60)

Here, the hoop is formed as a result of the physical injuries that Sycorax suffers during an attack by Kit and his crew: " . . . she was bent like a hoop and could only shuffle forward, raising her head, like a turtle poking out of its shell" (164). In the eyes of her captors, she becomes more and more like the Sycorax of *The Tempest*, a two-dimensional character from a story not her own: "When they peeled off her incinerated clothing, they were surprised to find that she was a woman, and an old woman at that" (132). Barely recognizable as a human being's, Sycorax's situation in the novel dramatizes the problematic nature of racial categories with which Kit's twentieth-century descendants, Miranda and her father Kit, will struggle, coming up against reductive nicknames and descriptive terms like "touch of the tarbrush" (22), "awfully swarthy" (237) and "musty" (249). Both characters call into question the dividing lines of racial and cultural identity by providing a challenge to the whitewashed narratives of their family's past. At the same time, as Ariel and Sycorax are transformed from human beings to caricatures that more closely conform with Shakespeare's play, the interaction between Warner's novel and *The Tempest* highlights the dehumanizing nature of racist labels.

But Warner nuances that dilemma further, illustrating the way in which these female characters are already circumscribed by the patriarchal hierarchies extant upon the island long before the arrival of Kit and his crew. Living in exile from the rest of the Caribs because women with power are untrustworthy in the eyes of the rest of the tribe, Sycorax's blueness—which also mirrors Shakespeare's "blue-eyed hag"—is evidence of the dyer's trade she must adopt in order to survive away from the village. At the same time, her witch status is not purely a fiction of Kit or of Prospero. Instead, her rescue of Dulé sparks a reaction from some of the other islanders that is prompted by a fear of race and gender difference: they believe that she had effected the rescue by "witchcraft" and that perhaps "she'd mated with one of the animals she tamed and this was the progeny" (86). Thus, Warner's Sycorax occupies a position in two intersecting stories of oppression, one marked by her status as a woman, the other characterized by her racial difference in the eyes of her captors.

Stephen Orgel writes that

> Power, as Prospero presents it in the play, is not inherited but self-created: it is magic, or "art," an extension of mental power and self-knowledge, and the authority legitimizing it derives from heaven—"Fortune" and "Destiny" are the terms used in the play.[15]

In *Indigo*, the extent to which female characters are legitimately allowed to practice that "art" on any level is bounded by a whole series of inherited, rather than self-created, rules and codes that stem from a destiny that Warner argues is common to all women: a life circumscribed by subservience to a longstanding patriarchal order. Indeed, female power must exist and define itself away from overriding narratives of patriarchal "Fortune" and "Destiny" in which a woman's silence is implicit.

In the figures of Sycorax and Ariel, Warner demonstrates the way in which the colonial experience is, for her indigenous female characters, merely a transition from one colonial mode to another.

> Go make thyself like to a nymph o'th'sea. Be subject
> To no sight but thine and mine, invisible
> To every eyeball else. Go take this shape,
> And hither come in't. (1.2.303–06)

The shape-shifting nature of Prospero's servant, commanded to do his bidding, becomes a general symbol of the position of the colonized woman, contained within the limits of patriarchy on one level and within the racist gaze of the white settlers on another. Importantly, through Dulé, the son of an African, and Ariel, the daughter of an Arawak, Warner depicts a society that, although it is ultimately destroyed by the arrival of the English, defies the label of "new" world, existing as a thriving international community with its own hierarchies. Indeed, Warner is writing against what Edward Said describes as the tendency among western scholars to approach the "whole of world history as viewable by a kind of Western super-subject, whose historicizing and disciplinary rigour either takes away or, in the postcolonial period, restores history to people and cultures 'without' history."[16] Warner avoids that tendency, and her indebtedness to Peter Hulme's varied and multi-sided account of early Caribbean history is certainly marked. In this sense, her feminized Ariel also dramatizes the female experience of empire-building. Here, she is forced to make a choice between practicing the healing arts her adopted mother has taught her and exploring her own developing interest in the world of love and sexuality. She is depicted as a young woman struggling to create an identity for herself in a society where a strong gender divide is already in place and in which language is equally polarized along male-female lines:

> ... Sycorax warned the girl, when men and women spoke to one another, they were required to control the danger of their exchanges with honorifics and periphrases that might keep the distance between them ... (114)

Through Ariel, Warner opens up the curse of language that plagues Caliban to portray the way in which non-white female characters are doubly cursed, not simply by Prospero, but by patriarchy in general. The language that Kit finally teaches her—the English language as well as a new, sexual language—engages the young girl in a different power dynamic that is both racial and sexual. The birth of their child, Roukoubé (whose name means Red Bear Cub) further relegates her to a life of female servitude, meeting the needs of her child and her sick mother: "she had no more words, indeed it seemed to her that she no longer owned a voice, but only a hollow drum for a head on which others beat out their summons" (173). Ariel becomes symbolic of the island's new face, sustaining hybrid children, shape-shifting with the desires of each new master.

In illustrating the slippage between Shakespeare's play and the view of early Caribbean history that the reader is offered in the novel, Warner explores the dehumanizing nature of the master-slave, male-female hierarchies of colonialism. In using the female voice to nuance that power structure, Warner makes this first point of contact between two civilizations a catalyst for her discussion of the way in which the categories of race and sex gradually come to reduce and to consume women.[17] As a monstrous symbol of the conflict between the British colonial machine and women, the mythical figure of Manjiku resurfaces periodically in the mythology of the islanders and, later on, in Serafine's stories:

> Manjiku specially likes to eat women: juicy, dark women full of blood, the way we are when we get old enough to be mothers. Manjiku thinks he'll have

a baby himself if he eats enough women, especially women with babies inside them waiting to be born. (221)

The voracious appetite of the empire is represented by this threatening white succubus, a pale, needy mass that hungers for dark, fertile women to compensate for its barren state. At the same time, the dominant stories of the past, from *The Tempest* to the textual evidence contained in the books of the Everard and Warner families, either omit the stories of women, indigenous islanders, and slaves or they completely skew that history in order to legitimize violent acts.

But the search for El Dorado that fuels the expanding empire gives way to Warner's own search for regeneration in *Indigo*. Turning the image of Manjiku around, Warner herself integrates the voices of many different women into her novel in an effort to renew the past and her role within her own family's history. Carol Thomas Neely, in her essay "Remembering Shakespeare, Revising Ourselves," comments upon the strength with which women writers have responded to Shakespeare's elegiac romances and the particular significance that this genre has lent to their own creative endeavors:

> Shakespeare's romances and feminist elegiac romances are similar in their mourning for difference, loss, rupture, death, and their working through these to painful reconciliation, to a blend of renunciation and exhilaration. Their focus is on generation and generations and especially in the appropriation of the past—familial, literary, historical—in the service of renewal.[18]

Warner's re-vision of *The Tempest* merges the familial, literary, and historical elements of which Neely writes at the same time as it contains the possibility that Shakespeare's play, in itself, can act as a site of renewal and reconciliation. Her complicity in her family's past—a fact of her birthright—is important in this sense as she uses male-generated textual histories to confront the literalized monsters of her family's past. From the white demon, Manjiku, to the refracted colors of the novel itself, Warner is reinscribing herself onto a new family history, in which non-white, feminine voices are not consumed by the author but articulated and, ultimately, set free. In rebelling against circumscription by merit of her ancestry, Warner is opening up her role as an author to include a myriad of voices and perspectives, moving away from what Wilson Harris calls the "static polarizations of cultural identity" in order to destabilize and interrogate her position as a white, British daughter of the Empire.[19]

So, while the Everard and, in turn, the Warner family legacies provide their female heirs with warped and discordant family narratives that are marred by loss and breakage, the alternatives that the author provides through *Indigo* exist in her efforts to articulate that past in creative terms and in her protagonist's ultimate ability to recognize her complicity in the repetitive plots that have defined her family history. Shakespeare's text is central to this endeavor. The notably loquacious Miranda, who drifts from one meaningless relationship to another, finds that she is unable to center herself in relation to the stories of the past. Using Shakespearean comedy as a touchstone for her own experiences as a woman in modern-day England, she muses:

> She wasn't living inside one of Shakespeare's sweet-tempered comedies, nor in one of his late plays with their magical reconciliations, their truces and appeasements and surcease of pain. No garland of marriages at the fall of the curtain would draw her into its charmed circle. In her world, which was the real world at the end of the century, breakage and disconnection were the only possible outcome. (391)

The distinction Miranda is making between the "real" world of the twentieth century and the contrived, "magical" elements of Shakespeare's drama serves to draw attention to the meta-fictional nature of *Indigo*. What links the different levels of narrative in Warner's novel—her own family story, Shakespeare's play, and the fictional history of the Everards—is this sense of "breakage and disconnection." Miranda sees only one side of *The Tempest* in her vision of the late plays—the "truces and appeasements"—and is unaware of the other stories inherent in the play itself, the story of subjugation and slavery implicit in the struggles of Caliban, Ariel, and the off-stage figure of Sycorax. Although she cannot hear their voices on Enfant Béate, their experiences are made available to her through the play itself.

In the end, it is a performance of *The Tempest* that becomes a vehicle for reconciliation for Miranda not because of its "tidy" ending or because it represents reconciliation, but because it contains and memorializes an alternative version to a past that she has always viewed through the eyes of her ancestors. If the future for Sycorax lies in her conscription to the reduced and fossilized form of her Shakespearean counterpart, then for Miranda, escape from that type of fabulation rests in her ability to recognize and to move beyond such conscription in a way that is impossible for her cousin Xanthe. Xanthe's nickname, "Goldie," links her to the Everard legacy of greedy exploitation; similarly, she is unwilling to recognize and accept her family's wrongdoings. As she tells her cousin: " . . . how can you feel guilty about something you had nothing to do with? All that stuff about oppression . . . Miranda! It happened three-and-a-half centuries ago!" (279). While, on one level, Xanthe's question seeks to deny her culpability in the sins of the Everard past, on another level it reveals Warner's grappling with a major question about the nature of responsibility and Miranda's role in *The Tempest*. If postcolonial criticism seeks to examine the power dynamics of Prospero and Caliban, then the function of Shakespeare's play in *Indigo* pivots upon both Warner's and Miranda's ability to acknowledge the degree to which they are still partially contained within the plots of the past. Thus, *The Tempest* has a dual function in Miranda's movement toward a recognition of and, ultimately, a reconciliation with her familial legacy. Janus-like, it provides a window onto the past at the same time as it contains the possibility of transformation within the new context of a postcolonial reading.

The production that Miranda witnesses takes place in a deconsecrated church, a space that has been reinvented beyond its original ritualistic purpose. Miranda arrives while the cast is rehearsing act 1, scene 2, in which Caliban rails against Prospero and Miranda, and Shakespeare's Miranda expresses her disgust at Caliban for trying to rape her. Shaka Ifetabe, as Caliban, lies prostrate on the stage in this production, his ankles tied together:

> The actress bent down to Caliban's eye level, presenting her breasts to his face, and spat at him,
> "Abhorred slave,
>   Which any print of goodness wilt not take,
>   Being capable of all ill!"
> The young woman was ranting the speech, she was taunting him with smiles, with seductive looks which then turned to scorn, and she was wiping tears from her eyes in horror at the memory of the ingratitude he'd shown her care for him. (387)

The Miranda onstage recalls the domination-subjection connection between Ariel and Kit, as this actress thrusts herself sexually in Caliban's face while simultaneously denying the possibility of a sexual encounter between them. In watching her Shakespearean counterpart interacting with Shaka onstage, Miranda is able to recognize and to posit alternatives to the narratives of shame that have characterized her family history. Watching Shaka perform, she interrogates the nature of her own gaze:

> You're trapped in the fantasy that someone like him could melt you and take you down to the thing you've lost touch with—the longed-for, missing Primitive. . . . I am such a fucking racist, she was thinking. . . . (389)

A mirror for Miranda's experience, the play prompts her to acknowledge her role in a colonial legacy marred by racism and warped and tangled relationships between men and women. In questioning the way in which she is trapped in a "fantasy," Warner's Miranda undergoes an awakening through her encounter with Shakespeare's play, unlike her namesake, who remains asleep during her father's account of the island's pre-history. *The Tempest* might not be a new story, but it prompts Miranda to posit the existence of a new language that functions beyond the curses of her family's past and beyond the dynamics of guilt and shame.

Ultimately, in the offstage union of Shaka and Miranda, black and white, male and female, the chessboard codes of the past are finally relinquished in favor of a new game. Echoing the union of Ferdinand and Miranda, Warner writes:

> They had begun play. Their openings were well-tried, unadventurous. But these same familiar moves would take them in deep: face to face and piece by piece they would engage with each other so raptly that for a time they would never even notice anyone else outside looking in on the work they were absorbed in, crossing the lines, crossing the squares, far out on the board in the other's sea. (395)

Here, the space of the water becomes the ultimate symbol for Warner's encounter with her family's past, a place in which Manjiku—the ominous, guilty monster of her family's sins—lurks dangerously, but also a place where limits and borders can be escaped in favor of interplay, negotiation, and a sense of human connectedness. As in the stories of Serafine, in whose tales "everything risked changing shape" (4), Shakespeare's play and Warner's family ties are renegotiated and subjected to a sea-change inherent in the act of re-creation through the writing process. In many ways, the shipwreck with which *The Tempest* begins becomes a catalyst for Warner's approach to British history in *Indigo,* as she searches through that wreckage, moving away from the island that has shaped her past, into the unknown and often unsafe waters that surround it. While an island is the primary means by which Prospero can choreograph his return to power in Europe, Warner's foray into her family past is characterized by a sense of empowerment that is achieved through confrontation rather than denial or omission. For her, the space of the water, with the truths it contains—"full fathom five" with the sins of her forefathers—becomes a site of retrieval and, the final sea-change, escape.

## Notes

1. Marina Warner, *Indigo or, Mapping the Waters* (London: Virago, 1992), 122. Further references to this work will appear in the text.
2. William Shakespeare, *The Tempest,* in *Complete Works* (Oxford: Oxford University Press, 1988). Further references to this work will appear in the text.
3. Adrienne Rich, "When We Dead Awaken: Writing as Re-Vision," in *On Lies, Secrets, and Silence* (New York: Norton, 1979), 35.
4. Quoted in Aucher Warner, *Sir Thomas Warner: Pioneer of the West Indies* (London: West India Committee, 1933), 57.
5. Warner, *Sir Thomas Warner,* 38.
6. Ibid.
7. Marina Warner, "Between the Colonist and the Creole: Family Bonds, Family Boundaries," in *Unbecoming Daughters of the Empire* (Sydney: Dungaroo Press, 1993), 200. Warner has also commented on the contribution her family history made to the writing of *Indigo* in Chantal Zabus, "Spinning a Yarn With Marina Warner," *Kunapipi* 16 (1994): 519–29.
8. The title of Ant's book echoes the title of one of Sir Pelham Warner's many books on cricket, *How We Recovered the Ashes* (1905).
9. This description was inspired by a portrait of John Luttrell by the Tudor artist Hans Eworth. Painted in 1550, it depicts Luttrell, naked to the waist, rising triumphantly from the sea being led by the allegorical figure of Lady Peace. Notably, there is a shipwreck taking place in the background. Warner has added the image of her ancestor's island to her own version of the portrait, adapting the painting to tell the story of her family's history in the same way that she uses *The Tempest.*
10. Kate Chedgzoy, *Shakespeare's Queer Children: Sexual Politics and Contemporary Culture* (Manchester: Manchester University Press, 1995), 96.
11. George Lamming, *The Pleasures of Exile* (Ann Arbor, MI: Michigan Press, 1960), 245.
12. Hélène Cixous and Catherine Clément, *The Newly Born Woman* (Minneapolis: University of Minnesota Press, 1986), 40. She also writes:

    So all the history, the stories would be there to retell differently; the future would be incalculable; the historic forces would and will change hands and change body—another thought which is yet unthinkable—will transform the functioning of all society. We are living in an age where the conceptual foundation of an ancient culture is in the process of being undermined by millions of a species of mole (Topoi, ground mines) never known before. (40)

13. Peter Hulme, *Colonial Encounters: Europe and the Native Caribbean 1492–1797* (London: Methuen, 1986), 124.
14. Ibid.

15. Stephen Orgel, "Introduction," *The Tempest* (Oxford: Oxford University Press, 1987), 37.

16. Edward Said, *Culture and Imperialism* (New York: Alfred A. Knopf, 1993), 40.

17. The conflict between women and fiction is a predominant concern in much of Warner's work, especially in her nonfiction, in which she has dealt extensively with mythical female figures, from Joan of Arc to The Virgin Mary. See *Alone Of All Her Sex: The Myth and the Cult of the Virgin Mary* (London: Weidenfeld and Nicolson, 1976), and *Joan of Arc: The Image of Female Heroism* (London: Weidenfeld and Nicolson, 1981) in which she writes of the saint:

   In the transformation of her body, and in the different emphases of different times, we have a diviner's cup, which reflects on the surface of the water the image that the petitioner wishes to see, its limits and extensions drawn, as in all magic operations of this kind, according to the known qualities shared between diviner and petitioner. (*Joan of Arc,* 7)

18. Carol Thomas Neely, "Remembering Shakespeare, Revising Ourselves," in *Women's Re-Visions of Shakespeare,* ed. Marianne Novy (Urbana: University of Illinois Press, 1990), 245.

19. Wilson Harris, *Fossil and Psyche* (Austin: African and Afro-American Studies and Research Center, University of Texas, 1974), 2.

# 13

---

# Claribel at Palace Dot Tunis

## Linda Bamber

Dear Claribel,

You will have heard by this time from more official sources that Alonso is dead. Prospero sends his regrets, but I really loved your father and will miss him very much.

Although we held private services for Alonso yesterday, the state ceremonies will be delayed until you arrive. I am looking forward, Claribel, to meeting you at last. I hope you don't mind, but I have always thought of you as an alter ego and wondered very much about your life. It's not hard to guess why. Our fathers, rivals who became in-laws, were at the exact same moment marrying off their daughters for their own political advantage, you to the King of Tunis and me to your brother. Prospero, of course, wanted me to fall in love with Ferdinand first, whereas Alonso had no such scruples; but what would have happened if I hadn't obligingly done so is something I don't like to think about. Perhaps I knew I had no choice. It's all worked out for the best; but sometimes when Ferdinand and I quarrel badly I wonder if my "falling in love" was not just another of my father's magical effects. At such times I feel quite futile; and at such times, Claribel, I think of you. Would it have been better or worse, I wonder, to have it out in the open, as it was between you and Alonso? You, at least, got to say no, even though it didn't stick. On the other hand, our marriage didn't feel, as yours did, forced. Which of us did well?

The funeral, as I said, is being delayed until you arrive in Naples; but it is also being delayed until we ourselves return. At the moment we are back on the island. The place is now a major tourist attraction, and the archipelago of which it is a part has become quite prosperous. Its people serve tourists from Asia, Europe, and the Americas; from everywhere, in fact, but your part of the world, Claribel. Africans don't come. They are not interested in our story because the one (part) African in it, Caliban, was a slave. His mother, Sycorax, was black. These are matters I think more and more about. I seemed to have woken up in the middle of an ugly racial drama, and I don't like my role one bit.

You are wondering, no doubt, why Ferdinand and I have chosen the occasion of your father's death for a holiday. In fact it is because of his death that we are here. Prospero, who never wanted to set foot on the island since the day we left it, seems to think there's something here he needs to find before *he* dies. Of course, my father has been expecting to die ever since we left here 23 years ago, but Alonso's death has given him new conviction.

For my part, I would have refused to come. I thought it disrespectful to Alonso to leave at such a time. But Ferdinand, who worships Prospero and is afraid of him, took my father's side. I remember very well how Prospero produced *that* effect. First insane accusations; next terror and enslavement; finally a shower of gifts, including me. It was the wedding masque that put the cap on it, goddesses, mowers, reapers, and what have you. Iris slid down a wet sunbeam as an immense rainbow opened up like a parachute behind her. Juno's blue peacocks fanned their tails. Ferdinand didn't know whether he was coming or going, and where Prospero is concerned, he never has.

Please note what goddess *wasn't* at the masque: Venus. My father had her refuse to come. When he "gave" me to Ferdinand all he could talk about was what we deserved if we didn't wait. He said he hoped we'd hate each other! Isn't that nice?

Well, Prospero doesn't control me directly any more, but I must admit that through Ferdinand and Tanzo he still does a pretty good job. Ferdinand, as I said, immediately sided with Prospero about the trip. Then Tanzo caught it from them. I have always wanted Tanzo to love his grandfather in spite of everything, so when they form an alliance I just do what they say.

So here we are. Of course it is very disturbing for me to be here after such a long absence, 23 or 400 years, depending on how you measure time. The place is both familiar and strange, with a rocky coastline and poor soil. The vegetation is incoherent. One side of the island seems mainly tropical, with banana and tamarind trees; the other has olives and citrus just like home. Sometimes we try to find the exact location where the climate changes, the way you try to catch the old year turning into the new; but the low ridges are too jumbled, and we lose our way. There are also some areas where both forms of vegetation are mingled together, and others with plants that don't fit into either climate. But in fact nothing grows here in much abundance.

I'll say one last thing before I close. Everyone always asks about Caliban, and you must be curious too. Caliban lives in the ducal palace in Milan. That is, he lives in an attic room of the palace, and my father seems to live there with him. All his imperiousness toward Caliban is gone, but Caliban couldn't care less. Prospero almost never comes to Naples, and when we go to him we spend half our time in the dark attic while Prospero tries to teach Caliban how to play chess. Caliban can't learn to play chess and doesn't want to, but sometimes, by force of will or by wheedling or waiting for his moment, Prospero gets him to play a few moves.

"Wonderful, marvelous," cries Prospero and launches into an analysis meant to inspire further efforts. Naturally, it has the opposite effect. Caliban still leers at me from time to time. Do you wonder, Claribel, that I am not eager to visit Milan?

Oh, Claribel, please write to me. I am nervous, of course, that you will find this letter offensive, or, worse, boring. From years of thinking about you I feel an intimacy that you may not feel with me. But if you don't, it's high time you did! Write to me right away!

Dear Claribel,

Hello, hello, this is Miranda. Is that you? Claribel@palace.tunis? Alonso's daughter, Ferdinand's sister, the Queen of Tunis? This is Miranda, your sister-in-law, Ferdinand's wife. My address is mirnfer@island.temp. Please answer as soon as you can.

Dear Claribel,

So it was you! I knew it! Claribel, I mailed you a long letter a few days ago. What I must repeat are my condolences on the death of your father. Let me know if it comes.

It was Trinculo who suggested I try e-mail. Do you remember Trinculo? He was your father's butler and a terrible alcoholic in the old days. Now he's been sober for years, unless you count cyberspace as an addiction!

Dear Claribel,

Have you really been thinking of me all these years, as I have of you? What vindication! Nobody knew I had made you my imaginary friend, of course, so there was no one to mock me for it; but I imagined disapproval from the usual suspects, Prospero and Ferdinand. So now I'm gloating.

But what was keeping us from writing each other? I want to say "patriarchy," and that's always true, of course; but blaming things on "patriarchy" is never very satisfying, don't you agree? Why didn't I write to you all these years? Even my father, with all his magic, had to find the right moment to conjure up his dramatis personae. He said he depended on an "auspicious star." I don't know about the stars, but you seem more accessible from here. I'll write tomorrow, or later today.

Dear Claribel,
     Thank you so much for your long message. It is very moving to hear news at last about what feels like my own life; that is, my life in you.
     First of all, about your marriage. Yes, we knew the reason you fought your marriage. Of course we knew! I can see how far in the past all that is for you and how exhausted it makes you to talk about it at all. But it's so important to have you do so! It gives me hope that I, too, will some day be emancipated from racial categories and feel as exhausted as you do when called upon to revisit them. Thank God your marriage has worked out so well.
     Secondly, about Alonso. You say he starved you into submission, and I believe you. But is this the same man I knew? The man who named my son? He thought the word "Abuntanzo" would honor my father and please me, too. Abundance and prosperity were all Alonso ever wished for me; but I admit that I have seen, in his encounters with Ferdinand, the man you describe. The two of them just fought to a draw, so I turned a blind eye.
     Once, years ago, Alonso and I were walking together on a path by a sea wall, chatting. We stopped to look at the sea, and I noticed a terrible sadness on his face. On an impulse I said, "Alonso, are you thinking of Claribel?" He stared at me, paralyzed, and I thought in alarm that he was going to cry or choke. Then he walked sharply down the road. I stood there waiting to see if he would come back, horrified to have caused this rupture in the fabric of things. I remember seeing a lizard zip into a crack in the sea wall and thinking that the disappearing lizard was my only contact with the former world. When I caught up with Alonso he was composed but severe, and I understood I wasn't to allude to what had just happened.
     It is hard for me to put together the painful sympathy I felt for him at that moment with the anger I feel now. And for you the conflict now that he is dead must be overwhelming.

Dear Claribel, Dear Ear, my dearest listening Ear,
     I can't get over the happiness of telling you things. It is as if an occluded star has revealed itself and is listening attentively to my messages. And I am the astronomer who always knew it was there!

Today's message has to do with our visit to the park. The National Park of Prospero is what they call it here. It is the area of the island where our story took place in the old days, and these days it is crowded with tourists. Of course we went incognito, arriving on a tour bus like everyone else. Everything is tastefully fenced and signposted in imported redwood, and the names of the various locations are carved and painted in gold: "Prospero's Cell"; "Caliban's Cave"; "Here Ariel Appeared to Alonso as a Harpy"; and so on. The park is unified by oleander bushes, all blooming, all white. They camouflage the toilets, line the paths, encircle the Visitors' Center. After a while I began to doubt their reality, as I began to doubt my own.

Claribel, I am having a very weird experience here! Things are so different—and so much the same. The pine tree, for instance, where my father found Ariel imprisoned when we first came to the island. It was old to begin with and it's old now, with a longitudinal fissure in its trunk. Until I was about nine I could squeeze myself in there, and I used it as a hiding place for my skeletons, stones, some dry pith I had saved from a dead tree. I can't help thinking what Tanzo would have put in it if it had been his hiding place instead of mine. Small, dirty plastic objects, I think: aquamarine-colored combs, miniature cycling rabbits, mismatched dice. But there it was, my tree, the original of which my memory kept a permanent, perfect copy even though I didn't think of it for decades. Of course there's also something disappointing about its reality: it's just a tree, shedding a little, peeling a little, going nowhere. Meanwhile it's labeled "Pine Tree from which Prospero Freed Ariel," and there's an informational pamphlet explaining how Sycorax ruled the island before my father came, how she tortured Ariel, and so on. I stood in front of it, stirred by memories. The different selves that I was growing up were all churning inside me, murmuring and complaining like ghosts. Well, anyone can have that experience, I suppose; but not everyone goes through it to the accompaniment of strangers having their own experience of one's own experience! Near me was a group of people in thick black shoes, the men in beards, the women in bonnets. I think they were members of a sect. I could hear them saying that the tree was the same or different from what they had imagined. Was it "realler," one of them asked, in reality or in imagination? My question exactly. I seemed to be shedding and peeling to nothing as I stood there; whose life was I living, exactly?

I need to think more about Sycorax. She was Caliban's mother. The pamphlet in the case next to the tree follows the official pro-Prospero line: Sycorax was revolting and bad, and her replacement by Prospero was a big improvement for all. The worst thing Sycorax did was torture Ariel; but I can remember my father threatening, at least, to torture Ariel, too. And then of course Sycorax was black. It's interesting how my father never seemed to focus on her blackness, only on her disgusting femininity. But the blackness she passed on to Caliban was part of *his* disgustingness. I see it all so clearly now for the bullshit that it was. And yet Sycorax, or rather the idea of her, still terrifies me. I grew up hating and fearing her; the idea that her black magic was no different from my father's—which was "white"—is truly an impossible thought.

Dear Claribel,

Prospero and I spent the day at the National Park. The others went to the beach. It is difficult for me to spend that much time with Prospero under the best of circumstances, and these were pretty bad. First of all, he doesn't know what he's looking for, so whatever we see just upsets him because that isn't it. We move on to the next thing, which disappoints him in its turn. As usual, the question of whether I want to stand still or move on or jump off a cliff never comes up. I wouldn't expect that. But it's exhausting to be with him when he's relentlessly discontent.

Moreover, I feel somewhat responsible for his agitation, since I was the one who insisted that we leave Caliban at home. I felt it would make the trip impossible if Caliban came along, but now I wonder if it doesn't make it impossible *not* to have him along. Prospero seems to need him, although I don't know why.

We spent the day revisiting together scenes that were significant to both of us from the past; but there were two pasts, his and mine, and he is quite clear that there was only one. He keeps assuming I remember particular spots that are important to him because of interactions that he had with elves and spirits there: storms he raised, promontories he shook. Remember when I shook this promontory? I was, in fact, the audience for many of his feats, but not always a very engaged audience, and most of them have gone completely from my mind. Whatever little shreds and glimmers of memory I do have are effectively drowned out by his loud demands for me to witness him again, this time in the act of his revisiting. We saw a huge oak that Prospero had split with lightning, and Prospero evoked the night he had done it as if I remembered every detail. In fact I did remember feeling excited and proud; Prospero did seem god-like to me in his power. But do I remember how I tried to mimic his spells and potions, how I ran three times around his book, how I raised my childish arms to the skies and pointed, as he had, to the tree? Of course not. The whole point of these memories is how empty and powerless my gestures were in comparison to his. Suddenly Prospero was back in that moment, thunder and lightning coming more and more under his control. "I could direct it!" he cried. "East, west! I could feel it first in my body and tell it where to go!" Tears came to his eyes. We staggered to a bench near a massive tree, Prospero leaning on me a bit theatrically, and I fed some birds while he recovered. The tree was labeled "Jove's stout oak rifted with his own bolt." I heard one of the tourists say, "Spondaic. Check the consonants. Late style."

One scene, however, I certainly do remember. It is the glen in which I proposed to Ferdinand, a small grassy area near the cell we lived in. There were no tourists, no oleanders, no pamphlets, so it took me by surprise. This insignificant-looking place was the navel of my universe, Rome, Delphi, and Piccadilly Circus rolled into one! It all came back in a painful rush. Ferdinand had been hauling logs for my father, a useless and humiliating task. I had come to find him because I was in love out of my mind, and I wanted to touch him. Instead I rushed at the logs to carry them myself. I actually picked up three large logs, a weight of over 50 pounds. I can feel their rough skins against mine, clumps of dark earth sticking to them and smelling like the forest. I could have carried them up a mountainside, running. But instead Ferdinand took them from me, and we talked. I had to know if he loved me, so I asked; but it was awful. The sky threatened and pulsed as if it might cave in on me. "Do you love me?" I asked him. If he didn't, I was dead; if he did I was an everlasting angel. Yes, he said, yes, yes, I love you, yes.

Prospero said, "I was watching the whole time, you know. I was hiding right there," and he pointed to some large poinsettia bushes. I wanted to kill him. It wasn't exactly news to me that he had been watching; I've heard about it dozens of times. His will encircled us as the bushes encircled the grove. But if anything has ever happened to me, if I've ever done anything, it was that. And those two lovers, Ferdinand and Miranda, had stirred and reawakened and lived in me, which was thrilling, horrifying, disturbing, and sad. As far as Prospero knew, it was the place where one of his many plans had come to fruition, and not his favorite or most interesting plan, either.

Well! If he wants to come back again tomorrow he can come by himself. I'm going to the beach with the others. We'll be coming back over the weekend for some special show they're going to put on; something they call a "reenactment"; but I've had more than enough of this for now. Write to me when you get this, even if it's just a line.

Dear Claribel,

The re-enactment turns out to be a big deal. Everyone promises it will be the high point of our visit. It seems they go through our whole story in a year, focusing on one key scene per month. This month it's the masque, of all things. I'm very relieved it's not something more intense. What if I had

to sit through the engagement scene? Or, God forbid, Prospero rifting oaks
with Jove's own bolts? The posters show Juno landing in a kind of Busby
Berkeley chariot; swans instead of peacocks, and white feathers everywhere.
Apparently people plan their trips around these events, often returning until
they've "collected" all twelve.

Prospero seems calmer. We're playing a lot of chess these days, and I think
that mollifies him. In the evenings we put the pieces in a sack and walk to
some beach or grove where we draw a chessboard in the dirt. First we quarrel a bit about the state of play; then we arrange the pieces and pick up where
we left off. Prospero and I have the best memory for the game; when we dis-
agree the others arbitrate. It's nice to have our quarrels down to an evening
ritual—for now, at any rate.

Dear Claribel,
   It's evening now. This is the second time today I've tried to write to you.
This morning I sat down and typed "Dear Claribel" when I had the odd
sensation that someone else was in the room. I turned to look, but my vision blurred. Suddenly I could hear a whole array of sounds at once: birds,
insects, the town, the sea. . . . Everything jangled, then everything
hummed. When it was over it seemed I had moved, because I was sitting
on the edge of the bed, listening to a normal, desultory, midday bird. And
then I saw Ariel. He was sitting at the table where I had been. His face was
boyish, but his skin had softened, and his thinning hair stuck out here and
there in a kind of punk way. There was an impression of elegance, fluidity,
and a little weariness. Oh, yes, the most important thing: he was looking at
me. He knew who I was. He didn't seem surprised, but he didn't seem un-
surprised, either. He seemed to be saying hello. Hello Miranda. And then
he was gone.
   I rushed downstairs, but of course the courtyard was empty. Next door to
the inn an old man was standing in his garden looking up into his pomegranate tree.
   "Did you see anybody?" I asked him.
   "I've seen everybody!" he laughed, gesturing toward the street. I went
into the village looking for Prospero.
   "You've seen Ariel?" he said sharply when I found him in a cafe. When I
heard the grabbiness in his tone all my defenses went up.
   "Not . . . really," I hedged. "I just thought about him, and I wondered if
you had too."
   "I think of him all the time," said Prospero simply. "You know that." He
met my eyes, and for a moment it seemed as if he knew what had happened

without my telling him. As if he knew everything, in fact. Some promise hung in the air; something to do with him and me; an offer of love.

"Ariel . . ." I began hesitantly, feeling a fatal desire. "Just now . . ."

"What?" said Prospero, leaning forward. "What? What?" He was speaking softly, but I happened to glance at his eyes. They were all but emitting jagged voltage symbols, will and mastery gone berserk. My confusion dropped away. "Nothing," I said clearly. "I just remember him, that's all."

Prospero stared at me for another moment with insane intent, but then he saw that I had changed. He would learn nothing. He sat back and picked up his coffee cup, trembling. Suddenly a spasm of rage came over him, and he smashed the cup on the floor.

Claribel, what possessed me to think I could tell Prospero? Will I never learn? I don't know if I'll ever see Ariel again, but at least I didn't lose the sight of him I just had, his greeting. I could tell that Prospero thought Ariel might be what he had come for. Maybe he is and maybe he isn't; but this time he came to me.

I know I saw Ariel, but since we got here I've had some trouble distinguishing other perceptions from my dreams. One day I kept thinking of a dream I'd had about a beach entirely made of smooth, flat, gray stones. The shore was sloped so that each wave picked up the stones and floated them free. Then the dropped stones made a long, slow rattling sound like a rain stick, going on and on long after you'd think it would end. It was a beautiful sound. I wanted it to go on forever and was afraid it would end, as it always did. It all seemed particularly mysterious and significant until the other day Tanzo said he'd been back to the rattling stone beach.

"What?" I said.

"That beach we saw the other day," he said. "The one with the all those stones." And then I remembered we had been there together.

Dear Claribel,

Today Ferdinand and I went to the Park by ourselves. It occurred to me that Ferdinand might be finding it as disturbing as Prospero and I do to be here and that I might pay some attention to that. I said something like, "So. Do you find it disturbing to be here, Ferdinand dear?" and he said something like, "No. Well, yes. Well, I don't know." Introspection has never been Ferdinand's strong suit, which is fine, but I was suddenly impatient and bored with our outing. I walked ahead irritably.

We came out at the famous "yellow sands," which were neither very yellow nor very sandy. In fact, they looked like the rubble left over on a construction site after a sloppy crew has gotten through with it. There was a wonderful park sign, though, a tank of clear water with coral and pearls drifting slowly through it, propelled by a circulating pump. On the back of the tank Ariel's song was printed:

> Full fathom five thy father lies;
>     Of his bones are coral made;
> Those are pearls that were his eyes;
>     Nothing of him that doth fade
> But doth suffer a sea change
> Into something rich and strange.

I said, "OK, let's go back now. That's enough for today."

Ferdinand said, "Let's just see what's in the gift shop." Of course there was a little redwood gift shop, decorated with white oleanders. Inside were spiky coral necklaces and egg timers filled with bright yellow sand. Ferdinand seemed more and more distracted; when we got outside he set off at a pace I couldn't keep up with. Finally we came to a bank by the sea.

Out of the blue Ferdinand said, "I wish I had been nicer to Father." I looked at him, startled. He looked very sad. "I know he couldn't help the way he behaved," he said.

I suppose I should have said, "Alonso knew you loved him," or "You did your best just as he did," or something like that, but I didn't. I stared at him for a minute, my memory jostled by this first display on his part of filial grief.

"I know where we are!" I burst out. "This is the bank you were sitting on when Ariel came to you! Isn't it? 'Sitting upon a bank, weeping again the king my father's wrack'?"

"What's Ariel got to do with it?" he snapped at me, as well he might have. But I realized that he had been dousing for this spot all morning, and now he had found it. Decades, centuries ago he had sat exactly here, looking at the sea in which he believed his father had drowned, "weeping again the king my father's wrack." Now he was here to do it again. I went down to the beach and lay in a sheltered rocky space. The frigates and pelicans circled above me. They had done their morning's fishing and were just passing the time until they got hungry again, riding the thermals, flying for flying's sake. Thoughts of Alonso drifted through my mind, mostly from Tanzo's childhood. When I went back up Ferdinand was in another mood entirely, focused and calm.

"You're right," he said. "It was Ariel who led me away from here; who led me to you." And he smiled.

Tanzo joined us for lunch in the cafeteria at the Visitors' Center. Everything seemed to be made of chickpeas. In the afternoon we gave him a little tour: the glen where I proposed, the scene of our first chess game, and so on. At first he was interested, but soon he started yawning politely. He kept his mouth as closed as possible, arching his palate and flaring his nostrils.

"Had enough?" I asked.

"No, no," he insisted. "This is interesting." Ferdinand thought he meant it, so we forged on, Tanzo fighting off sleep and Ferdinand enjoying himself more and more. By the time we were in the cove where Prospero had renounced his powers before leaving for Italy, Ferdinand had become truly eloquent. About half a dozen tourists were eavesdropping on his lecture.

"His magical powers," Ferdinand said, "his astounding creative force—he was served by most delicate elves, he plucked up huge trees and made fierce storms. Then he made a single thing of us all: your mother and me; Caliban, who wanted to kill him; Trinculo, who was drunk; Sebastian and Antonio, who wanted to kill Alonso; and Alonso himself, who thought I was drowned and it was his own fault for marrying off Aunt Claribel against her will. All of us, everybody, stirred up by greed and guilt and lust and thirst, all warring inside ourselves and at odds with each other; he made us all into a single wave; and calmed it, as Ariel calmed the waters. But what he had created needed him in it. He gave up everything and joined us in the ordinary world, an ordinary man."

Tanzo said resentfully, "Who was this Sebastian person?"

"A friend of Uncle Antonio's," I said quickly. "A creep. He died years ago." I was uneasy, and not just with Tanzo's boredom. The tourists were listening with keen interest to Ferdinand, and in a minute they would suspect who we were. Ferdinand, meanwhile, seemed to have actually become Prospero. He stood facing the sea; suddenly I was caught by his performance.

"'I'll break my staff,'" he said deeply, from within my father's spirit. "'Bury it certain fathoms in the earth, And deeper than did ever plummet sound, I'll drown my book.'" The deep deliberateness of his voice made him sound like a man cutting off his own arm, sane, sober and wide awake. The tourists were amazed and moved, and I was close to tears myself. Tanzo, on the other hand, was going nuts. His face twisted with humiliation.

"Dad, stop it!" he shouted when he couldn't bear it any more.

"What! What is it?" shouted Ferdinand, violently awakened. We got out of there as fast as we could, a few tourists hurrying after us for more information. I told Tanzo that he didn't have to come to the Park any more for the rest of the visit. He's made friends with some local teenagers, and they pick him up in the evenings on their motor scooters. I don't know where they go, but it doesn't matter. Sometimes I wish someone would pick me up on a motor scooter. I wish you were here, Claribel. You see how things are.

Dear Claribel,

Thank you for all your messages. You are always with me now; it's as if the background of my life has changed to a more beautiful color. And then sometimes you are in the forefront of my mind, as you were early yesterday morning as I walked on the beach. From one end to the other, all I thought about were things we have said to each other, our perfect understanding. The waves came up on the sand in huge, smooth, flat semi-circles, arriving and vanishing indistinguishably. After a while I realized that Ariel was walking beside me. It was misty, and at first he was just a sensation; but then there he was, taller than I remember him because he was walking above me on the slope of the sand. I was surprised, but this time not overwhelmed.

"Ariel!" I said delightedly.

"How's your father?" asked Ariel—just like that.

"Fine, great," I raved, thrilled to hear him speak. "We're all fine."

"I'm free now," said Ariel, "and I like that. But I enjoyed working with your father." He smiled, and I realized he looked younger than he had last time I saw him.

"Stay with me," I said on an impulse, and he did. I told him everything that has happened, Alonso's death, Tanzo, how crazy Prospero is about Caliban, everything. At one point we even had a conversation about Sycorax.

"Have you seen the pamphlets next to the pine tree?" I asked.

"I'm not much of a reader," said Ariel.

"Well, the bibliography for further reading lists articles that say she represents archaic matriarchy and also the despised and repressed female body." Ariel liked that a lot.

"That's very good," he laughed. I couldn't tell why.

"Was she vile?" I asked.

"Vile? No. She was difficult. But your father was difficult, too. I enjoyed working with them both."

When Ariel left I didn't feel the slightest need to tell anyone what had happened; certainly not to tell Prospero. Now, of course, I'm telling you. But that's different.

Speaking of Caliban's mother, the man himself is here with us. I should have known Prospero would never have come without him, no matter what promises he made before we left. Trinculo has been looking after Caliban in secret. They are installed in a motel across the causeway from the Park. But the one thing Trinculo has to do is get to AA meetings, and he's been taking

Caliban with him. The way it all came out was that Caliban, who'd been in any case making a habit of cutting his toenails at meetings, yesterday stood up on a chair and pissed in an arc. A member of the meeting called the local constabulary, and Caliban had to spend some time in jail. Prospero went and sat near him, alternately demanding to see the governor and comforting Caliban. Of course Caliban didn't give a damn.

The worst of it is that now they know who we are. Prospero told them as a way of assuring leniency for Caliban, although nothing the least bit bad was going to happen to him. So now they want to put us up in the governor's mansion, which we've refused, and to sit in a special box at the Re-enactment, which we've accepted. They've also organized a gala reception after the show at which we are to be the guests of honor. I find it all depressing. This place depends heavily on tourism for its economic success, and we—or rather, the idea of us—is crucial to the tourism industry. That's fine, but it's unpleasant to be the target of so much economic smilingness. We suddenly have representational responsibilities, like royalty, and it makes me feel nonexistent. And old, Claribel! Because the Miranda everyone wants is not this middle-aged woman but the dazzling girl I once was. I keep feeling that she's right behind me, a flower without a speck on her petals, and I need to step aside so the others can speak with her. Where did she go?

I see that I've capitalized the word Re-enactment. Clearly I've been infected by the reverence and patriotism with which this event is always discussed. But there is an undercurrent of something else, especially among the younger people. I think preparations are underway for something subversive. Last night a group of local kids called Tanzo aside for a private, keyed-up conversation. They stood near some buildings in the dark, and we could hear an occasional snirt of laughter. When they parted there was an I'll-do-this-and-you-do-that feeling to things. I'm sure it was something to do with the Re-enactment.

"What was that all about?" Ferdinand asked Tanzo. Tanzo just laughed.

"Do they know who we are?" I asked.

"No," said Tanzo. "Not yet, anyway."

"Well, don't do anything physically dangerous," I said. "Okay?"

"Whatever you say," said Tanzo airily. There was a smell in the air as of saltpeter around illegal fireworks.


Dear Claribel,

I have discovered I can summon Ariel any time I like simply by thinking of you. I've tried it twice already today. Each time Ariel appears, he looks younger. The last time he came he was just what he'd been in the old days:

quick, compliant, energetic, and androgynous. He offered to turn a little bush into a fairy for me just out of excess of good spirits, like a dog who can't contain himself and suddenly gives you a kiss.

"Sure!" I said. "Why not!" So a small fairy appeared, curtsied, danced, curtsied, and went back to being a bush. I was overjoyed. Now I'm really enjoying the vacation. Prospero, Caliban, our duties, the Re-enactment—it's all noises off. All I care about is doing things with Ariel.

Dear Claribel,

Today I had a conversation with the old fellow next door. He told me there's a guerilla theater group that performs something scatological or obscene every time there's a Re-enactment. So that's what Tanzo's friends are excited about. I'm relieved it isn't something worse, although of course it's embarrassing to think of them probing our story for its scatology and obscenity. My friend told me it can get pretty rough; but fundamentally it's a play, so I can't imagine anyone will get hurt. Tanzo's old enough to see whatever he wants to now. My friend and I ate a pomegranate together, sitting on chairs in his overgrown yard.

Ariel is showing me special parts of the island and I'm meeting the spirits that live here. It's the most fun I've ever had.

Dear Claribel,

I am writing to you from the Visitors' Center during the intermission of the Re-enactment. The whole thing is a pain in the neck. First of all, it's unexpectedly cold, and I'm only wearing a sundress. They brought me here because I was shivering, so I'm briefly 1) warm and 2) alone. I'm in an employees' lounge with lots of beige upholstery, a coffee machine, and a workstation. At first I couldn't get into my e-mail account, but Trinculo came by and figured it out.

The performance itself began well enough. We are in a natural amphitheater, with woods and hills all around us. At twilight suddenly gods and goddesses, dressed mostly in white, began to be visible moving among the trees, appearing and disappearing. We turned every which way in our seats to watch them. They were having a murmurous conversation you could almost hear. Some of the gods and goddesses were human-sized, but some of them turned out to be large puppets manipulated by several people at once. Perspective effects kept appearing and dissolving; you couldn't tell whether you were looking at a large god far away or a small god close up.

So that was great. But then came a combination of an overdone ballet blanc and the most boring lecture you've ever heard in your life. Swirling chiffoned goddesses; potted white oleanders in huge clumps; a booming-voiced Prospero; Ferdinand and Miranda standing there like dolls with exaggerated looks of surprise. And all this was constantly interrupted by talking-head lectures on every little point of textual and interpretive scholarship imaginable. The worst was at the end. Ceres and Juno sang their song, and then an awed Ferdinand said to Prospero, "Let me live here ever! So rare a wond'red father and a wise / Makes this place paradise!" At which point the action, such as it was, stopped, and we heard a panel discussion on the recent graphological scholarship showing that Ferdinand actually said "wife," not "wise," the f and the s in those days having been graphologically similar. The panel was falling all over itself to make a feminist point out of this. A wife? A father and a wife, one of each? Excuse me, but where is the feminism in this? I leaned over to Ferdinand and whispered, "Out with it. Did you say 'wife' or 'wise'?" but he just frowned in irritation. Of course, he has no idea what he said; moreover, he was involved in his public function and wholly unwilling to be ironic with me at our hosts' expense. Then I felt irritated myself.

But the real problem is that the guest of honor, Prospero, the Really Big Guy, isn't here. Neither is Tanzo. The whole government of the Archi is in attendance on our account; we are sitting in a raised, specially constructed box where everyone can watch us; and the speakers and actors, who haven't been told about Prospero's absence, occasionally make graceful references to him, glancing through the footlights in our direction. At first I pretended to be worried about him, but when I realized they were preparing to search for him I had to backtrack.

"This often happens," I begged them. "He's overtaken by his own creativity and forgets everything else. He'll have something wonderful for us, perhaps, when he returns." Ferdinand joined me, and we finally persuaded them; Ferdinand seemed convinced by our story. I was, and am, disgusted. How many times have I vowed never to cover for my father again? But I can't just leave; and if I stay I have to be polite and tell lies. So here I am once again. And where is Tanzo? I don't even know if he's safe.

Dear Claribel,
   My last message ended abruptly because I heard them coming back for me. I haven't written since for reasons that will become clear.
   The performance dragged on interminably. By the time it was over I was chilled to the bone. Then we went to the governor's mansion for a gala reception, *Hamlet* without the Prince of Denmark. After a while, the big guy did indeed appear—at which point things got worse.

Ferdinand, Trinculo, and I were standing in a reception line in the foyer of the house, near an odd, asymmetrical staircase. We seemed to be shaking hands with the entire population of the Archipelago. Even Stephano, Trinculo's dopey friend, was in demand. At about 11:30 Prospero appeared. He burst in the doorway, ploughed over to me, and shouted,

"I raped you! I raped you!"

"What?" I said, completely stunned. I tried to pull him out of the crowd but couldn't. He kept waving his arms and shouting, "I raped you!"

Out of the corner of my eye I could see Tanzo's stricken face, and I knew as if I had been told what had happened. Tanzo had taken Prospero to the underground re-enactment, and it had had to do with the time Caliban tried to rape me. I knew it because I had been rehearsing and repressing this scenario all along. The one thing I hadn't wanted Tanzo to see was the attempted rape.

"Tanzo," I said urgently. "What happened?"

"They did the attempted rape," said Tanzo miserably.

"Obviously," I said. "But why is Prospero claiming credit?"

Tanzo gave me a nasty look. He will never go along with irony where Prospero is concerned.

"They did it as wish fulfillment," he said resentfully. "Caliban was supposed to represent Prospero's forbidden wishes." Meanwhile Prospero stood there yelling, "I raped you," over and over.

"Go away," I finally shouted at him. I was mad at him for the evening he had just put us through and for this current atrocity and my childhood and everything else.

"I raped you!" he shouted, his face an inch from mine.

"I don't care what you did, just get away from me! I hate you!" By this time I had completely lost control.

"I raped you!" said Prospero.

"I hate you, I hate you," I shouted. Finally Trinculo dragged him a couple of feet away. Ferdinand put his arm around me and said, "Everything's okay."

"I hate you!" I shouted, this time at Ferdinand. Trinculo shook Prospero by the shoulders and tried to establish eye contact. Prospero said, "I raped you" a few more times and then let Trinculo take him away. Ferdinand said calmly,

"I'm going to address the group. Don't worry about a thing."

Then he went up a few steps of the crazy staircase and made an inspired speech. It calmed even me, and by the end everyone relaxed and laughed at his jokes. Ferdinand really is a genius at public speaking. He managed to imply that he saw everything, understood everything, and took responsibility for it all. Fathers, sex, power, he said, we're all in the soup together. He was urbane and sincere at the same time, and I've never been more grateful for his talents.

Oh, Claribel. Did Prospero rape me? I don't think so. But what did happen? I've been sick ever since, trying to remember. Prospero has taken Stephano and gone off to an abandoned island at the northernmost point of the Archi. Tanzo is impenetrably angry, guilty, and shocked. He won't talk about it—which is just as well, because I have no idea what to say. People his age have a kind of mental trash masher they can use to get rid of inassimilable experiences, and I presume he's mashing up the experience of having seen a play in which his mother gets raped by his grandfather. Or almost raped. I still don't understand exactly what went on. Ferdinand and Trinculo bring food.

Dear Claribel,

The whole island is waiting for me to make a statement. Their future, as they see it, depends on what I say. Half the people here think Prospero should be exposed for sexual abuse and the Park redesigned around that issue; the other half are appalled at the thought of what that would do to the tourist industry, which is, after all, the basis of the Archi's economy. It's not just a local issue, either. We are besieged by international journalists, photographers and TV crews. Someone is making a documentary and keeps asking us to repeat our entrances and exits. As you can imagine, we try to make as few entrances and exits as possible. It has become clear that since "the Accusation," as they call it, was made in a play, I'm supposed to answer in a play. All sorts of facilities have been put at my service: musicians, actors, stagehands, and a lighting crew. I've never written anything for the stage before, nothing but a few little poems. Moreover, I don't know whether Prospero raped me or not, so I don't know what the play should be about. Someday I suppose this nightmare vacation will be over, and I'll be safely back in Milan; I can imagine no greater happiness.

And how are you?

Dear Claribel,

Ariel is helping with the play. First of all, we're using spirits, not the experts provided by the Archi government. Secondly, we think the plot may involve chess. There was chess in the old plot, and there it felt both archetypal and underused. Ariel says this may be a chance to exploit its possibilities.

Claribel, I have a gift for chess. I am far better at it than other people, better than anyone I've ever known but Prospero. It was Prospero who taught me in the first place, which wasn't fun. "That pawn is pinned," he'd shout. "Can't you remember anything?" Usually when he yelled at me I shut down; but not about chess. I think chess was the one thing from his former life that he couldn't do without, and I was his only hope of a game. It must have made me feel powerful. By the time we left the island I could beat him about half the time. I still can, and he still gets a kick out of it when I do.

Ferdinand and I were playing chess when Prospero revealed us to your father. Ferdinand was down by a knight, and I was mad because I thought he had let me take it. Why should he assume I couldn't play as well as he could? So I played as hard as I could, and soon I had two more pawns and a bishop in exchange for a single pawn of my own. I will never forget the feeling that came over me when I realized that Ferdinand was no match for me at chess. It was like losing altitude too fast in a plane. Who was this feeble person I was about to tie myself to for life? Did he expect to lollop behind me in all our endeavors, half-dragged, half-hustled? But when I looked up, Ferdinand was looking straight at me, smiling. I could see he was amused by how seriously I was taking things, and I could also see how much he loved me. Utterly confused by the gold flecks in his brown eyes, I messed up the next few moves, and he hooked two pieces with his remaining knight.

Dear Claribel,

They've sent word to the ranger station on the North Island to tell Prospero the play will go on in a week. I don't know whether to hope he comes or hope he stays away. Will he be mad if I say he raped me? Will he be mad if I say he didn't? Will I be mad if he doesn't come? Is this what they mean by the creative process?

Dear Claribel,

Okay, this is the best I can do.

At the climax of the play Caliban bursts into the cell and attacks Miranda, who kicks and shouts, "Father, Father!" Prospero rushes outside for something to beat him with, but his face appears in the window of the cell, watching, not rushing. He's interested, to say the least. Miranda shrieks in a prolonged, despairing way: she realizes that Prospero partly wants this to happen. Suddenly the lighting changes, and Ariel is revealed to be sitting in the cell. Everything is silent except for Caliban grunting around. Into the silence Ariel says quietly,

"Pawn to Queen's Knight four."

This refers to a game of chess that Prospero, in the absence of an opponent, has been playing with himself. When Ariel says, "Pawn to Queen's Knight four," Miranda suddenly realizes that this is the beginning of a combination 16 moves deep. If she assumes the role of Prospero's opponent, it will win her the game. Still struggling against Caliban she shouts,

"Pawn to Queen's Knight four!"

At that the faces of the spirits hanging all over the stage slowly change. They had been mirroring Prospero's guilty interest but now are variously confused, frustrated, and awakened.

"That's good," Prospero says involuntarily. "That's an amazing move." At that moment he looks down and sees that he has in his hand a large stick, suitable for beating Caliban. He rouses himself and rushes in. Caliban is quelled, and Prospero produces a masque in which the gods act out the moves of Miranda's astonishing play. Both the white queen and the black one are played by Juno in a virtuoso turn. The pawns are peacocks, folding and unfolding their tails.

As I say, that will have to do. The play goes on tomorrow. Ariel kept reminding me to please myself first, but I am extremely nervous about whether or not this will please all the interested parties. Does it please you, Claribel?

Dear Claribel,

One thing I needn't have worried about was Prospero's reaction. He came, and so did Caliban. Caliban actually *asked* to come. Trinculo got him into some kind of ill-fitting mottled woodman's garment, brown and green. It seemed quite clean. When the play was over Caliban looked at Prospero, who looked back. I saw it in a flash, so I didn't know which one of them was interrogative and which one nodded yes. But I knew they had agreed that my play was the literal truth of what happened. I was relieved and angry at once. If Prospero thinks that's what happened, shouldn't he apologize? Meanwhile my play has been mistaken for the simple representation of an actual event. What about my artistic decisions? What about my suffering? And so on.

Oh, well. There you have it. Things will never be right between Prospero and me, no matter what. Caliban, however, seems different. I didn't see him at the party after the play or all day yesterday. But last night as we were sitting down to supper Caliban came along, pulled out a chair and sat down. We were at a small cafe on the beach with rickety tables and chairs. I was too wrung out even to be surprised, much less to be on duty in case of disaster.

But there was no disaster. Caliban stayed in his seat and ate like a normal person. We had a local fish with tangerines for dessert. No one wanted to get up when it was over, so we just sat there talking while a huge, transparent moon rose over the water.

Tomorrow we go home. Tanzo surprised us by suggesting that Prospero should make some kind of farewell speech in the renunciation cove, but Prospero barely knew what he was talking about.

"Renounce what?" he asked.

"Your powers," said Tanzo. Ferdinand and I exchanged glances.

"Don't talk nonsense," said Prospero, and left to go bowling with Caliban and Stephano.

As it happens, the one who is tempted to elegiac farewells is me. I wouldn't mind delivering myself of some remarks in the cove. But I'd like Ariel to come with me, and I can't find him anywhere. By the way, I think Ariel played himself in the play. I mean, I don't think it was one of the spirits we were using as actors who said to Miranda, "Pawn to Queen's Knight four." I think it was Ariel himself. What a devil he is. How I shall miss him.

But Claribel, when I come home I'll see you! So much has happened since Alonso's death that I no longer associate it with your visit, although of course for you there still is that sadness. Claribel, my dearest Clare, come early and stay late. I have so much more I want to tell you; and I want to show you everything in Naples and Milan.

Dear Claribel,

It occurs to me that there is no particular reason not to write to you. When you didn't come for the memorial service I was afraid for your well-being and contacted the Foreign Office. They said you were fine. But if you're fine, why don't you answer my mail? I still don't understand, but I know I won't hear from you as long as I'm in Italy. Someday, perhaps, I'll go back to the island, and then we'll see.

The big change since we left is Prospero's relationship with Caliban. The two of them are simply friends. Caliban had the operation on his back that we had been urging on him for years, and now he stands up straight. Prospero doesn't try to get him to play chess any more, or indeed to do anything at all. Both of them seem to have forgotten their former differences. If I allude to the past, they look first blank and then quite irritated.

Prospero, meanwhile, is inflamed by a new passion. He has learned that race is an arbitrary category, merely designating ancestry, and he talks of nothing else. I don't know what the thinking is in Tunis, but in Italy this idea has been around for decades, mostly in academic circles but now sometimes in the popular press. I just never expected *Prospero* to take up the project of deconstructing whiteness. He's involved in a vast research project to show that the entire nobility of Italy, including himself, is "black." We're all sick to death of it by now. Recently I dreamed that he went out on the balcony with a megaphone and bullied passersby with the good news. People muffled themselves, hunched their shoulders and hurried on.

Caliban knows that the project is largely, if not entirely, undertaken on his account, and he's touched. But even Caliban gets fed up. Last week, for instance, we went to Rome to interview an old lady whose grandfather might or might not have had an African mother. She had on a black dress and lived with her daughter's family in the front rooms of a once-grand apartment. She fascinated me, a seated figure in black drinking a red Campari, undisturbed at being and having been. But Prospero never knows when to stop, and eventually I'd had enough of her long, insignificant life. So, it seems, had Caliban, because I saw him discreetly flick his cigar ash into the lady's Campari. Then he strolled to the front windows and gazed down at the street.

But that kind of thing is the exception now rather than the rule. Prospero and Caliban are such good friends they've started to look alike. I saw them once on the street, both wearing sunglasses, soft loafers and pleated pants. I thought, "Two clean old gents walking and talking slowly together." Perhaps it's all this talk about genealogy and race, but for a moment I thought the darker one was my father. A brilliantly clean shop window behind them caught the sun, and then they were gone.

I'll stop now, Claribel. I miss you very much. Remember the beach with the rattling stones? As long as the stones are falling down the berm, sequentially coming to rest, all is well. But then it stops. The stones float in a vague and disconnected way, each unsure of its place. My place is near you, Claribel. I won't pretend I'm not anxious-hearted here without you.

I have planted all the terraces of the palace with white oleanders. And perhaps I'll write again.

*Love,*
*Miranda*

# Contributors

ISKA ALTER is Associate Professor of English at Hofstra University, where she teaches both American literature and the drama of Shakespeare and his contemporaries. In 1995–96, she was Fulbright Teaching Fellow at the University of Hong Kong. She has published *The Good Man's Dilemma: Social Criticism in the Fiction of Bernard Malamud* and numerous articles on modern drama, Arthur Miller, Jewish-American fiction, detective fiction, and Shakespeare.

LINDA BAMBER teaches at Tufts University. She is the author of *Comic Women: Tragic Men: Gender and Genre in Shakespeare,* and has published fiction and poetry in *Raritan, Ploughshares, Tikkun, The Kenyon Review, The Harvard Review,* and elsewhere.

DIANA BRYDON is Director of the School of Literatures and Performance Studies in English at the University of Guelph. She has published extensively on postcolonial literatures, criticism, and theory and is currently investigating the interdisciplinary history of the critical concept of postcolonialism with funding support from the Social Sciences and Humanities Research Council of Canada. Together with Irena Makaryk, she is also co-editing a collection of essays on Canadian Shakespeare.

CAROLINE CAKEBREAD recently received her Ph.D. from the Shakespeare Institute, the University of Birmingham. She writes on Shakespeare, contemporary women's literature, and feminist literary theory. At present, she lives in Toronto, Canada, and is working on a book about spinsters and single women in contemporary literature and culture.

PETER ERICKSON is the author of *Patriarchal Structures in Shakespeare's Drama* and *Rewriting Shakespeare, Rewriting Ourselves,* co-editor of *Shakespeare's "Rough Magic": Renaissance Essays in Honor of C. L. Barber,* and editor of Harry Berger's *Making Trifles of Terrors: Redistributing Complicities in Shakespeare.* Having in recent years turned to cross-disciplinary work in visual art, he is currently co-editing, with Clark Hulse, a new collection called *Early Modern Visual Culture.*

PENNY GAY teaches in the English and Performance Studies department of the University of Sydney. Her publications include *As She Likes It: Shakespeare's Unruly Women* and a study of *As You Like It.* She is currently working on a book on Jane Austen and the theater.

BARBARA HODGDON is the Ellis and Nelle Levitt Professor of English at Drake University. She is the author of *The End Crowns All: Closure and Contradiction in Shakespeare's History, The First Part of King Henry the Fourth: Texts and Contexts,* and *The Shakespeare Trade: Performances and Appropriations.* Currently she is at work on the Arden 3 edition of *The Taming of the Shrew.*

PATRICIA LENNOX has a master's degree in English Literature from Hunter College, CUNY, and is a doctoral candidate at the Graduate Center, CUNY. She currently teaches English and world literature at Baruch College, CUNY, and is a member of the editorial production staff of *Renaissance Quarterly.* She has written on the stage history of Shakespeare's *Henry VI* for a forthcoming volume on the play edited by Thomas Pendleton, and is working on a book examining women's roles in Shakespeare films.

BARBARA MATHIESON earned a joint Ph.D. from Stanford University in Dramatic Literature and Humanities. After teaching for four years at Stanford in the Culture, Ideas, and Values program, she moved to a small farm with peacocks, fruit trees, and flowers in Ashland, Oregon, where she is an Associate Professor of English at Southern Oregon University. Her teaching interests include Shakespeare, early modern British literature, and world literature.

MARIANNE NOVY is professor of English and Women's Studies at the University of Pittsburgh. She has written *Love's Argument: Gender Relations in Shakespeare* and *Engaging with Shakespeare: Responses of George Eliot and Other Women Novelists,* and has edited *Women's Re-Visions of Shakespeare* and *Cross-Cultural Performances.* She is currently writing on adoption in literature and culture.

SUZANNE RAITT is Associate Professor of English and Women's Studies at the University of Michigan. Her books include *Virginia Woolf's To the Lighthouse, Vita and Virginia, Volcanoes and Pearl Divers: Essays in Lesbian Feminist Studies,* and, with Trudi Tate, *Women's Fiction and the Great War.* She has also edited Katherine Mansfield's *Something Childish and Other Stories* and Virginia Woolf's *Night and Day.* She is currently finishing a book on May Sinclair.

FRANCESCA T. ROYSTER, Assistant Professor of English at the Pennsylvania State University, is currently completing a book manuscript entitled "Becoming Cleopatra: Cross-Cultural Appropriation and Shakespearean Tactics." Her recent publications include "The 'End of Race' and the Future of Early Modern Cultural Studies," *Shakespeare Studies* (Fall 1998).

JANE SMILEY is the author of nine works of fiction, including *The Age of Grief, The Greenlanders, Ordinary Love & Good Will, A Thousand Acres* (which won the Chicago Tribune Heartland Prize, the National Book Critics Circle Award, and the Pulitzer Prize), *Moo,* and *The All-True Travels and Adventures of Lidie Newton.* She lives in northern California.

# Index